On Hell's Perimeters
by Don Klotz

Pacific Tales of
PBY PATROL
SQUADRON 23
in World War Two

EAKIN PRESS Fort Worth, Texas
www.EakinPress.com

*It is with humble gratitude
that I dedicate this book
to my wife and family,
my comrades,
Lt. W. Boardman Jones, Jr.,
and my niece,
Patricia Roche.*

Copyright © 2002
By Don Klotz
Published By Eakin Press
An Imprint of Wild Horse Media Group
P.O. Box 331779
Fort Worth, Texas 76163
1-817-344-7036
www.EakinPress.com
ALL RIGHTS RESERVED
1 2 3 4 5 6 7 8 9
Paperback ISBN 978-1-57168-782-1
Hardback ISBN 978-1-57168-690-9
eBook ISBN 978-1-68179-235-4

ALL RIGHTS RESERVED. No part of this book may be reproduced in any form without written permission from the publisher, except for brief passages included in a review appearing in a newspaper or magazine.

Contents

Tribute to VPB-23... v
Preface... ix

FIRST TOUR: 1940–1941
1   A Bittersweet Omen...................... 1
2   Prelude to Pearl......................... 5
3   The Japanese Attack...................... 11
4   The Radio Tells Us....................... 22
5   Wake Island.............................. 27

SECOND TOUR: 1941–1943
6   The Battle of Midway..................... 43
7   The Solomons............................. 52
8   The Lost Crew............................ 78
9   Return to the Solomons................... 89

THIRD TOUR: 1943-1945
10   Joining the Navy........................ 113
11   Naval Air Technical Training Center..... 125
12   Naval Air Gunners School (NAGS)......... 132
13   Operational Training Unit (OTU-1)....... 136
14   A New VP-23............................. 143
15   Destination: Kaneohe.................... 152
16   A Return to Midway...................... 157
17   Eniwetok................................ 162
18   Saipan—Tinian........................... 178
19   Guam.................................... 190

20	Ulithi	199
21	Peleliu	206
22	Iwo Jima	220
23	Going Home	232

REUNITED: 1941-1995

| **24** | The Reunion | 259 |

Index ... 265

Tribute to VPB-23

To the men of VP/VPB-23, welcome aboard! We come together by common bond and distant memories, reflecting upon deeds done on Pacific atolls in a war fought half a century ago. We meet as comrades who shared that special moment in history.

Come on board! Grab the ladder! Give a strong hoist up and over into the blister, contorting head and body to maneuver forward through sharp-edged compartment hatchways, along a narrow catwalk, to man your stations for takeoff. Experience the coughing start-ups, the smell, the roar of Pratt & Whitneys. Feel full-throttle speed and surface bounce and batter to the final release from Neptune's holding grasp. Then upwards, airborne ... and on to the airy drone and drudge of missions too numerous to mention.

As FDR so aptly foresaw and defined, we were the generation that would have its rendezvous with destiny. An early Sunday morning in December of '41 would assure that premonition.

That we, the survivors of America's last world war, have come together in commemoration some fifty-plus years later, gives just cause for celebration and testimony.

It seems not so very long ago that we left the war behind us. We returned to work or school as old young men with determined effort to get on with our lives. We married, raised children, and achieved a measure of success in business or other endeavors.

There were those who did not return. We are here to pay special tribute to them, as well as comrades who have since gone off on the last patrol. We miss them. We salute them.

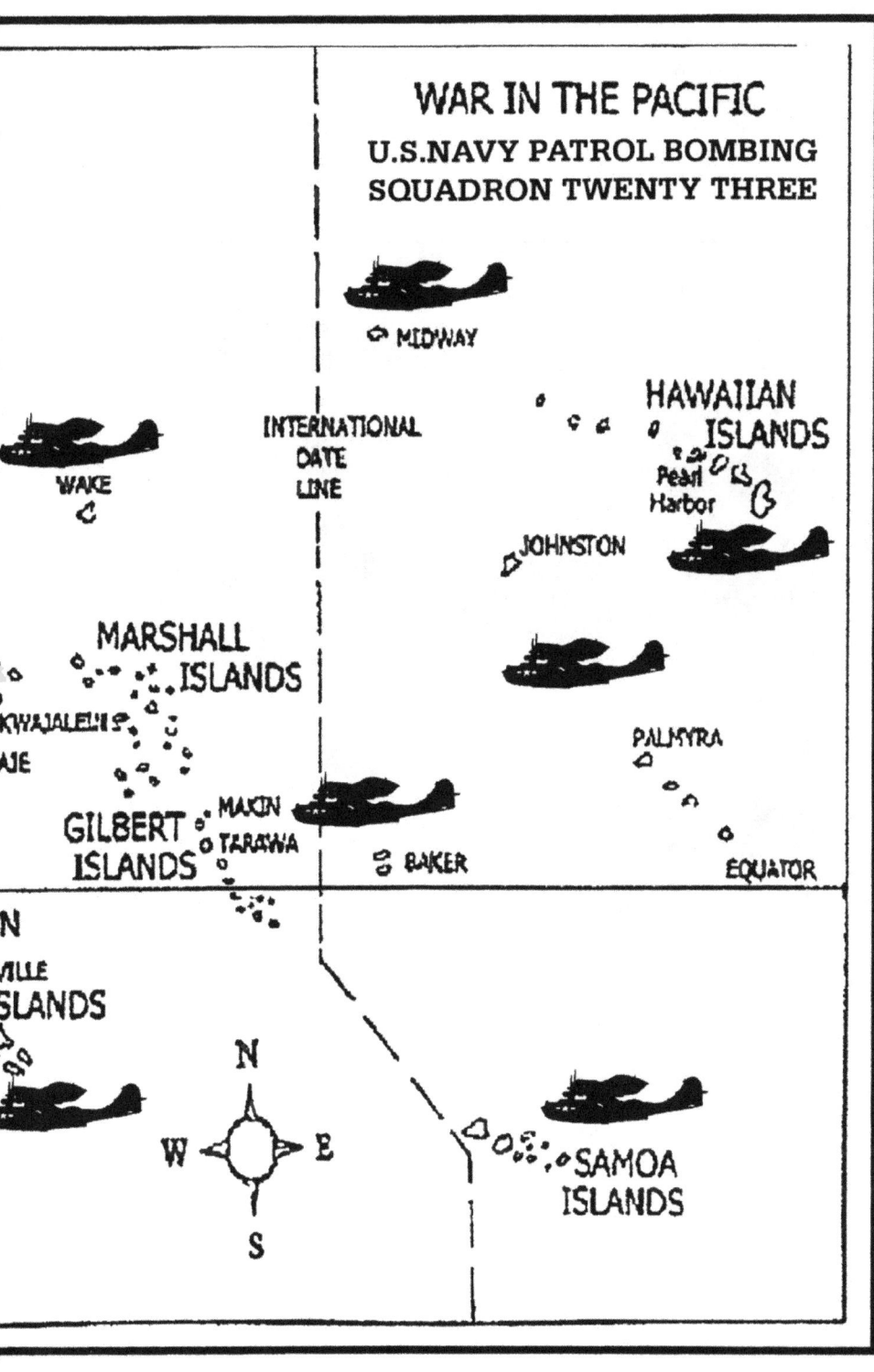

PBY attacking Japanese war ship.
(Artist rendition/newspaper)

(R. Reed Collection)

Preface

In 1994, as the fiftieth anniversary of the end of World War II approached, I began a search for my VPB-23 comrades by placing a notice in American Legion and VFW magazines. I also wrote Admiral Kelso, Chief of Naval Operations; Admiral Baker, Chief of Information; Captain Vance, Deputy Director of Naval History; the Naval Academy; and the National Archives. The U.S. Navy responded admirably, sending me a microfiche listing of VPB-23 officers and enlisted men, its "log" of plane disbursements and quarterly action report, and the squadron's War Diary detailing its missions and tours of duty.

The wealth of material inspired me to write a book about the little-known exploits of the Navy's valiant PBYs and the Black Cats of VP/VPB-23—the Navy's oldest patrol squadron serving three tours of duty from pre-Pearl Harbor until the end of World War II.

To aid in searching for surviving members, I decided to publish a newsletter, "U.S. Navy VP/VPB-23 Black Cat Log," for WWII pilots and aircrewmen who flew PBYs in the Pacific in U.S. Navy Patrol Bombing Squadron 23.

The newsletter, "Black Cat Log," has a twofold purpose: to bring together comrades in an annual reunion of camaraderie, and through their letters and stories to write our squadron's history.

You may ask why such a story was prompted some fifty years after WWII. While half watching television in my home at Wilton, Connecticut, I suddenly became aware that the program was showing a travel film journey of a refurbished PBY Catalina flying boat. The craft was flying over the pyramids of Egypt, across the Sudan, and continuing into Africa on an airborne safari. Intrigued, I requested an itinerary of the "Flying Boat Tour," only to realize it was not the prospect of adventure but rather the sight of the "Old Cat" that would be the impetus to my beginning another journey.

There's an incongruity about writing from memory events that happened some threescore years ago—particularly by someone who has suffered a couple of heart attacks, was brought back from sudden death less than two years ago, recovered from triple by-pass surgery and is now monitored by a metal defibrillator. Add to that a right arm affected by Parkinson's disease and macular degeneration that has negated vision in my left eye.

Sitting before an old Mac IICi, it is that younger person in me that I am reaching back for. And just as I did as a radioman in a Catalina flying boat, I hunt and peck at the keys before me to write a story of a time long ago ... one man's journey that began in the depression, carried into the Second World War, and covered a vast remoteness of Pacific Ocean to fly the perimeters of hell and islands of death.

I flew with Black Cat Squadron VPB-23 as a radioman-gunner in Lt.(jg) W. Boardman Jones' crew. We flew Reconnaissance, Air-Sea Rescue, and Dumbo missions in the Central Pacific from March 1944 to August 1945.

At war's end, I returned to school in my hometown, attending the Chicago Academy of Fine Arts. I then went on to work as an art director in a Chicago advertising agency and over the years in others located in St. Louis, Missouri, and in New York City.

At the outbreak of the Korean War in 1950, my career was suddenly interrupted by my recall back into service. I joined U.S. Navy Patrol Bombing Squadron 28 (VPB-28) for an eighteen-month tour of duty. My PB4Y squadron flew out of Itami Air Force Base in Japan and was involved in patrol and mine-laying operations off the coast of Korea.

Afterwards, I resumed my career in advertising and in 1965 started my own package design firm in Wilton, Connecticut. Among a distinguished list of clients were General Foods, Nestle, Richardson-Vicks, and PepsiCo.

My wife, Ann, and I were blessed with and raised four sons and a daughter and are proud grandparents of seven granddaughters and three grandsons.

But back to the journey. How ironic that after some forty-nine years, a TV video would touch something inside me and start me off on a nostalgic journey to search for a group of former Black Cat comrades, who for many years since have distinguished themselves as Gray Cats!

Actually, an earlier meeting that took place on a street in St. Louis in 1956 was the first step in my literary journey. It was in passing him that I suddenly recognized my Navy patrol plane commander, Lt. W. Boardman Jones, Jr. Though we exchanged embraces and salutations, we were both in a hurry to get to meetings. Promising to get together soon, we went our separate ways.

Another thirty-eight years would pass before I would receive a package of old crew pictures and a biography of two tours in the Pacific from W. Boardman Jones, Jr., with an offer to help find old shipmates.

I especially want to thank all of those VP/VPB-23 comrades who shared so generously with me their written memories and/or oral reminiscences. And also historians Jim Mooney and Jim Morrison, for their input and encouragement.

And special thanks to Keith Guthrie, author and VP/VPB-23 comrade, who introduced me to Eakin Press and its knowledgeable staff. Their patience and professional guidance helped bring this book to publication.

Thanks to my good friend and renowned illustrator Bernie Fuchs for his dramatic painting (on the cover) of a lone PBY flying in unsettled skies toward its Pacific mission.

VP/VPB-23

FIRST TOUR
1940-1941

1
A Bittersweet Omen

"In ROTC we trained with Enfield Rifles until they were taken from us to give to the Army."

In 1925 the U.S. Navy engaged in routine maneuvers in the Pacific under the code name of "The Battle of Hawaii." Marking an ominous beginning in naval history was the inclusion of the first aircraft carrier, USS *Langley*, as an operational unit of Aircraft Squadrons, Battle Fleet. That same year two Navy PN-9 flying boats made record-breaking news by flying non-stop from the West Coast to Hawaii. The flight was commanded by "Navy Aviator Number Two," CMDR John Rodgers.

Significant as these events were, another should be mentioned. Some 6,000 miles away, on February 4, 1925, this writer was born.

My "first flight" was up the stairway leading to our third-floor apartment in Chicago. I was brought home from the Lying-in Hospital on Valentine's Day. My older sister, Gen, to this day reminds me that she could hear me crying all the way up. She also remembers that Dad was carrying a red, heart-shaped box of chocolates.

It now seems a bittersweet omen: 1925 was also the year that Hirohito succeeded his father as emperor of Japan. Only four years before, Mussolini had been appointed premier of Italy. And only eight years from the time that Adolph Hitler would become chancellor of Germany.

In January of 1939, as war clouds darkened the horizon, we

were a family of six, and just barely coming out of the "Great Depression." Having made a number of moves, we were not alone in the national crisis that enveloped us.

Mid-semester that February, I graduated from the eighth grade at Hawthorne Elementary Grade School. Mom was working at Morton Company, planning and cooking meals for the employees. Dad, now separated from Mom, lived with his parents not too far away. My older sister, Gen, was working for the Chicago Rapid Transit, and my sister Anna Mae was working as a typist in a National Youth Administration job up at Great Lakes. My brother, Jack, was in school and also working part-time as an usher at a nearby theater.

We all turned over our pay, no matter how small, to Mom. It was she who paid the bills, shopped for the groceries, managed the household, and allowed us to keep a small portion of our earnings. It was Gen who was the biggest breadwinner.

That summer, when I was fourteen, Mom got me an apprentice summer job through her uncle, who lived in Downer's Grove, Illinois. The position at Curt-Teich Lithography Co., an established lithography firm, would provide me with some firsthand knowledge of printing methods, as well as a little prewar intrigue.

It took some spunk for Mom to make a call to her "Uncle Charlie" (who was at odds with my dad), but it landed me the summer job at Curt-Teich on Chicago's south side. My portfolio consisted of several poster paint drawings on shirt-card cardboard. One, a smiling, bell-bottomed and bright-blue-uniformed sailor in white cocked hat, already revealed my nautical leanings.

It was my first real job. As an artist apprentice, I sat at a drafting table and painted skies and landscapes on postcards of famous hotels and tourist attractions, and sharpened up ill-defined photos for color-plate reproduction. The technique was special; today the company's postcards are collector's items. The pictures served as my introduction to famous places all over the USA, and I loved my work.

The men around me were all craftsmen, friendly though very gothic. Many had German accents, as engraving was a trade mastered in Germany. My gentle-faced foreman and mild-mannered mentor was a large but most accomplished engraver named "Hans." He wore a journeyman's apron and would patiently guide me

CHAPTER **1**   *A Bittersweet Omen*   3

through each day's work, giving me tips on handling a brush, painting techniques, and helping me in many ways.

One day in the summer of 1939, two men wearing felt fedoras pulled down over their eyes came in and walked over to Hans, talking very quietly to him. It was like watching a black and white "B" movie. He smiled back nervously, then his face grew grim as they put him in handcuffs. Grasping him by the arm, apron and all, they quickly pulled him right past me and out the door. We were told later that he was a German spy! I felt sorry for him and can still see that kindly face.

At summer's end, I returned to Oak Park High School, eager to start my freshman year. Though a poor student in academics, I excelled in art and soon was drawing for the high school yearbook, sketching with friends and even taking part in intramural sports and a gymnastics show.

In 1940 the papers were full of wolf pack attacks on allied convoys. H. V. Kaltenborn was, along with accompanying radio static, broadcasting overseas reports of the fall of France. Edward R. Murrow came in nightly describing the London Blitz, the valiant Brits, and the RAF fighting against Luftwaffe odds.

After reading that the British Navy was accepting fifteen-year-olds for sea duty, I asked Mom for permission to join up, and got an emphatic "OVER MY DEAD BODY!" and an argument that convinced me to stay in school a little longer.

I joined the Sea Scouts instead, just long enough to get a uniform, a barely basic knowledge of seamanship, and a grand cruise down Chicago's Drainage Canal and up the Chicago River.

Austin High School was a happy move. In 1941, back in school as a junior, I became actively involved with the school's newspaper, *The Austin Times*, and drew cartoons promoting scrap drives, bond drives, and victory gardens.

I also joined the ROTC unit in school. We wore khaki uniforms with blue lapels and white web belt and brass buckle. I spent a lot of time polishing that buckle and my brass buttons with jeweler's rouge, while spit-shining my black shoes. We trained with British Enfield rifles until they were taken from us to give to the Army, which in some cases trained with wooden rifles. I missed my big chance to fire my rifle. I was disappointed to not have been given another chance to fire that British Enfield. The rifles were quickly replaced for fake wooden ones and the old Enfields given to Army inductees who desperately needed them. We were a country not yet prepared for war.

While the attack on Pearl Harbor came as a surprise in 1941, the flames of war had been burning from the start of the Spanish Civil War. At that time the first young Americans went off to fight for the Republic against the Fascist General Franco. They were also volunteering in the French and British forces. Others "hired out" as paid flyers to Chiang Kai-shek's Air Force and would be the first to fly against Japan and achieve fame as the "Flying Tigers" under an American, General Chennault.

The Rape of Nanking would shock the world, and the bombing of the Panay by Japanese planes gave a sober view of what was soon to come.

Prelude to Pearl

America, at the tail end of the Great Depression, wanted no part of another war.

In 1940, Europe was deeply embroiled in war. Germany had invaded Denmark, Norway, Holland, and Belgium. Then Hitler's generals went through Luxembourg and France, and in short time forced a British evacuation at Dunkirk on the English Channel.

Radio commentators reported nightly from abroad. The radio waves were filled with eloquent prose from grim-voiced Winston Churchill extolling valiant Brits, and urging the RAF to fight to the finish against overwhelming Luftwaffe odds.

There were war clouds in Asia, too, as the Japanese extended their grip on Manchuria and the Dutch East Indies. There had been the Panay Incident, where Japanese planes bombed an American gunboat in Chinese waters. And American volunteers had answered General Chiang Kai-shek's call to engage the Japanese in the air war over China, winning fame in General Chennault's "Flying Tigers."

On the island of Oahu in the Territory of Hawaii, it was a "good life," Robin Larson, a pilot in VP-23, reflects:

I was an Ensign then. We were young men—simply enjoying an island paradise that had existed before only in our imaginations.

I joined VP-23 in September of 1941, arriving at Pearl and to a warm reception. We were gradually learning the ways of the islands, and thoroughly enjoying the experience. We even worked tropical hours, 0700 to 1500—seven to three. You could take your surf board and have six hours at the beach, or play eighteen to twenty-seven holes of golf—after work. Watta life!

This doesn't mean that our new lives were not being used to good effect during the duty hours. We had ground school classes to teach us the aircraft, and instructional flying each day. Life was so peaceful and idyllic that we could not believe that the relations between the U.S. and Japan could deteriorate so fast and so soon.

It is difficult for me to commence any statement about Dec. 7, 1941. As young officers recently arrived in Hawaii, none of us were expecting any such thing to happen.

Ens. Robin Larson would go on to serve in all three VP-23 Pacific tours and as executive officer of the squadron its last tour of duty.

C. James Watters, from Texas, remembers:

In June of 1941, after graduating from USNR Midshipman's school, I was commissioned an Ensign. I was ordered to active duty with VP-25, based at Ford Island—when the squadron was redesignated VP-23.

Being a deck officer, I was one of the first non-flying officers assigned to a PBY squadron. LCDR Massie Hughes was skipper, and Lt. Bob Winters was Exec. My first duty assignment was personnel officer with collateral duties involving navigation and bombardier training. I took my turn of being OOD—and whenever feasible, I was assigned to a flight crew for a training hop, or a patrol to practice navigation or use of Norden Bomb Sight.

As the squadron had barely enough pilots to fill the seats at that time, I frequently had the opportunity to do some "uncertified" piloting. Ensign Glen Steward, a pilot with whom I flew on occasion, was often my mentor. Glen was killed attempting a night landing at Pearl with no lights. His plane had been damaged in the coral reefs off Palmyra, temporarily patched, and he was bringing the plane back for major repair.

I was usually included in the advance base operations such as Hilo Bay or Palmyra. This was a great on-the-job training and I could not get enough of it. It really was exhilarating for a 21-year-old ensign.

Saturday mornings were frequently used for "full dress" inspection—sometimes with gloves and sword for those officers not assigned to patrol duty. Hangar, work stations, and offices were also inspected on Saturday prior to permitting the crews to go on liberty at 1300.

Fleet Air Wing Two was under the command of Admiral Patrick N. L. Bellinger. My contact with wing was with the flag secretary—or wings operations officer, CDR Logan Ramsey. Wing operations assigned sector patrols to various squadrons based at Ford Island and Kaneohe.

When not on patrol, squadrons participated in training exercises or simulated war operations with the Pacific Fleet.

Aerial gunnery was practiced on towed target sleeves and water bombs were dropped on floating targets towed by fleet tugs. This was much of the routine prior to the Japanese attack.

The squadron was a close knit organization in off duty hours. The social life was parties, dances, and times at the beach surfboarding and spear fishing. On occasion the officers and enlisted personnel enjoyed a big luau hosted by Hawaiians. The music and hula dancing was the best. The attack on Pearl Harbor was to bring an abrupt change from the pre-war life of the squadron.

C. James Watters' story is one of distinguished service and of unique contribution both on the ground and in the air, as squadron personnel and maintenance officer while serving under the command of CO James Ogden.

Holder of American Defense, Asiatic-Pacific, Victory, and American Theater medals, Jim also cites two Oak Leaf clusters and a few other medals that may have slipped his mind.

After the war, he returned to a family business in Southern California, where he and his wife, Mary, lived for thirty-eight years before moving to Texas.

Aviation Radioman First Class Glenn Pennock from Bellvue, Colorado, recalls when he was assigned to Navy Patrol Squadron VP-23 based at Ford Island Naval Air Station:

> I began flying patrols in a PBY ... a glorified glider which lumbers along at about 100 MPH. Navy Dept. lack of cash limited our patrol excursions typically to just over three hours instead of the 12 to 14 hours and long distance performance range the plane was designed for.
>
> Even so, we knew the Jap subs were out there. We would frequently find Japanese fishing boats slipping in closer than the three-mile limit allowed. We drove them back by strafing across the bow and dropping waste bags the crew used in its commode!

As early as January 16, 1941, Adm. "Pat" Bellinger made his views known to Admiral Stark, Chief of Naval Operations: "The international situation is critical—more so in the Pacific. After taking over command of Patrol Wing Two, and looking over the situation, I am surprised that such an important advanced naval outpost as the Hawaiian Islands is operating on a shoe string—and the more I look, the thinner the shoe string appears to be!"

Arriving in Washington that month, Rear Admiral Bellinger received the following message: "Atlantic Operations *first* priority—America and her allies in the Pacific must *remain on the defensive* until men and materiel are ready for offensive operations."

Admiral Bellinger then set about doing what he could in preparing for the coming conflict and reported that 50 pilots and 250 enlisted men in each of his squadrons were carrying out 300-mile patrols seven days a week.

In July of 1941, he reported five patrol squadrons in operation on the West Coast: Patrol Squadrons 22, 23, 24, 25, 26—including Patrol Squadron 27, newly commissioned in June of 1941. Patrol Wing One was transferred to Kaneohe from San Diego.

In 1941, Pat Bellinger, commander of Patrol Wing Two, was holder of many "firsts." Beginning his flying career as Navy Aviator No. 8, he piloted the first Navy plane to come under fire at Vera Cruz in 1914. He made the first catapult test and first nighttime seaplane flight, and also set a record for seaplane altitude flight. He helped to establish the first Naval Aviation Training Center at Pensacola, Florida.

He was commanding officer of the Aircraft Tender USS *Wright* in 1928; the Aircraft Carrier USS *Langley* in 1933; and the USS *Ranger* in 1936. In 1940, after serving as CO of NOB, Norfolk, Virginia, he was assigned to PatWing Two—by that time earning the title "Father of Naval Seaplane Aviation."

Now under Adm. James O. Richardson, commander in chief of the Pacific Fleet, Admiral Bellinger wore many hats and bore the following responsibilities:

1. Commander Aircraft Scouting Force, Pacific Fleet, based at San Diego.
2. Commander Hawaiian Based Patrol Wings.
3. Commander Patrol Wing Two, in addition to those seaplane tenders assigned him by the Fleet Commander.
4. Commander Task Force Nine, which included Patrol Wings One and Two.
5. Commander Fleet Air Detachment Pearl Harbor (all aircraft at NAS Ford Island!).

6. Liaison with Commandant 14th Naval District Adm. Claude E. Bloch, for Aviation Developments within the district including Midway, Wake, Palmyra, Johnston Islands, and Australia.
7. In addition, he was Commander Task Force Four, home based in Seattle, Washington, rotating its squadrons of VP-41, 42, and 43 on station in Alaska, Naval Base Defense Air Force.

In 1940 LCDR Francis Massie Hughes assumed command of Patrol Squadron 25 at Pearl Harbor. The squadron of PBY-2 flying boats would soon be redesignated Patrol Squadron 23. (Massie's crew would be first to get airborne during the December 7 Pearl Harbor attack by the Japanese Navy.)

VP-23 had just received brand new PBY-5s from San Diego in early November, and prior to the attack they were being flown for checkout and training.

Lt. Howard Ady, Jr., recollects:

> We flew our old PBY-2s back to San Diego to pick up new PBY-5s. After a week's wait, we were finally able to take off, and on November 22, 1941, with the help of marginal winds, headed back. Unable to make it to Pearl, we landed at Hilo on the big island and waited there for a fuel barge before returning to Ford Island. [Editor's note: Ady was back at Pearl Harbor on the morning of the attack.]

Gale Burkey, VP-23 Enlisted Naval Aviation Pilot, writes:

> About mid-1941, we doubled up our "readiness" status—someone out there knew we had a Japanese threat on our hands.
> We went from one section of four on duty for 24 hours—to two sections on alert status—actually sleeping in the hangar and next to our planes. Even our food was brought to us. That's where I was at 0800 December 7, 1941.

On that Sunday morning of December 7, Admiral Bellinger reported that forces under his command were disposed as follows: Patrol Squadron 21 at Midway; Patrol Squadrons 11, 12, and 14 at Kaneohe; Patrol Squadrons 22, 23, and 24 at Pearl Harbor; all seaplane tenders except the USS *Wright* were at Pearl Harbor. The Seaplane Tender USS *Wright* was en route to Pearl Harbor from Midway.

Condition Readiness was "Baker 5" (which put 50% of assigned aircraft on four hours' notice) with machine guns and ammunition in all planes except those undergoing maintenance work.

This was augmented by specific duty assignments on December 7 which required six planes from Patrol Squadrons 14, 24, and 12 to be ready for flight on thirty minutes' notice. However, general orders were modified that morning by circumstances and planes actually ready for flight, which, in fact, left Patrol Squadron 23 with only eleven planes ready on four hours' notice—among the total of seventy-two planes ready for flight from Patrol Wing Two!

In this condition, Bellinger noted that four-hour notice was primarily to permit rest and recreation of personnel, and was in no way a criterion of material readiness. One plane of VP-23 theoretically on four hours' notice was actually in the air forty-five minutes after the first bomb dropped.

To summarize, Admiral Bellinger went on to say: "... from the moment the first bomb dropped, aircraft of this command were in the following condition: 14 were in the air, 7 on search at Midway, 58 were on the surface ready for flight in four hours or less; and 9 were undergoing repairs."

The urgent necessity for conducting daily searches after December 7 and for putting all planes back in commission, together with an urgency for immediate operations, have precluded an exhaustive analysis of the events of the day. Certain highlights, however, may be of interest:

- All planes in commission had guns on board, together with full allowance of service ammunition.
- Days and weeks prior to the attack, VP-23 was involved in patrol "sector" flights from Oahu. In the predawn hours of December 7, 1941, Adm. Pat Bellinger's Catalinas were out there—but the patrol emphasis was on the southern and western approaches to Oahu, not the northeast sector! There were not enough planes to cover the 360 degrees. In short, a hole was left in the patrol curtain.

In a later report, Pat Bellinger would point out that the wind coming from the northeast actually facilitated recovery of returning Japanese aircraft!

The Japanese Attack

"Climb Mt. Niitaka"—radio signal that sent 353 Japanese carrier planes at dawn on December 7, 1941, to bomb the American fleet at Pearl Harbor.

At 0745 the first wave of Zeros made their attack. At 0758 Operations Officer LCDR Logan C. Ramsey, Fleet Air Wing Two, was in the radio room. After a hurried call to Admiral Bellinger, he began broadcasting the terse alarm on all frequencies: "Air raid, Pearl Harbor—this is no drill! Air raid, Pearl Harbor—*this is no drill!*"

Adm. Pat Bellinger would later report:

Japanese dive bombers concentrated on parked planes at Ford Island destroying most of the squadron's PBYs in less than a minute. Two bombs hit VP-23's PBYs lined up wing to wing outside the squadron's hangar, knocking out eight planes.

One plane got airborne during the attack ... three others would get airborne after the attack. A VP-23 plane returning from early morning patrol was involved in the sighting and destruction of a mini sub outside the entrance to the harbor.

During the first attack, fire was opened from the guns mounted in the planes. When it was discovered that these were not effective for fire from the ground due to structural interference, many personnel removed these guns from the planes together with full allowances of ammunition, and set them up on benches in vises—opening up effective fire against the second attack.

In another report, Admiral Bellinger praised the actions of VP-23 Commander Massie Hughes, who was also in command of all squadrons at Pearl and Kaneohe. Both Commander Hughes and LCDR James Ogden, Executive Officer, had quarters on Ford Island.

Wrote the Admiral: "... Even as the second wave was about and the sky was filled with anti-aircraft fire, Commander Hughes took off in the only undamaged plane at Ford Island—to search out Japanese carriers. He did not have to do so, but he seized the opportunity and flew off. I take my hat off to him."

C. James Watters of VP-23 wrote:

When the attack started, I was in BOQ with my assigned roommate Ensign Hal Lough (later killed in a PB2Y accident on the Atlantic Coast). We were shaken by tremendous explosions—and looking out our window, we saw a Japanese plane making a low strafing run right over adjacent officers and BOQ. The pilot had his canopy pushed back—and we could look right into his face!

We pulled on our khakis and hailed a ride to the hangar area. Enroute we saw the USS *Utah* overturned, and upon reaching our aircraft parking area, we found several of our planes burning. All hands were trying to move aircraft not yet burning, from burning ones. Some men removed machine guns from the burning planes, firing them without any support.

Eleven of twelve aircraft were damaged, three planes were pieced together and four planes were flyable before the day was over. The hangar area had bomb craters and shrapnel everywhere. Our casualties from the attack were very few and it is unbelievable, as all of us were moving around in this area under siege.

The four days following the attack were spent living at the hangar, sleeping on a cot, with mosquito netting an absolute necessity. Meals were served twice a day with drinking water brought from the swimming pool.

For the first few hours it was presumed that invasion was a real possibility. After a couple of days, that thought was dispelled as patrols had ascertained that no enemy units were anywhere near.

Clean-up and repair of operations could be formulated. Sector patrols and courier trips to Johnson Island, Canton, Palmyra and Midway Islands for the movement of personnel, supplies and operational plans made up the daily routine until VP-23 was directed to proceed to Midway Island and subsequent Battle of Midway ...

I was flying with Executive Officer Lt. Hugh Winters, Ensign Bucky

CHAPTER 3 The Japanese Attack

Earnest, and Chief Aviation Pilot Bill Chase. (Actually the PPC was CAP Bill Chase, assigned to the crew because Lt. Winters was not the best pilot.) We flew our patrols as ordered, and could not believe that we had missed the Japanese fleet. Of course, we found out later that their carriers and attack force had come from the northeast—and not the west!

Coming back into Pearl Harbor was another story. First of all, we had no real recognition or radar recognition signs as they do now. The only thing they could think of for the returning planes was to instruct pilots to make a right turn off Diamond Head on the even hour and a left turn on the odd hour. As you can imagine this left a lot to be desired. We made our turn and headed toward Pearl Harbor—so far, so good. It was dusk as we were landing and we knew that the Pearl Harbor channel was filled with debris, and even a contact with the smallest log at our landing speed would tear the bottom out of our PBY, and that we would crash and probably flip over. Most of this kind of accident in our type of airplane resulted with the loss of the whole crew. Again the Lord was with us. We landed without hitting anything, and safely taxied back to our ramp—and pulled up by our beach crew.

As we relaxed for a minute before heading for our hangar, some hundred yards away, a flight of three aircraft came flying over. Suddenly, someone had decided this was another enemy attack—and everyone let loose. We threw ourselves to the deck as flat as a person can be, and laid there for several minutes. I have never seen so many bullets heading in so many directions!

Our people were "trigger happy." They had survived a terrible experience only a few hours before and they wanted to shoot at someone and they did! All three of *our* carrier planes were shot down. One crash landed in a corn field, one bailed out and one went down in the channel but amazingly they all survived.

When this was over Lt. Winters and I went to the BOQ to see if we could get clothing. On our way, along the west side of our airfield, there were road entrances into various hangars—where sentries with loaded guns were posted. At the first one we came to the sentry challenged "Stop or I'll shoot!" as we started to pass. And shoot he meant. He had not been briefed properly. He was to guard the entrance to the hangar, NOT the road around the field, but he represented the feeling of desperation that night—some ten hours after the attack!

What we did not know until we arrived was that families of married officers living on Ford Island had been taken to BOQ because it offered a safer building than their frame houses. It also gave them a better sense of security to be with other families. And so they were assigned to our rooms. Squadron officers would be living at the hangar for a few days.

We also did not know that the many survivors from ships that had been sunk were also taken to our BOQ—and told to help themselves to our clothing. Most of them had nothing except whatever clothing they might have had on at the time of the attack—and in some cases that was very little! We were happy to share what we had with them. We took a few items of clothing and toilet articles and went back to our hangar and our cots.

Next day was most interesting as you could see every conceivable combination of clothing possible. Enlisted men with officer's shirt, coat cap, tuxedo shirts and pants—anything at all that could be worn. After a few days, this was taken care of by opening Navy clothing shops and providing money and checks to those who had lost billfolds and pay records, as well as their clothing. It was a time of great confusion, and it could have been really humorous, if it hadn't been so serious to our nation.

That morning, resident voyager and outer island worker Jim Powlison and his poet wife Nani had a grandstand seat from which to give an eyewitness account of the Pearl Harbor attack. Some years earlier, the newlyweds had journeyed to Hawaii fresh from college to find and build their dream house. Nani Powlison writes:

> It was upon one of the highest points on the Island of Oahu that our "Hilltop House" sat—a stone's throw to the water's edge one hundred and seventy-five feet below. Eight little offshore islands came within the range of vision; and on many days Molokai, Maui and Lanai, large islands of the Hawaiian group, loomed up in the ocean southeast of their home. Honolulu was but fourteen miles away. Dividing that distance, one could look up to the world famous Pali gap in the lush green mountains of the Koolau Range. People from far away are forever asking us if on that fateful morning from our Hilltop, we were aware of the attack while it was happening. We were all awake despite the early Sunday morning hour— we were up with a weekend house full of friends, having savored a full night of light-as-day moonlight.
>
> Hearing a heavy booming, we speculated the explosions were to carelessness of some sort, that first focused our attention to Kaneohe Naval Air Station, a short distance from the bay. In the dense black smoke and flames rising high in the sky, we saw no airplanes. Then suddenly flying low, for they met no resistance, and coming straight at us in formation, was a whole squadron of unfamiliar planes.
>
> As they zoomed by close to our windows, some at eye level and some below us, so clearly visible were insignias of the rising sun, glinting on the bright metallic blue wings. We could also see who was piloting them, and its impact—that it was they who had destroyed Kaneohe Naval Air Station.

CHAPTER **3**   *The Japanese Attack*   15

Then came a sudden awareness of how our hilltop might appear to them—like a bit of fortification! As if our fear took form, one fighter plane dropped out of formation, and as we almost ceased to breathe, circled our home.

We will never know to what we owe to the fact that he did not fire, but he went on his way to the Army Air Field at Bellows with other planes. It may be that the few articles of laundry on the line, obviously feminine and color of pink, may have been the reason.

After minutes more and Bellows Field wiped out . . . we were again in the beeline of the attackers roaring back towards their carriers to the northwest of our island. An Army plane did succeed in getting into the air, but without ammunition and riddled with enemy bullets, we watched at our windows as it journeyed in our direction a scant two miles, and then plummeted headlong into Kailua Bay. It was another soul shaking emotion added to a list of unfamiliar ones of that hour!

And our plunge from normal living and perfect peace to complete blackout and wicked war had been almost too rapid for our own survival. But we did survive—and so did Puuhonua, despite the fact that the Army, a few days later, asked us to move out of Hilltop House and turn it over to them for the duration.

Although we were moved out, Hilltop House must have symbolized a special place to the men in the service assigned duty throughout the war at the observation point, and they took beautiful care of it. Not one initial or heart was carved in the wood, nor did they chip the rocks. And we would return again to our little house on the hilltop to resume our peaceful lives.

Glenn E. Pennock, S1/C ARM, VP-23 aircrewman, tells it this way:

I will never forget that 7th of December Sunday morning in 1941—when the Japanese attack on Pearl Harbor killed 2,403 people and shook our nation from its isolationist slumber dragging it into another bloody world war.

On the morning of the attack on Pearl Harbor, I was in a sweet, deep slumber after a Saturday night's celebration at a Waikiki Tavern—when I was abruptly shaken awake by thundering explosions.

I was astounded by the onslaught of Japanese bombers—and to see aircraft with the red meatball flying down the channel so coolly searching for targets. The dive bombers were screeching down dropping their bombs—and their wingtips were smoking from the humid air.

I remember leaping into the bow of a seaplane to get its .30 caliber into action, only to discover the sights had been removed to protect them from rust. Using tracers, I managed to hit three aircraft—putting perhaps 10 rounds into one Zero that just kept flying around as if nothing happened!

I also remember a radioman in my squadron who, grabbing a gun from another seaplane, carried it to a tail elevator and somehow, shooting from the hip, downed a Zero.

The Japanese torpedo planes knew the location of their targets and executed their runs with cool precision. The Zero fighters were strafing everything in sight. An ammunition magazine was hit on the destroyer *Shaw* across the bay which was in dry-dock. The explosion went 500 feet in the air.

I could not believe how colorful a battle could be! In the early morning during the first attack, the only easy-access ammunition was colored practice ammo. The whole sky was covered with puff balls of orange, red, brown, green and yellow instead of the white puffs left by regular ammunition.

And sailors were showing up wearing bright, colorful Hawaiian sports shirts taken, we learned later, from a haber-dashery shop in town whose wall had been blown out. One vivid but grim reminder the day after the attack was the bright orange rusty ruin of the USS *Arizona*, and other ships that had burned and exposed the metal to salt air. Not so colorful were the remnants of the previously new PBY Catalina seaplanes which were nearly melted into the ground.

Nevertheless we were out the next day as survivors doing what we should have been doing earlier—conducting extended reconnaissance missions! For rations we had only hard-tack, candy bars and swimming pool water. (The Japanese had also damaged the water system, forcing survivors to drink the only remaining water available.)

The mess hall was out of commission—now used for holding the 900 bodies of Marines and civilians all laid out in neat rows. Passing through the mess hall morgue, I realized that war was a deadly business and later wrote in my diary:

"Be it ever resolved:
1. We must make every effort to get enough food to sustain life.
2. We must make every effort to stay alive.
3. We must not go to Waikiki Tavern on Saturday nights and do battle the next morning.
4. We must stop drinking swimming pool water!"

Such scarcity, however, prepared me and my crew for the dangers and deprivations we would continue to suffer.

CHAPTER 3 The Japanese Attack

A Pearl Harbor survivor attached to VP-23 from 1941 to 1943, Glenn won a promotion for his heroic conduct in action against the enemy and is holder of the Distinguished Flying Cross and four Air Medals.

Gale Burkey, then an enlisted Naval air pilot in VP-23, remembers:

> I think I saw the very first bomb before it hit the ground! Needless to say, I was quite upset about the whole thing. The reason I saw it is because I was on alert in the hangar that morning having coffee and getting ready for a flight.
>
> We had twelve planes on the ramp, warmed up and ready to go on a few moments notice. Four more were inside the hangar undergoing maintenance. At 0800 sharp, hearing a low flying aircraft pulling out of a dive, looked out the hangar door and got my first close up view ...
>
> At that point it became shockingly apparent that this was no drill. Bombs were exploding in our formation of ready airplanes—which were soon wiped out completely.
>
> With a lot of sky-gazing, we could see much of the ongoing attack taking place about us. Large formations of Japanese planes flying horizontally high in the sky, torpedo planes pulling up low overhead—having just dropped their fish on the battleships moored next door to our ramp!
>
> Many fighters were buzzing around, firing at anything that moved. It seemed an eternity before any of our guns started shooting back, and we saw none of our own aircraft in the air. We didn't want to take cover in the hangar—it seemed their next logical target. Actually, only one of the three PBY hangars on seaplane point was not destroyed.
>
> Finally we were heartened to see some return AA fire ... and a couple of "rising suns" bite the dust. Then, after a half hour or so we saw some of our own aircraft, but wish we hadn't. The Navy carrier planes, flying low and slow in a landing configuration, were attempting to land at Luke Field next door.
>
> In retrospect, they had been launched by our own carriers at sea—and presumably had been ordered to land at Ford Island. I don't know why, but they were being shot down while in a landing pattern ... and on the runway, by either Japanese fighters or worse—maybe by our own AA batteries!
>
> Then there was the flight of B-17s arriving from the U.S. West Coast into the center of this mess. They were low on gas, had no apparent communication with the ground and appeared to be trapped at the low altitude against the Pali mountains. I don't know if any of these were shot down.

Back at our own hangar during the next two hours all available hands, or half of the squadron, was working feverishly to get the four planes undergoing maintenance into shape. By 10 A.M., Lt. Kellam and I with a pick-up crew commandeered the second plane to get "buttoned up" into flight condition. I think the skipper, CO Massie Hughes, took the first one. Our beaching crew soon had us in the water (a flaming, oily cluttered mess!). Our orders: to seek out and destroy the Japanese carriers!

Our bombardier reported, "Skipper, we have no bombsight—the bombsight lockers were locked and no one had the key."

Our Patrol Plane Commander Lt.(jg) Joe Kellam responded, "Never mind, we'll dive bomb the carrier when we find it!"

Airborne by 10:30, we proceeded northeast looking for the Japanese carriers ... with no idea of where they were ... to my knowledge none of the three or four planes that got airborne ever discovered the carriers that day.

The search bearings given us were nowhere near the location of the Japanese forces. We did sight a surfaced enemy sub at the mouth of the Pearl Harbor channel on our departure, but he was not our target for that day.

Anyway, we searched for some nine hours that day and into the night with negative results. Actually, we felt quite comfortable to get away from the early morning dive bombers, but were uneasy about having a place to come back to.

It turned out that the worst part of the flight was in trying to get back into Pearl Harbor in the dark that night. Ground gunners were shooting, not only at falling stars but at moving PBYs too! To make matters worse, we had a landing light stuck down, so we made a nice target. It took three or four passes over Ewa before we could be identified, but fortunately our landing was uneventful except for logs and debris in the oily waters.

So much for Dec. 7th 1941 except for a sleepless night in the only hangar that was still there. Thinking back to those years, I'm grateful to have gotten through so many battles and to have successfully flown missions totalling 10,000 hours.

Initially, Burkey was on the scene as an enlisted naval air pilot. Then, winning a war promotion to ensign, he flew with VP-23 through Pearl Harbor, participating in the Battle of Midway and the Solomon campaigns. In 1943 he was assigned to the European theater of war and flew Liberators out of England. Capt. Gale Burkey is the recipient of two Distinguished Flying Crosses and six Air Medals.

Frank Shacklett, ARM 3/C PHS, VP-23 ('41-'42), said of squadron Skipper Massie Hughes:

CHAPTER **3** *The Japanese Attack* 19

I was on the beaching crew that Sunday morning, and we launched him to go look for the Japanese carriers.

Later, we were very happy to learn that he did NOT find any part of any fleet—for we could well visualize a catastrophe resulting from the confusion, where those two war horses might have tried to go at each other. (I know how mad Massie Hughes was, and I heard later that Admiral Halsey was in a frothing rage.) ... and I'm pretty sure that the PBY would have lost out against squadrons of SBDs and F4Fs.

Will start here and mention things that come to mind that really don't belong in my history. I came out of ARM school at San Diego Air Station in June of '41 and was assigned to a squadron (don't recall which one) and then was transferred out to Pearl to VP-23 within weeks.

So I must have been almost a plank owner. At Ford Island I did a three-month stint of mess cooking, then got off of that on Dec. 1st, when I made third class, and turned 19 years old. I thought I had it made.

A week later came the 7th of December, and I was assigned to a flight crew to fly many of the 12 to 15 hour patrols for the next few months.

Glen Rickard, AMM1/C, VP-23 ('41) had this memory:

I was stationed at Ford Island with VP-23 and was a tractor driver for the beach crew when Pearl Harbor was attacked on Dec. 7th.

That morning it was my job to drive the tractor, so I hooked up to the rear of a PBY waiting for the pilot to arrive. A gray sedan pulled up along side the airplane ... and to my surprise out jumped Commander Hughes in red pajamas, a robe and slippers! He proceeded on into the airplane, taxied down the ramp and took off. He returned several hours later wearing the same clothes! Thanks for the memories.

Albert L. Brown, aviation chief radioman at the outbreak of WWII, flew with Lt.(jg) Winters' crew along with ACRM Julian Parker and recalls:

I was having breakfast with Julian at the Navy exchange the morning of Dec 7th when the attack began. During a lull, we looked around for a machine gun to set up, but we couldn't find any, so we ran over to the armory. No luck there either, so we asked for a couple of rifles. They told us they were out of them, too. As we started to walk away, we had another thought. A shake of the head told us that there were no pistols either!

I remember Chief Parker throwing up his arms in exasperation and shouting: "Let's go get us some rocks! At least we'll have something to fight back with!"

M. Chuck Hubbell, LCDR, USN Ret.:

As a Seaman 2/C, I arrived at Pearl Harbor November 19, 1941, and was assigned to Patrol Squadron Twenty-three. Home port was NAS Ford Island in the middle of Pearl Harbor. On the morning of Dec. 7th, I mustered with the duty section at 0745 and assumed "first hangar watch"—as the rest of the crew returned to barracks. At 0755, I heard the whine of aircraft diving—and went outside to observe two 3-plane sections which I recognized immediately as Japanese. Watching in disbelief for a few seconds I saw VP-21 and VP-22 Hangars were hit hard—as well as the many parked PBY-5 aircraft.

Dashing back into the hangar, I tried to go out the rear door—but was knocked down by a bomb explosion. I then picked myself up and proceeded diagonally across the hangar to the front, fully expecting to be killed. I was lucky because this was the only hangar that did not get hit.

Upon going outside, I remember a drainage ditch was nearby and attempted to take a line tied to a nearby pad-eye, and lower myself into the 10-11 foot deep trench. However, due to strafing by low flying planes and with machine gun bullets hitting inches from my head I let go and fell heavily, injuring my left knee.

After about ten minutes, I recovered from my initial shock and was able to proceed to the front of the hangar to assist a few of the duty section personnel who had made it back from the barracks. We set up fifty caliber machine guns on tripods, normally utilized to clean the weapons.

A senior PO 1/C did the firing and I fed the ammo. We had no luck, because on every shot the gun mounted on the tripod kicked back, making accuracy impossible. In fact one Jap, in an open cockpit, actually thumbed his nose at us on one pass! After an hour of low level attack we had a short lull, soon followed by high altitude bombing (10,000 feet).

Watching our ships fire back and cheering when they scored hits was about all we could do. Our skipper soon appeared and as I was on the beach crew, I went into the harbor to remove the Port side mount and stow it for their return. It was during this time that the USS *Shaw* munitions blew up, knocking me down with a large wheel—further hurting my left leg.

One of the most stirring sights was the Battleship USS *Nevada* proceeding towards the channel and after many hits, the Captain beached her so that the ship's 16-inch guns covered the entrance to Pearl Harbor.

The next twenty-four hours was spent filling sand bags and setting up gun crews. I was given a .30 caliber, which I had never fired but fortunately had field stripped as part of practical factors to making S 1/C. There was no sleep due to depth charging of Midget subs and the firing at anything that flew. Unfortunately, the USS *Enterprise* sent her planes

CHAPTER 3 *The Japanese Attack*

in to land and as we were not informed some "friendly fire" hit a few of them.

I could write a book on the Pearl Harbor attack, which was the most memorable 24 hours of my 28 years as a gunner and aviator, of many other combat situations I would participate in.

Lt. Clarence Mykland ('44-'45) summarizes his experience on December 7, 1941:

I was on a destroyer task group escorting Bull Halsey's USS *Enterprise*, and heading back to Pearl Harbor after escorting a group of Marine fighters to Wake Island in November of '41.

Our destroyer ran into rough water and had to slow its pace. The ship was about 150 miles from its destination on Sunday Dec. 7th, when Pearl Harbor was bombed. The USS *Maury* was able to make it into the harbor the next morning only to witness utter devastation. Oil was spilled everywhere, and ships were burning and turned over.

We were given orders to immediately refuel, restock supplies, and head back to sea to look for Japanese subs. To this day, I can't believe how they got through and bombed Pearl Harbor.

After two more years of Destroyer duty, I was given the opportunity to apply for flight training. I was sent back to Tacoma, Washington, where I married my sweetheart, Barbara. Then moved to Florida where I won my wings, became a flight instructor, witnessed the birth of our first child and then sent to the South Pacific to join—Patrol Bombing Squadron Twenty-Three!

4 The Radio Tells Us

"A day that will live in infamy."—FDR

In the days of deep depression, the nation took spirit and was kept in laughter by radio.

Daytime radio included such soap operas as Myrt & Marge, Ma Perkins, Life Can Be Beautiful, Road of Life, The Goldbergs, and One Man's Family. It was George Burns & Gracie Allen, Eddie Cantor, Fibber McGee & Molly, Fred Allen, Red Skelton, Amos & Andy—and so much more!

As kids, we listened to Tom Mix and his Ralston Straight Shooters, Little Orphan Annie, Jack Armstrong—the All-American Boy, Dick Tracy, and Flash Gordon. There were multitudes of "radio clubs" with secret passwords, boxtop badges, and whistles to send away for. Radio was our nation's—and our family's—main source of entertainment.

There were also newspapers, magazines, and movies. The Saturday morning matinee was for us kids, and the give-away dish and games lured the adults. But radio was prime entertainment—and the family binder.

With the election of Franklin Delano Roosevelt in 1932 and his frequent "Fireside Chats," our family's radio listening took on a new dimension of hope and promise as our president rallied a despairing nation. National news had become a daily prime source for

CHAPTER 4 The Radio Tells Us

instant information as war clouds loomed closer and added a strange urgency to everyday life. It was the radio that brought the nation, and my family, into World War II.

In Chicago, Illinois, on December 7, 1941, a broadcast some 6,000 miles away informed listeners of a bombing attack on an unfamiliar place called Pearl Harbor in Hawaii, and sent shockwaves through a nation.

A startled and discomforting family reaction came as our Sunday's radio entertainment was suddenly interrupted by a scratchy and static-filled overseas news broadcast of a tragedy occurring in a place we had never heard of. Gathered in our small living room, we listened to a crackling radio broadcast as a news commentator excitedly fed us short spoonfuls of startling information. In rapid succession, the radio voice from that faroff place told of a disaster: "The Japanese have just bombed Pearl Harbor! The president and his cabinet are meeting! The president will be making an announcement soon... Stay tuned! And now, back to Jack Benny!"

Looking at faces around me for some explanation, someone asked: "Where is Pearl Harbor?"

"Quiet! Listen to the radio. They'll tell us!" was the reply.

It might have been radio commentator Robert Trout, or Edward R. Murrow, or H.V. Kaltenborn, but the voice coming from overseas told us: "Pearl Harbor... a Naval Base on the island of Oahu... in Hawaii... a surprise attack by the Japanese Navy and Air Forces on American ships anchored along 'Battleship Row'... sunk and decimated... an undisclosed number of dead—and more trapped or lost in the burning inferno of thick oil on waters, blackened clouds of choking smoke, and bombed wreckage of sunken iron hulls."

The radio voice continued with reports of other enemy aggression in the Philippines, and of calling up the nation's armed forces. Soon the president would make the inevitable declaration of war.

I remember the worried face of my mother as she looked up from her sewing and glanced at my brother and me, saying: "Well, thank God, my boys are too young. They won't be going off to any war!" The faces of my two older sisters, Genevieve and Anna Mae, showed immediate concern. Both had prospective husbands of draft age. The selective service boards would be put into high gear.

The next day, at Austin High School in Chicago, I joined other classmates around stairwells, hall lockers, and in classrooms in excited dialogue that took priority as teachers relaxed scheduled procedure to allow student reaction.

Then, sitting at desks in our homerooms, we heard the president's voice piped over the school's sound system: "Ladies and Gentlemen: The President of the United States..."

Not a sound was made as classmates exchanged nervous glances and looked up at the speaker to hear Franklin Delano Roosevelt's words resounding over every classroom. The static-filled radio broadcast only accented the gravity of the situation. President Roosevelt began speaking in short, terse sentences. Detailing events of this tragic "day of infamy," the nation's commander in chief reflected the common mood of the nation's surprise, anger, and outrage and accented a pledge to seek out and strike down the enemy. He continued: "... a deliberate attack upon the United States ... unprovoked and dastardly ... by Japanese Imperial Forces at Pearl Harbor."

As I glanced about the room, I saw my classmates and teacher in seriousness never quite seen before. Some heads were angled upwards to the speaker; others had hands cupped to their ears. The president continued: "There is no blinking from the grave danger that we are in, but I am confident that with unbounding determination, we will gain inevitable victory!"

His words rang true and would be remembered: "Yesterday, December 7, 1941, a date that will live in infamy, the United States was suddenly and deliberately attacked by the Naval and Air Forces of the Empire of Japan." He went on to list the areas attacked by the Japanese on the same day and night: Malaya, Hong Kong, Guam, Philippine Islands, Wake, and Midway, reiterating: "No matter how long it may take us to overcome this premeditated invasion, the American people in their righteous might will win through to absolute victory ... with confidence in our armed forces—with the unbounded determination of our own people—we will gain the inevitable triumph, so help us God." He then asked Congress for a declaration of war.

To those of us attending school that Monday, December 8, of 1941, his words would make an indelible mark and begin a perilous journey into four catastrophic years of a decimating war which in the end would exact over 400,000 lives. Among those would be classmates sitting at the desks surrounding mine.

Others were those whose lives were already at risk as pilots and aircrewmen of VP-23 stationed at Pearl Harbor in the squadron I was destined to join.

Many seniors had already enlisted and were on the school's "In Service" Honor Roll. It would be a war wreaking havoc in all forms—swallowing the lives of desperate men lost at sea or killed on beachheads littered with decimated tanks, in sunken amphibs, and in planes whose crews went down in flames while flying the perimeters of hell.

At age fifteen, a sophomore at Austin High School, and a kid who had never ventured but a few miles from home, I could only wonder: "Where *is* Pearl Harbor?"

Pearl Harbor. It would become a name and a place the nation would never forget—and a time-mark in history of what was the beginning of more catastrophic consequences to come. Just as "Remember the Maine!" was a battle-cry in the Spanish-American War and "Remember the Alamo" the call to arms for Texas independence, "Remember Pearl Harbor!" united a troubled and divided America together in common bond. The surprise attack abruptly ended the lethargy and isolation of an America struggling out of the muck of the Great Depression—and hurled it into a world war.

So the radio told us: Pearl Harbor.

ooo

At Ford Island, the aircrews of U.S. Navy Patrol Bomber Squadron 23, with most of their planes decimated, were angrily regrouping. After fighting off two waves of enemy air attacks with machine guns and small-arms fire, fighting fires, and somehow managing to get their few flyable planes down the ramps and into the water to take off after the enemy, the squadron personnel were now salvaging damaged PBYs and getting back to operational order as they, too, listened to radio reports of an advancing enemy. An enemy they would be called upon to hold at bay—in a defensive action to buy more time for an unprepared nation that would fight a war on two fronts.

These were the men of VP-23. Some of them I was destined to meet. Overseas they would be listening to "Tokyo Rose," who played nostalgic music and engaged in defeatist chatter to bring down American morale. While in the United States it was radio music that was sending the boys marching off to war: "Better Buy Bonds Today"; "Remember Pearl Harbor"; "The Army Air Corps"; "Off We Go—Into the Wild Blue Yonder"; the Marines hymn; "God Bless America!"

Just by turning the dial listeners could enjoy the music of Glenn Miller, Artie Shaw, Tommy Dorsey, Fred Waring, Kay Kyser, Clyde McCoy, Dick Jurgens, Paul Whiteman, and Duke Ellington. These and others provided music to dance by as the boys trained for war—while the radio "Hit Parade" of favorite songs kept morale up and hopes high with songs like "Don't Sit Under the Apple Tree" to tug at the heartstrings of so many boys gone to war and the girls they would leave behind...

When the Lights Go On Again

When the lights go on again ... all o'er the world,
And the boys are home again all o'er the world,
And rain or snow is all ... that may fall from the skies above,
And a kiss won't mean "good-bye" ... but" hello" to love;
When the lights go on again ... all o'er the world,
And the ships will sail again ... all o'er the world
Then we'll have times for things ... like wedding rings,
And "Free" hearts will sing ... when lights go on again
All o'er the world!
When we have our victory ... and we've added to history
We'll be right there to see ... how sweet and simple life can be.
When the lights go on again—all o'er the world.
—1942 PORGIE MUSIC CORP
Bennie Benjamin Music, Inc.

Wake Island
DECEMBER 8, 1941

On December 18, Ensign "Murph" and his VP-23 crew were assigned the task of slipping into Wake.

On December 8, 1941, the Japanese Invasion Force attacked Wake Island. Thirty-six bombers flying out of a rain squall from Roi in the Marshalls bombed and strafed Wake Island, the most "heavily defended" U.S. atoll in the Pacific.

Lacking radar, the Marine garrison had but fifteen minutes' warning—little time for the anti-aircraft gunners to man their guns or for pilots of the F4F fighters, recently delivered by the USS *Enterprise*, to scramble into action. Explosions destroyed seven of the precious fighters; fires consumed the large gasoline storage tank; and twelve Marines died along with six staff members of the Pan-Am Hotel.

Only a few years earlier, the U.S. Navy had begun construction of an air and submarine base on tiny Wake Island, a two-and-a-half-square-mile island lying in a horseshoe-shaped lagoon.

Now a Marine defense force of 447 men commanded by Maj. James P. Devereux, together with a small contingent of Army and some 1,100 construction workers under the command of CMDR W. S. Cunningham, USN, first repulsed the enemy. Then for the next fifteen days, the gallant defenders held world attention until December 23, when forced to surrender. Some 1,616 Americans became prisoners of war and most were taken to Japan and China.

Pan Am's flying boat *Philippine Clipper* escaped with only twenty-four bullet holes and was able to take off with seventy airline personnel and wounded from Wake. As Captain Hamilton piloted his course northeastward, he radioed back that a Japanese cruiser and destroyers were headed for tiny Wake.

On December 18, Ens. James "Murph" Murphy and his VP-23 crew were assigned the task of slipping into Wake before the anticipated invasion attacks took place. It was to be one last mission to deliver needed equipment, get intelligence information, and bring a Marine communications officer off the beleaguered island.

Ensign Murphy and crew carried out their mission and took off just ten minutes before the enemy invasion fleet arrived. They were: Flight Crew #1: PPC Ens. James J. Murphy; 1st Pilot Ens. Francis C. Riley; Ens. Howard P. Ady, Jr.; NAP J. A. Spraggins, RM1/C; Glenn E. Pennock, RM3/C; Art Hampy, AMM1/C; and Cheney. The following personal reports are from four crewmembers of that flight.

PPC Ens. James J. "Murph" Murphy, VP-23:

First Day: Dec. 18, 1941—EST Departed Pearl Harbor 0610 in 23-P-4. Proceeded to Midway. The plane was beached on ramp, refueled and prepared for next day's flight. Mail and equipment (Radar) was delivered to CO on Midway. During the night at approximately 2100, an alarm was sounded over the island and our crew, 23-P-4, was ordered over the side to moor in the lagoon. Part of the crew returned to the beach.

Second Day: Dec. 19, 1941—HST. At first light departed from Midway for Wake Island. Proceeded on uneventful trip to Wake. On approaching the island 23-P-4 was immediately scrutinized by the one remaining Marine fighter plane. Landing was made in a rainsquall and plane was again prepared for next day's flight and moored in lagoon. CDR Keene would allow no personnel to remain on plane. All crewmembers slept in dugouts this night.

Third Day: Dec. 20, 1941—HST. Departure made this day was made considerably more difficult after first light but no delay was encountered and arrived at Midway in early afternoon. Midway's Radar picked up planes a considerable distance out. It was reported that dive-bombers a short time had attacked Wake Island after departure of 23-P-4.

Major W.L.J. Bayler USMC was carried as passenger under verbal orders from Wake Island. Plane was refueled and prepared for next flight.

Fourth Day: Dec. 21, 1941—HST: At first light departure was made for Pearl Harbor. The boat crew was supposed to be at the dock to take

CHAPTER 5 Wake Island

us to the plane but they were not there. We waited and waited ... but apparently they didn't get the word on the time we were to be picked up. We were getting pretty itchy, because we wanted to get away before the Japs arrived—but the boats finally came—and we lost no time getting the engines started, warmed up and taking off.

Lt. Francis C. Riley, USN (Ret.):

After the 7 December attack on Pearl Harbor by the Japanese Attack Force, Wake Island was being regularly bombed and shelled by the enemy. Wake Island Defense Forces were badly in need of equipment and reinforcements. The CINCPACFLT needed a more accurate picture of the conditions on Wake and also had a replenishment plan under way that he wanted hand delivered to the Defenders of Wake. He requested CDR Massie Hughes, CO of VP-23, to send someone to Wake to deliver his message—and bring back a first hand report of conditions from Wake Island Base Commander, CDR Cunningham. He also wanted a report from Col. James P. S. Devereux—the officer commanding the Marine detachment.

CDR Hughes assigned the flight to Ensign James J. Murphy. I was assigned to the crew as first pilot. Other crewmembers were: Ensign Howard P. Ady, Jr. and NAP J. A. Spraggins, RM1/C. After briefing by CinPACFLT, we proceeded the next day on the 19th of Dec, from Midway to Wake, landed in the lagoon, tied up to a buoy—and were taken to a welcoming party that was waiting.

The Marines have written two versions of what was said when we reached the dock. One version was that we asked where the "Wake Island Hotel" was, and the other version is that we asked for the "Pan American Airways Hotel" there. I'm sure both versions are correct ... and I'm not sure there was a PanAm Hotel there.

PanAm had at one time people there to service the "Clippers" and PanAm did have a hotel at Midway. Our squadron had done advance base training at Wake in May 1941, but "our hotel" was a fleet tug modified as a Patrol Plane tender—and we slept under the tarp on deck!

If there were any sleeping facilities for the plane crews below deck, they were too hot to sleep in.

We delivered CINPACFLT's message to CDR Cunningham at his bunker command post. There were a large number of civilians on the island doing construction work, but I don't recall where their housing facilities were.

I am sure I ate my evening meal, but unable to remember the details. That night we slept in a dugout. Knowing the Japs liked to make early morning calls, we got up early on Dec. 21st, so we could take off not too long after daylight.

We pilots, the Plane Captain, and probably a couple of other crewmembers met at the dock. Also with us was Major Bayler USMC—assigned to Wake on temporary duty to set up a communication system for the Marine aircraft and having completed his mission he had orders to return to Pearl Harbor. (He was author of the story "The Last Man Off Wake Island," which was published in the *Saturday Evening Post*.)

Ensign Murphy told me to get in the port seat and make the takeoff, which I did. We got off about 7:00 A.M. and headed for Midway staying low for some distance because we didn't want to be spotted by the Japs if they were coming in.

Right after take off we gave the Wake Island base radio our "over and out" departure report which also was sent to Midway to let them know we had departed Wake.

We proceeded to Midway without incident. They had never received the message from Wake and they were surprised to see us. We learned that the Japs had hit Wake before base radio got the departure message we sent. The attack that morning was the first of several attacks that culminated in the capture of Wake by the Japanese.

On 22 Dec. we flew from Midway back to Pearl Harbor and the next day gave CINCPAC-FLT the reports and messages that the people on Wake sent back—along with our own observations.

I guess our flight to and from Midway to Pearl Harbor must have been watched over by Providence and our lucky star was shining very brightly on us because we were extremely fortunate to get in and out of Wake between attacks. Apparently CINCPAC took a calculated risk by sending us in—and won. I'm glad!

Capt. Howard P. Ady, Jr.:

On the 17th of December, Skipper Massie Hughes called "Murph" and me in and told us to get our gear together—that we were going on a special flight. I was still wearing the clothes I had on since Dec 7th, except for what others I could scrounge, so I went home and got some fresh clothes—and we left the next morning for WAKE.

This was probably one of the biggest "fiascoes" at this time in the war. There was obviously nothing anyone could do out there. They had already turned the USS *Saratoga* around, and except to satisfy some morbid curiosity of someone on CINCPAC's staff, that would be all that could be accomplished!

Glenn E. Pennock, ARM3/C:

On 18 Dec. 41 (this was Dec. 19 across the dateline) at 0600 we

CHAPTER 5 *Wake Island*

loaded four boxes of radar parts, orders, and bags of mail received from Pearl Harbor for delivery to Wake Island.

We arrived Midway 1530 to find they had been under some bad shelling. A power plant had been hit, though with 6-foot reinforced concrete, without damage. But the shelling had ruined the hangar. Men had "camouflaged" all three buildings with sand paint and had also put "trees and flowers" on the power plant. Someone had put a sign "Do not pick the flowers."

In the evening there was an air raid warning and we headed back out to sea but it was a false alarm, so we came back in and tied up to a buoy. The pilots slept in bunks. Cheney and Hampy slept on the wing, I slept in the plane's tunnel hatch.

The bombing raids on Wake came at us like clockwork—1000 to 1100 and 1600 to 1700. This never failed except for two days due to bad weather. The Japs would come in with 18 to 48 planes ... and they destroyed everything—all clothes, buildings and aircraft!

The Wake garrison was left with one tattered fighter that they were trying to patch up in the underground hangar, and another that they were using for spare parts. We heard so many heroic stories. They should all be given medals.

Two Marine pilots, Hank Elrod and another whose last name of Tharin, must have been a two man defense of the island. They tried everything—from carrying a 100-pound bomb in the cockpit and rolling it over an enemy ship. Elrod and Tharin would get airborne before an air raid and stay high while Major Devereux would shoot with his 5 and 3 inch guns ... and then when the bombers would leave, some smoking ... then those two would dive down and attack them. There were few small arms and the 1,200 contractors wanted something to fight with.

We took off 20 December (21 Dec. Wake Time) at 0630 with Major Bayler, a Marine pilot and Communications systems officer. He was needed to install more Communication and Radar gear at Midway. We also took much mail and packaged valuables back to Pearl Harbor to mail home for the people on Wake—who knew they were going to be taken prisoner by Japanese Forces. We landed on Midway at 1800 departing the next night, arriving at Ford Island after an eleven hour flight.

For Air Raid Drills at Ford Island and Pearl Harbor—the stations would send 090, 090 ... and repeat. You couldn't miss this, as it sounded like a series of dashes. The VP-23 Radio Shack used the old railroad type "clicker" for non-priority messages from COMPATRON. It was different learning telegraph clicker code sound.

The Wake Island defenders held out for 15 days—and had all America and her allies "rooting" for them—but alas, there would be no reinforcements to send.

VP-23 Aircrewmen Herbert Horstman, S1/C AMM, and Richard Jacobs, S1/C AMM, sent early to the island for Temporary Attached Duty would be among those taken prisoner on Wake Island.

In October 1941, Charles I. Imus, S1/C, was in a draft of AMM School graduates reporting for duty in U.S. Navy VP-23. Also included were shipmates Herbert J. Horstman and Richard W. Jacobs. Seaman Imus writes:

Soon after reporting to the squadron the group of us were sent on TAD (Temporary Assigned Duty) to the USS *Curtis* for training in seaplane handling. Our task completed, we returned to squadron headquarters where yet another TAD request called for two seamen to be transferred to Wake Island. As I was last on the list, Horstman and Jacobs were selected and assigned to duty at Wake. Herbert Horstman and Richard Jacobs represent the only VP-23 crewmen taken prisoner when the island was over-run by the Japanese Landing Force.

A few years after the war, Charlie Imus was driving through Cottonwood, Idaho—Richard Jacobs' hometown. Stopping for gas, he asked the attendant if he knew Jacobs. "Yeah, he died at Pearl Harbor. I think either the Cottonwood VFW or American Legion Post was named in his honor." Charlie told him, to the best of his knowledge, and from information he had learned from the Wake Island Defenders Organization, that Richard Jacobs must have died at Wake. On the plus side, Charlie had learned that Herb Horstman did survive his imprisonment and was living in the San Diego area. Location notices posted in the *Navy Times* have thus far not succeeded in locating the surviving POW.

Charles Imus: "I've always believed that fate had a hand in choosing those two seamen that got caught on the Wake Island draft." [Editor's note: The squadron roster indicates that Richard W. Jacobs died of wounds 10 DEC 1941 (WIA DEC 41).]

Historian Jim Sawruk writes:

Richard W. Jacobs Sea 2 Serial No. 3686270 was Wounded in Action on 8 December 1941 and Died of Wounds on 10 December 1941 at Wake Island while assigned to the Wake Base Detachment. I believe he was TAD to them from VP-23 or else the paperwork did not catch up in time before he was lost. He is erroneously listed under the USN Pearl Harbor Casualties in the official records.

CHAPTER 5 Wake Island

At the Punchbowl National Cemetery in Honolulu, there is a 5x10-foot flat marble gravestone—the largest in the cemetery—listing the names of 178 men. This common grave holds the remains of all of the unidentified military and civilian burials repatriated from Wake Island in proper burial and identification. Of these names, ninety-eight were executed by the Japanese in October of 1943. To our knowledge Richard Jacobs' name is not among them. (An article in *Naval History Magazine*, "Massacre at Wake Island," gives an account of the Japanese occupation.)

Hollywood lost no time in dramatizing the gallant defenders of Wake, and in doing its patriotic part to boost the country's low morale and encourage enlistment in the armed forces.

The movie *Wake Island* was quickly produced in 1942 to portray the brave defense of the small U.S. Marine garrison fighting against impossible odds to hold tiny Wake Island. Academy Award nominations and Oscars that year, including Best Picture, Best Director, and Best Screenplay, were given to the film, which starred Brian Donlevy, William Bendix, Robert Preston, and MacDonald Carrey.

It was patriotic, moving, soul-stirring, and I am certain it was a major impetus for a new influx of recruits volunteering to serve their country. When I saw this movie back in Chicago, it certainly brought me closer to my own decision to get into the war!

First Mass Trans-Pacific Flight from San Diego to Hawaii by VP-10, soon re-designated VP-25 and finally VP-23. (Ricketts Collection)

(Left) *25-P-10—One of Trans-Pacific PBYs that made history. Gunnery Officer and Pilot Jones in foreground. Plane check on Canton Island. Note VPB insignia under wing.* (LaPlant Collection)

(Below) *Crew of 10-P-9 (L-R): Gragg, 1st Mech., AVCAD Drill, L. LaPlant NAP, LTjg Greenlee, Mason radioman, Drake plane captain.* (LaPlant Collection)

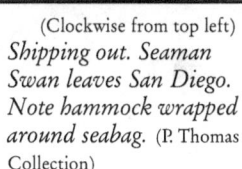

(Clockwise from top left) *Shipping out. Seaman Swan leaves San Diego. Note hammock wrapped around seabag.* (P. Thomas Collection)

Ernest Pederson on lawn in front of Queen's Palace, Honolulu. (Luberti Collection)

Honolulu photo booth memories. Eddie Rochester was later lost at sea with Lt. Baxter Moore's crew. (Luberti Collection)

Posing near the Pali (l to r) *P. Williams, H. Luberti, W. Chase, Maslanski, unknown, Stillwell.* (Luberti Collection)

(Middle) *Jack McGarry, ARM3/C.* (Reed Collection)

(Above) *World-famous Waikiki Beach, 1940.* (Luberti Collection)

(Middle) *In his merry Oldsmobile–Pres Thomas on liberty, Honolulu, 1941.* (P. Thomas Collection)

(Below) *Playing on the Pali* (l-r) *Binkley AP3C, "Doc" Redhage AMM1/C, Frank Sustae AMM1/C, and Jerry McBride ARM1/C, on liberty in Oahu.* (P. Thomas Collection)

(Clockwise from top right) *Dress whites and looking bright. Ensigns C. James Watters and Hal Lough.* (J. Watters Collection)

Ready to roll: Ensigns James Watters and Hal Lough on liberty in Hawaii. (J. Watters Collection)

Barbed wire on beach at Waikiki no deterrent for Ensign Watters. (J. Watters Collection)

(Clockwise from top left) *Marion "Lee" Hofheins in photo booth on liberty in Honolulu. He was in VP-23's "Lost Crew" on patrol the night before the invasion of Guadalcanal.* (R. Reed Collection)

Harry Knight ARM3/C (left) *and Robert Reed ARM3/C on liberty in Honolulu. (Knight was killed in action.)* (R. Reed Collection)

On the Town! (l-r) *VP-23 aircrewmen Lee, Weiss, Landry, Hubbell, and Wilkerson on the beach in Honolulu.* (P. Landry Collection)

"Striker" Pres Thomas AMM and Ed Riepl (right) *of San Diego 1940. Ed would join the Navy and be assigned to VP-23 in the South Pacific. Within a week Ensign Riepl would be missing in action with his crew in the jungle mountains of Espiritu Santo. Fifty years later, the crew would be found and brought home to be buried with honors at Arlington Cemetery.* (P. Thomas Collection)

(Clockwise from top left) *Warren E. Peterson Y1/C, VP-23, with WAVE friend at Quonset Pt., RI.* (P. Thomas Collection)

Jim Pearson AMM1/C with Jane Thomas (Pres Thomas' sister). His crew of 15-P-23 was lost in mountains of Espiritu Santo in the Solomons. (P. Thomas Collection)

Ens. Glen Stewart—KIA in January 1942 while returning from a mission and attempting a night landing in debris-filled Pearl Harbor during enforced island blackout. (Mary McMahon Collection)

Taras "Slim" Hallas ARM3/C was documented in this famous Pearl Harbor picture as he stood amidst the devastation, burning PBYs and thick black smoke coming from destroyer USS Shaw explosion nearby. Just returned from liberty, and still in dress whites, "Slim" rushed to the hangar area only to see his plane shot up—yet he managed to set up a .50 caliber and fire at the second wave of incoming Zeros. Four Japanese planes were shot down by Navy personnel. (Official U.S. Navy Photograph)

VP/VPB-23

SECOND TOUR
1941-1943

The Battle of Midway
JUNE 3-6, 1942

Japanese losses: four carriers—Akagi, Soryu, Kaga, and Hiryu (3,000 dead)
U.S. losses: Yorktown and DE Ballard (fewer than 1,000 dead)

"The problem at Midway is one of hitting before we are hit," wrote Rear Adm. Patrick Bellinger, who submitted a search plan worked out with Maj. Gen. Clarence Tinker of the 7th Bomber Command. It called for patrolling 700 miles out every day, covering the whole 180° west of Midway. Patrol Squadron 23 arrived at Midway Island on May 26, 1942.

Of 163 pilots and air gunners shot down in the Battle of Midway, twenty-seven were rescued from their life rafts by patrolling Catalinas. During the next ten days, others managed to attract attention of passing ships or even make their own way back to Midway.

Lt.(jg) Robin Larson remembers:

> I was on the six plane attachment that flew to Palmyra in February to cover the back of the first offensive action of our fleet. It was a nice assignment, but we lost a crew (a very good one) on their way back from Palmyra to Oahu. It was very hard on our skipper, LCDR Massie Hughes as he was very close to Bob Winters, one of the PPCs on the plane that went in.
>
> I was flying at Midway with the VP-23 crews that were sent out there. Lt. "Goat" Murphy and I sent the message "Many planes headed towards Midway." Lt. Howard Ady and crew were the next plane to us and the one that actually sighted the fleet and sent the message tracking their location.

Ens. Geoffrey L. "Blackie" Blackman sent this report:

Here's the "scoop" on the Midway Operation (VP-23) right out of my Log book. On May 19th—I flew from San Diego with Baxter Moore. A bunch of us had gone to San Diego to pick up new aircraft.

On May 29th, I was second pilot flying with CO Massie Hughes and Lt. ("Old Goat") Murphy (the real PPC!). We also had the Chief of Staff aboard with us. The story goes like this:

Late the afternoon before May 28th the Exec called us all together in the BOQ—told us to pack a bag for a week's stay, not to discuss this with anyone else and ordered us to stay in our rooms. He informed us that a truck would pick us up at 0300 and take us to the ready room.

When we arrived in the early morning, CO Massie Hughes was there with COMAIRPAC Adm. Bellinger—to give us a big pep talk and ... "GENTLEMEN, THIS IS YOUR CHANCE. GOD BLESS YOU!"

Then Massie told us we were going to Midway and we would be taking off in inverse order of rank and rendezvous over Kauai. We all know that one PBY is only about 5 knots faster than any other PBY. Anyway, when we got out to our aircraft they were all loaded with Torpedoes. To make a long story short we all joined up over French Frigate Shoals.

On June 4th Harold Lough was PPC and Gale Burkey was first pilot and Navigator. Our patrol was next to Howard Ady who spotted the Jap Fleet. On return that day we spotted a life raft and Harold dropped our depth charges and landed to pick up an SBD pilot and his crewman.

As we were returning to Midway we saw the *Yorktown* burning. Other pilots flying that day were: Lt.(jg) O'Dowd, Swede Theuson, and McKelven.

Ens. Horace E. "Nick" Nichols:

My first flight while stationed on Ford Island was to navigate for Lt. James Ogden, who was then Flight Officer of VP-23 and who was checking out Howard Ady as PPC. Lt.(jg) Bob Winters was our Executive Officer.

On May 7, 1942 we boarded an old four stacker destroyer, the USS *Detroit*, which took us to San Diego to pick up new PBYs. Bob Winters was to fly by Air transport to lead the flight back. Unfortunately, he was killed in the crash of the PB2Y that he was aboard. A very red letter day for the squadron.

Upon returning to Ford Island, we found that most of the squadron was at Midway. I was flying with "Cloudy" Riley PPC and Chuck Jones as Co-pilot. Massie Hughes took over our crew and we proceeded to Midway to join the rest of the squadron.

CHAPTER 6 *The Battle of Midway*

VP-23 and VP-44 were the only two complete squadrons at Midway. Several other squadrons were represented—but only by a few crews. Skipper Massie Hughes did not fly at Midway as he was an aide to Comdr. Logan Ramsey.

The day of the Battle (June 4th) we were assigned to fly the sector to the left of the sector from which the Jap Planes approached Midway. We flew over our entire sector and returned to Midway that evening. Massie wanted to return to Ford Island that evening to tell Adm. Bellinger first hand what was happening at Midway, so being the only PBY and crew available, we were elected.

The Japs had knocked out the fueling system on Sand Island, so we refueled the planes from drums, using buckets that we snitched from the defunct supply building. Our flight back to Pearl Harbor that night was uneventful. We returned to Midway on June 6th—and finally had a day off.

On June 8th I was flying with PPC Bob Slater on a search for survivors. For some reason we were late getting off that morning so we were searching by ourselves.

Approximately 107 miles north of Midway, we spotted two men in their life rafts. We landed as the seas were calm that day and we picked them up. These were the first two pilots off of the USS *Hornet*, that were rescued: Lt.(jg) Minuard Jennings and Ensign Humphrey F. Tallman VF-8. We took them back to Midway and were met by John Ford the movie director and the camera crew who took pictures of their rafts. Lt.(jg) Jennings had kept a log of their four days in the water, which was written on the top of his life raft. Years later I saw some of those pictures that were used in some Navy film.

The days following this rescue and using information obtained from these two pilots, the PBYs saved six more for a total of eight. Though the weather was deteriorating, we continued our search. Approximately eight to ten days after the battle, two more life rafts were spotted and though the crew that spotted them landed for the pick-up, no survivors could be found. We had approximately thirty PBYs circling the area and dropping float lights, but after the initial sighting we never saw them again. We could only assume that the men in the life rafts had tried to stand up—but were too weak—and possibly tumbled overboard.

After the search & rescue portion of the Midway battle, we returned to Ford Island and were given seventy-two hour R&R. However, I was called back to the squadron after only twenty-four hours and told upon arrival that we were leaving the following morning for New Zealand.

Two planes were to take Adm. Kelly Turner and his entourage on this trip. Lt. Jimmy Ogden was PPC of one—and Lt. Hal Lough, PPC of the other crew. Flying with Jimmy was Lt. Rob Larson who we once nicknamed "Magellan" for his navigating ability, and Lt.(jg) Del Ward as the other co-pilot. In our crew were Hal Lough and myself. I don't remember who the other co-pilot was—I think he joined us in New Caledonia later on.

We made the usual overnight stays at the various islands and eventually landed at the Tonga's, where we were detained for some three days because of a typhoon between the Tonga's and Auckland, New Zealand.

We eventually departed for Suva flying west of the typhoon to New Zealand. After the Admiral concluded his business, we flew to Noumea, New Caledonia. At the time we left Ford Island we were supposed to return but it was not to be. About a week or so later VP-23 crews began arriving in the South Pacific for what became the Battle for the Solomon Islands.

By late November of '42, we were relieved and proceeded back to Kaneohe where the squadron base had been moved while we were off in the South Pacific.

Shortly after arriving at Kaneohe, we were put aboard ship for the West Coast to bring back some new planes. Comdr. Massie Hughes was relieved by the new skipper, Frank Buck Brandley, who took command of the squadron.

Between Christmas and New Year's most of the squadron was on back to Midway in the new PBY-5As doing patrol and flying "dumbo" for Army Air Force B-24s bombing Wake Island.

It was at this time that I was checked out as PPC—and my two co-pilots were Ensigns Art McQuiddy and Mort Saylor. What a crew this was! If there was anything at all the crew wanted, which was mentioned in front of them, it had better be fastened down securely or those two had it!

I remember the "skipper" asking me about the "quality" of rations—because all of the crews were complaining. I told him that we had "no complaint"—so he asked what we were having for flight crew meals. When I related what we were getting, he was amazed. It seems Art and Mort had developed a friendship with the Master Sergeant in charge of crew rations, and had even taken him along on several flights. I later found out that "our crew's" rations were always set in another room—apart from the other rations. A testimony to the ingenuity of these two mavericks!

I believe we were one of the last crews in late Feb. 1943 to return from Midway.

Taxiing up to the hangar, we were met by Duty Officer Jim Watters—who told me to hurry it up for I was leaving for the States the very next morning—and had to be aboard ship by 1900 that evening. Today, I can't even remember if I had time to properly say "Good Bye" to all of my crew!

Only two of the pilots that I know of were returned to the States to form the first PB4Y squadron. Others were reassigned to the two PB2Y

CHAPTER **6** *The Battle of Midway*   47

squadrons that were organizing at San Diego; others went to PV squadrons that were forming at Alameda, CA.

To my knowledge Lt. Jimmy Ogden and Lt. Howard Ady, Jr. were never Skippers of VP-23. Jimmy acted as Skipper and Howard was SOP (Senior Officer Present) when crews were operating from the old *Mackinac*. Both Jimmy Ogden and Massie Hughes returned to the States with us and Massie remained Skipper until "relieved" by Buck Brandley.

On June 4, 1942 Lt. Maurice "Snuffy" Smith sighted enemy fleet—and reported details of Jap Forces approaching Midway. Three VP-23 rescues were to follow.

Aircraft from VP-23 actually made five pick-ups of downed pilots and aircrewmen in the Battle of Midway. Ens. William Jamieson participated as a member of Lt.(jg) August A. Barthes' crew in one or two of those rescues.

Ens. "Bill" Jamieson writes:

My log says that I was flying to Midway in Lt.(jg) Murphy's crew on May 29th with CMDR Massie Hughes. On June 1 and 2nd, I flew patrol with Murphy out of Midway. On June 3 our aircraft was damaged on the ramp at Midway and our crew was split up. I was transferred on June 4th to Ensign Barthes' crew and flew with him June 4-5-6-7 and 9th of '42. I left his crew to return to Ford Island with the crews of Lt.(jg) Brady on 6/11/42.

I flew with Lt. Murphy through most of the South Pacific Campaign up to October '42. Three of us, Lt. Reister, Lt. Spraggins, and myself were transferred back to the states to be with Cdr. Hughes, in the Operational Training Command at Jacksonville, FL.

After two years, I was ordered to the USS *Bon Homme Richard* as VD Division Officer and Flight Deck Officer—remaining on board until shortly before the war was over. Because of injuries, I received on deck (lost both legs) in a landing accident, I was retired in Oct 1946.

On June 6, 1942, Preston Thomas, ACMM, wrote this account:

My flight log shows that we left Kaneohe on 29 May 1942 under sealed orders. Once airborne, we opened them to find out that our destination was Midway Island.

Ensign Barthes was our PPC. I think he only joined VP-23 for this operation. He was one fine pilot. The other crew members I can remember were: Frank Sustae, AMM1/C, our bombardier, and Ensign Jamieson, who had lots of gear, including a tennis racket. We all wondered where he planned to play tennis.

The first night at Midway, we assembled in a bomb shelter with a lot of bunks and were addressed by Commander Massie Hughes. He told us the Japanese fleet was on its way to Midway and we must find it. He wished us all good luck and, as I remember, gave each of us a beer.

That night was a first time I had ever slept on an innerspring mattress! Being a boy from the hills of Wyoming, I had never experienced such luxury (funny—the things a person remembers!).

The day before we got there an electrician blew up the fueling system in attempting to wire it for detonation in case of evacuation. As a result, we had to fuel our planes from 55-gallon drums up to 1,400 gallons. We pumped it with a portable D.C. electric pump into a 5-gallon funnel with a chamois skin filter.

The fuel was so full of sand and filth from the drums that it wouldn't pass through the filter ... so we threw the chamois away and poured sand and all into the tanks. In flight we had to drain the AEL units often. Surprisingly we got out and back every day. Of course, that's a dependable PBY for you!

We flew the next few days at about 100 foot altitude in dense fog. The day NAP Lt.(jg) Willy Chase located the Japanese fleet, we came upon it a short time later—we saw lots of ships. Fortunately for us, their planes were bombing Midway at the time so our butts were probably saved.

Later in the day, we noticed dark specks behind us. As the specks closed in on us it became evident they were fighters moving in attack formation. Sustae and I manned the .50 caliber machine guns. As they closed in on us and I was but a split second away from firing, when I saw that big white star. Quite a feeling! So we sighed a bit and the color returned to our faces.

That evening we had no trouble at finding our way back to the islands—as big columns of smoke rose in the evening sky!

After the battle we continued our patrols. The sea was full of lifeboats, timbers and other debris. On 6 June, we landed and picked up an SBD pilot and his gunner. Both men were in good shape.

On 12 June we picked up another SBD crew that had been in the water more than a week. They had both hit the instrument panel when ditching and their noses and eyes were swollen. From the waste hatch they looked like Japanese to me, so I pulled down on them with my .45, but hearing good English—I did not shoot.

What a story! The night before, they had paddled close enough to Midway to hear the tractors pulling PBYs out of the water, then a big wind came up and blew them a long way back to sea. Sharks bothered

CHAPTER **6** *The Battle of Midway* 49

them—their feet and hands were swollen from the salt water—they had no drinking water or food and their noses were probably broken! They said they had discussed going over the side of their tiny life raft. But they didn't have to—thanks to the skilled piloting of Ensign Barthes and our good old PBY!

I recently learned the names of the crews that we rescued on 6 June 1942. They were Ensign Tony F. Schneider and Glen L. Holden ARM2/C . . . and on 12 June '42 Ensign Thomas W. Ramsey and Sherman L. Duncan AMM2/C. Both crews were from SBD squadron, VB-6, off the *Yorktown*.

The sea was running pretty heavy and on takeoff the Bombardier's sliding window cover was loose, but caused a problem on landing. We all felt pretty good after the flight.

Things slowed down after that, so we had a chance to rest and make friends and dance with the "gooney birds." There had been a lot of canned food stored in the hangar at Midway when it was bombed, so we were trying to salvage some of the canned fruit when an old CPO with a .45 and a hard hat on called us looters and ran us off.

The mess hall continued giving us flight rations that we had to cook on our Coleman stove out on the ramp. They eventually bulldozed the bombed food into the ocean. Needless to say, we were hungry for some variety.

We returned to Kaneohe on 14 June. The squadron deployed to Espiritu Santo on July '42 where my buddy Jim Pearson AMM1/c and other friends were lost on plane no. 23-P-15. I didn't make that trip. Anyone who lost their buddy can understand what a blow it can be to you.

Ens. Ken Hoagland graduated with the "first class" of aviators from Corpus Christi in November of 1941. Some days after the Japanese had struck at Pearl Harbor, Ensign Hoagland joined VP-23. He remembers:

At this time Massie Hughes was Skipper and I was flying with Swede Theuson in the Battle of Midway. We were in the sector adjacent from Howard Ady and requested to scout the Japanese armada steaming toward Midway. We were able to witness the bombing of the Jap fleet by planes from the carriers involved.

PPC Theuson flew along the line of warships sending information to fleet HQ. And as our plane had been on station for several hours and running out of fuel, we were prevented from making it back to Midway. Swede Theuson made a beautiful night landing in open sea far short of

Midway. We stuffed pencils into the many popped rivet holes on the seaplane's hull, and the plane stayed afloat that night.

The next morning we were spotted by units of the U.S. fleet, picked up by a tin can which then sank the PBY since the outcome of the battle was still in doubt. A couple of days later we were transferred to an oiler and much later arrived at Pearl Harbor.

Ens. Howard Dickerson reported into VP-23 at Ford Island, Hawaii, on April 28, 1942. He would get his initiation on June 4, 1942—the first big day of the Battle of Midway. He flew with several different Patrol plane commanders the week before June 4. His account follows:

On that day (June 4th) I was in Ensign "Swede" Theuson's plane, along with Co-pilot Ensign Child and Ensign Ken Hoagland . . . and myself doing the navigation. Being a junior officer, I was designated to do most of the navigation!

On June 4th, we took off around 0400 heading out at 286° sector. We had flown a couple of hundred miles when messages began pouring in of Japanese planes, ships, etc., heading for Midway. Our plane went out 680 miles and didn't see a thing!

When we got back to within 300 miles of Midway, we received orders to head for the Jap Fleet that had attacked our carrier planes. We soon saw three large ships on the horizon burning from stem to stern. The weather was hazy and foggy so we had to get fairly close to get a good view, and the ships turned out to be three first line carriers of the Japanese, later identified as the *Kaga*, *Akagi* and the *Soryru*.

We soon noticed black puffs of smoke all around us, which were coming from the guns of Jap destroyers circling the burning carriers and picking up survivors. We immediately scooted out of range and their destroyers took off to the north in the fog.

We followed them north and ran into the rest of the fleet. U.S. high altitude bombers were dropping bombs on the rear battleship and cruiser and it appeared to sink in five to ten minutes.

After circling the fleet for over two hours, all the while sending out messages back to our base, we got a surprise. A Jap Zero came out of the low clouds with his guns blazing! We dove to 150 ft. off the water, as he made his second attack from our starboard bow.

We did manage to get off shots from our guns—and I believe we got some hits—but we ended up with bullet holes on the trailing edge of the starboard wing . . . either from the "Zero" or from our own waist gun!

After this attack, we knew there had to be another Jap carrier in the

CHAPTER **6** *The Battle of Midway* 51

area. We were running low on fuel and decided we should head for Midway. With all the circling, etc. that we did, I knew we were in for trouble. It was getting dark and I started taking star sights, but with the fuel so low, it was a hopeless case.

Finally Midway gave us a course to fly to the North, assuming we overshot the base. With only ten minutes of fuel left, we ended up dropping a float light and landing in the open sea 100 miles from Midway—back in the direction of the Japanese fleet.

We hit the water bouncing about a 100 ft. high—and as I remember, five times!

When we finally settled, water came spurting through some 25 holes, where rivets had popped out. We quickly sharpened pencils, broke them in pieces, and stuck them in the holes.

The next morning we got up and sat on the wing of the plane, waiting for a rescue. It struck us then that the Pacific Ocean is some huge body of water and we were a mere speck. What a relief it was to see our fleet suddenly come out of the fog and haze—within a quarter of a mile of us! One of the destroyers saw us—I believe it was the *Monahan*—and they came over to pick us up. We left our plane floating.

After catching up with the fleet, we discovered no one had thought to remove the Norden Bombsight from the bow. The fleet commander ordered our destroyer back to get it. After retrieving the bombsight the destroyer was ordered to proceed and help convoy the *Yorktown* carrier which had been disabled by the Japanese.

We watched with dismay as the destroyer *Hammon* and the *Yorktown* sank, the only two ships lost in the Battle of Midway.

A couple of days later we were transferred by boatswain chair from the *Monahan* to the tanker *Cimarron* and finally a week later, we reached Hawaii.

A few days later our airplane was towed back to Midway. It was in good shape and the next month I flew in it to the South Pacific—a great testimony to the endurance of the PBY!

Lt.(jg) C. James Watters:

The first sighting of enemy units on June 4th beginning the Battle of Midway was made by Lt. Howard Ady Jr.—and through the battle and for several days after it was over, VP-23 remained on the scene rescuing downed survivors from the ocean. On June 30th 1942 VP-23 returned to Ford Island, Territory of Hawaii.

The Solomons
AUGUST–OCTOBER 1942

The next operation assigned the squadron was the initial assault in the Guadalcanal campaign.

The VP-23 Squadron's involvement in the Solomon Islands campaign began as outlined below:

- July 1942—VP-23 deployed to Noumea, New Caledonia, in support of the invasion of Guadalcanal relieving VP-71. Support provided by USS *Curtis* Seaplane Tender.
- July 15, 1942—USS *Curtis* moves to Espiritu Santo in the New Hebrides. VP-23 follows.
- July 25, 1942—VP-23 bombed Tulagi Island (the first target in the bombing campaign conducted by the squadron against Japanese-held positions).
- August 6, 1942—Lt. Maurice "Snuffy" Smith and his crew of seven are reported missing after a patrol flown out of Espiritu Santo. (*On January 14, 1994, a team of loggers discovered the remains of the aircraft and its crew where they had crashed on a ridge of a hill on Espiritu Santo.*)
- August 7, 1942—A nine-plane detachment of VP-23 was deployed to Malaita Island to support operations at Guadalcanal, with tender support from USS *Curtis*.
- August 9, 1942—Severe losses by the Allies at the Battle of Savo Straits forced the return of the detachment to Espiritu

Santo. Six planes sent to Ndeni, Santa Cruz Islands. This was rough duty!
- October 1942—LCDR James R. Ogden, USN, relieves LCDR Massie Hughes. VP-23 reports to Comdr. Aircraft, Solomons. LCDR attached to VP-25 at Ford Island. On December 7, 1941, it was Ogden in the cockpit aboard CO CMDR Massie Hughes' plane, which was first to take off to search out the Japanese Fleet. He also participated in the Battle of Midway. VP-23s flew cover for Solomon Island landings.

Lt. Horace E. "Nick" Nichols ('42-'43) remembers this about events at the Solomons:

During the Solomon Campaign VP-23 lost two crews—Moore and Smith. Bob Wilcox, one of the co-pilots flying with "Pappy" Reister, was killed while sitting at the navigation table when a Jap plane attacked us. Bob was my roommate for a short time before the Midway battle.

I can remember several planes being lost when hulls were damaged on coral reefs and then sunk. I think two were lost at Tulagi. "Bucky" Earnest and John Kosich were stranded on the island there for some time and endured the Jap shelling that took place every night. "Pappy" Reisler was evacuated shortly after losing their plane.

Lt. Francis C. Riley writes:

The next operation assigned the squadron was the initial assault in the Guadalcanal campaign. Lt. James Ogden was in charge of the detachment, and I was part of one of the crews. Our itinerary included overnight stops at Palmyra, Canton, Suva, Noumea and then Espiritu Santo where we joined the USS *Curtis*.

My duties were coordinating maintenance of our aircraft, ordnance requirements and fueling with our host tender and taking care of the needs of our squadron personnel. Some patrols required returning to the harbor in the forward area such as Nendi or Malaita—to rendezvous with the USS *Macfarland* and USS *Mackinac*. If we were not dodging AA fire on patrol, it was trying to keep a course in extreme weather.

At one time I took a drift sight which indicated in excess of 40 degrees. While at Nendi, planes from the Carrier *Wasp*, not recognizing the USS *Mackinac*, dropped a bomb which was a "near miss" off of the fantail.

In October 1942 Lt. Ogden was ordered to return to Pearl Harbor—and I was directed to return with him. A VIP passenger travelling with us on that return trip was Major James Roosevelt, USMCR.

Ens. Ken Hoagland gives this report:

The squadron was reassembled under the command of Lt. James Ogden. Our next flight prior to the invasion of Guadalcanal was to the USS *Mackinac* and Malaita. I was Co-pilot on "Pappy" Reister's plane when we spotted a Japanese Task Force approaching the Guadalcanal area. Our plane was suddenly attacked by what appeared to be three "float plane" Zeros. As we fled the area Ensign Robert Wilcox, a pilot on the plane, was struck by a bullet ricocheting off the armor plate of the pilot's seat, piercing his lungs—literally strangling in his own blood.

Capt. Robin Larson, VP-23, remembers the Battle for the Solomons:

It was a great honor when LCDR Ogden asked me to be Navigator for VP-23 detachment flying ADM Turner and his staff to where they were to plan Solomon Campaign.

On a later mission, we were ordered to go to a special lagoon with uncharted coral reefs. Our skipper "Massie" made the first landing—and then dropped smoke lights to give us a safe area to land in. Later that night, we learned of the Battle of Savo Island and our losses there—and were ordered to take off immediately. Our skipper Massie Hughes said, "No way—I got you in here safely—and I am not about to lose any of you by taking off in the darkness." We took off safely at daylight.

Later in October '41, I was ordered back to the states with an ear infection and grounded for a month or so. I then became XO of the Operational Training Unit of COMFAIR Wing 14 at San Diego.

Albert C. Snedeker, LCDR (Ret.) PHS, writes:

I flew out of a slew of islands—including Bougainville, Tulagi, Malaita, Savo, Ndeni and in and out of the Solomons. I also flew some special night recon with PT boats and rendezvous with coastwatchers. I started elimination training on 6 June 41 at Oakland, CA qualifying me for training as an aviation cadet at NAS, Jacksonville, FL.

Received my commission and wings on 28 APR. '42 and ordered to NAS San Diego, CA where within a day my orders were cut to report to VP-23 at Ford Island, HI. On 8 June '42, I was on my way to Hawaii aboard the USS *Grant* and on June 15th, I reported into VP-23. The day

CHAPTER **7** *The Solomons*

after, I was told to report to the Admiral's office at Pearl. In Hawaii for only 24 hours, I was trying to figure out why I was already in trouble! It turned out that the Admiral's aide was a Marine Col. James Snedeker, who saw my name on the incoming roster and wanted to meet me. Got a free lunch out of it!

My first flights in VP-23 were with Slater and Larson. Though "new ensigns" were relegated to navigation, Slater took pity on me and scheduled a few practice training flights enabling me to make a few landings and take-offs.

We moved out of Hawaii 10 July '42 with PPC Lt.(jg) Slater, 1st Pilot Ensign Elmer Laughlin and myself as 2nd pilot (Navigator). Also aircrewmen Gibson AMM1/C, ARM's three AMM's Johnson, Jones and Hampy, and two AOM's Larue & Harrison. We were in a flight of three—with Lt. Murphy in the lead. And as ours was the last plane in the water, I remember our squadron skipper, CDR Massie Hughes, giving us the old "Thumbs Up" sign!

Our first stop was Palmyra Island about 1,100 miles southwest of Oahu, covered with palm trees and lush tropical growth. The lagoon was in the center serving a natural landing and anchorage area. Next stop was Canton Island. Surrounded by white sand, coral reefs and very green water, it had only one small tree growing on it! We spent the night in a small hotel built by Pan Am for Pacific commercial flights.

On "Day Three," we flew on to Suva in the Fiji Islands and stayed at the GRAND PACIFIC HOTEL, where we were served (at least) a nine-course dinner in elegance by Indian waiters!

Lt. Al Snedeker recalls:

I can remember several planes being lost when hulls were damaged on coral reefs and then sunk. I think two were lost at Tulagi. "Bucky" Earnest and John Kosich were stranded on the island there for some time—and endured the Jap shelling that took place.

26 July 42—While on anti-sub patrol, we received a message that the Dutch ship Tjim Gara had been torpedoed. Locating the debris along with the remaining crew, we maintained contact until relieved by another plane.

29 July 42—We were sent on a mission to bomb Guadalcanal. Refueling at Efate, we went onto the Solomons—but because of lousy weather and low gas, we had to "abort," other planes went on and dropped their bombs, encountering very little hostile action.

1 Aug 42—We were briefed in "air conference" room on big push that was coming up. I was in group "A" (10 planes) that was to go all the way to Tulagi.

Aug 42—Aboard the *Mackinac* in the New Hebrides, I got O.K. for a day shore-visit with old friend Lt. Williams. Taking us by the bomber strip just completed (in only 28 days!), we stopped at a plantation for lunch. (This was owned by the Frenchman that was mentioned in Michener's *Tales of the South Pacific*. The volcano mentioned earlier was also in his novel as well as Harris of the Burns/ Phillip's store.)

7 Aug 42—On a return patrol to the *Mackinac* in Maramsike Channel near Malaita, Lt. Murphy hung our plane on a reef trying to find a "buoy" in the dark.

9 Aug 42—We received word that the Japs had damaged some ships at Savo Island. (We later learned that they were the USS *Quincey*, *Vincennes* and the Australian *Canberra*.) Consequently, we were ordered off the ship and back to our planes by the skipper of the *Mackinac*. A nervous chain smoker, the news made him over anxious to high tail it out of there. The weather was stinking and finally after milling around Marmasike harbor our eight planes all took off. We did some scouting north of the Solomons and then returned to Espiritu Santo. It was during these 2 or 3 days that U.S. forces landed on Guadalcanal and Tulagi, reinforcing our positions.

20 Aug 42—We returned to the *Mackinac*, which would continue to be our home, but the very next morning brought a huge explosion. Running up to the deck, we saw 2 SBDs circling just out of range. The pilots, mistaking us as Japanese, had dropped a bomb about 40 feet off our port side and did some strafing as they made their run. The OS2U float plane on the fantail (which probably prompted the attack) was totaled.

28 Aug 42—Spotted an enemy plane which did not see us ... and later that morning ran into another Jap plane, but fortunately we ducked into cloud cover and lost him.

6 Sept 42—One of VP-11 planes was down at sea and as the USS *Ballard* prepared to head out, I was one of the "non-flying" pilots drafted along with Slater and Watters to join the crew of the *Ballard* in the search. Weather was miserable with winds of 25 knots, the ship going about the same. It was then that I was very glad to be a flier! The VP-11 crew were sighted and picked up the morning of 8 Sept after 2 nights and a day and a half at sea. They were a happy bunch!

2 Sept 42—On the first leg back to Kaneohe. Spent night in Suva then ordered to take some electrical specialists to Tongatabu to work on the Carrier USS *Saratoga* which had been hit. The next day was Canton ... then on to Palmyra.

15 Sept 42—We were back home in Hawaii, then off to the States!

From San Francisco, we were flown to San Diego to test new planes from Consolidated. We started back to Hawaii in a five plane formation, but weather was so bad we lost one plane while another went high and was pushed up about 1800 ft before landing in Hawaii. I was in one of three planes forced back to San Diego, where we were to layover before trying again a few days later.

Al Snedeker would head back to the South Pacific and begin another tour of duty. His new assignments would take him to Funifuti, Tarawa, Tulagi, Naru, Green Island, Treasury, Rendova, Bougainville, and Suva, where he would outrun a typhoon to British Samoa.

Ens. Mike Cox writes:

I had the good fortune to fly in VP-23 as a member of Lt.(jg) Al Snedeker's crew from October '43 to January '44. At that time the squadron was based ashore—adjacent to Halavo Bay, and about two miles south of the village of Tulagi, on Florida Island. The squadron's primary mission was a Dumbo capacity. "Red" Leonard, who eventually retired from the navy as a captain, and I alternated seat and navigation time during our patrols. Although we had many interesting flights there were two that I remember quite vividly.

The first one involved picking up a coastwatcher on the east coast of the island of Chousel which is south of Bougainville. We were well covered on this flight by four P38s flying at our altitude, 500 ft—and four P38s cruising at 8,000. I presume they did not feel comfortable cruising along with us at 150 knots—because they were scissoring back and forth over us in a semi-thatch weave at all times.

We landed in a large cove on the southeast side of the island—about 40 miles south of Rekata Bay, a small seaplane base of secondary importance to the Japs and to ourselves. A native canoe carrying the coastwatcher and two of his men shot out of the heavily wooded coastline as rapidly as they could paddle. They hurried aboard, and Snedeker flew them out without mishaps.

From talking to the coastwatcher later, I learned that his name was "Seaton" and remarked that I had read several novels about collies and sheep dogs in Ireland written by Earnest Thompson Seaton. The coastwatcher acknowledged that he was a nephew of the novelist.

Seaton had been suffering from a toothache for approximately one year while he maintained a watch over Rekata Bay, reporting any activity in that port and additionally advising "Cactus" (ComAirSolomons) of any Japanese flights heading south that he could observe.

His two "boys" were native Melanisians of short, stocky and muscular build each carrying a Springfield 306—almost as long as they were! Coastwatcher Seaton was a man well over six feet in height. He was armed with a carbine which he carried as though it were a matchstick. The three of them were taken by boat across the slot to Guadalcanal where Seaton was to receive dental care. Although I heard no more of them, I am confident that they were flown back to Choisel to resume their coast watching assignment.

Admiral Nimitz has supposedly noted that the four most important factors in the winning of the Pacific War were: Submarines, the Carriers, the Coastwatchers, and the Bulldozers, but not necessarily in that order of importance.

Incidently, the coastwatcher organization of the South Pacific was initially organized as early as 1922 by Australian Naval Forces in anticipation of probable future difficulty with the Empire of Japan.

The other mission involving Lieutenant Snedeker and Ensign Cox was a rescue operation off Point Torikena. Midway up the coast of Bougainville the U.S. Marines had gone ashore against stronger Japanese resistance than intelligence sources had reported. Snedeker's instructions were to land and pick up two seriously wounded Marines. Ensign Cox writes:

These men were delivered to our PBY in a large landing craft. Getting a boat (LCD) of that size close enough to the starboard blister of a Catalina while rolling in an open sea is physically impossible without tearing off the starboard wing or its float—but we didn't know that.

Well! After a few "hairy" tries the coxswain did the trick, and we were able to get the two men in metal baskets aboard. Snedeker made a nice take off in the open sea, and with our escort of eight P38s returned us to Halavo Bay. The wounded marines were thence boated to Guadalcanal for emergency medical treatment. And that's the end of that tune.

A sidelight: During the invasion of Bougainville at Cape Torikena when the Marines had fought their way approximately 500 yards from the beach through heavy undergrowth, they were disturbed by the sound of heavy machinery. The obvious conclusion was that they were about to come under a counter attack by Japanese tanks. They immediately called for anti-tank weapons, and then moved slowly forward to observe a large clearing. There in the center of the clearing, was a battalion of Seabees— building an officers club!

Ens. Richard Doutt remembers:

The squadron (VP- 23) operated out of a strait between the south-

CHAPTER 7 The Solomons

ern end of Espiritu Santos and the island of Malo. I flew there from Efate with Lt. Kellam and his crew. We had Admiral McCain aboard who was to govern the operations.

Enroute from Efate, the Admiral told us to fly over an active volcano on one of the islands. It threw up cinders that hit the plane like anti-aircraft missiles.

Arriving at Espiritu, the place was empty except for a small DE type vessel that had hit a mine on the western end of the strait. The Admiral's flag ship, the seaplane tender USS *Curtiss*, had not arrived. We had left Efate hurriedly and our radio operator missed the flight so we had no one capable of sending or receiving messages. An Ensign in a leaky row boat rowed out from Espiritu and took the Admiral back to shore—where presumably they had some radio facility. Does this sound chaotic? It sure as hell was!

Eventually the *Curtiss* arrived—and so did our squadron from Noumea. I was put into Norm Brady's crew along with my old roommate from Corpus, Milt Cheverton. We operated patrols out of Espiritu, some of them night patrols and were waiting for the planned invasion of the Solomon Islands.

During this period, some PBY crew bombed the enemy air strip on Guadalcanal on a moonlit night to harass the Japanese. Also, during this period a "President" liner came in with armaments and troops. It hit a mine and though the Captain ran it aground, it sank rather quickly. Yes, it was a chaotic time.

I do not know whether Lt. Norm Brady and the rest of us (in his crew) were on patrol on the 6th, the day "Snuffy" vanished, but we probably were. Our squadron established our base on the island of Malaita in the Solomons the day of the invasion of Guadalcanal by the Marines. There was so much going on at the time that an overdue plane could have gotten lost in the shuffle.

Milt Cheverton and I flew with Brady all the time we were in the Solomon campaign. We operated for a while out of the Santa Cruz Islands flying patrols to the north to intercept any enemy convoys coming south from Truk to support the enemy forces on Guadalcanal.

"I vividly remember that August 23, 1942," writes Ens. Thomas Benton, continuing:

When we were flying patrol out of the New Hebrides islands to the East of New Caledonia. Our search area that day was north out of Espirito Santos and our seaplane tender was the USS *Curtiss*. We had a strong south wind all day so we arrived at the end of our patrol early and started back against the wind which reduced our "ground speed" to around 100 knots.

After we were on the homeward leg our Patrol Plane commander, Lt.(jg) Hal Lough had me take over command of the pilot's seat while he went back to the bunk for a rest after flying the plane for probably six hours. About forty minutes later, I heard a loud pop from the port engine. Looking out the window I saw that we were leaving a spray of oil—and number 13 piston was reciprocating outside the cowling which had been knocked off. A valve had become loose and had fallen on top of the piston, causing it to knock the piston clear off the crankcase. I immediately shut down the engine and feathered the prop, fortunately before we lost all oil pressure.

Hal Lough jumped to the cockpit asking why I feathered the engine. I just pointed out the window, because I was doing everything possible to keep that old PBY in the air on one engine. Both engines were past due for overhaul which meant we didn't have full power on the remaining engine. I asked Hal if he wanted to take over and he said "no, she's your baby." He then went back to the navigation table to find the closest island because we knew we could never get back to the *Curtiss* with strong head winds. Renell Island, some 80 miles away, was the nearest island.

We took a heading for it while I was trying to maintain our altitude, but even with full power on one engine we were still going down at a constant rate. Hal and the crew opened the bottom hatch and jettisoned our ammunition, mattresses and anything else that wasn't essential.

And all the time Bob Redhage, the head mechanic watching the engine gauges, was reading oil pressures and cylinder head temperatures to me. He began to caution me after about five minutes into this fight to keep the plane in the air that the cylinder head was climbing—which meant we would have to reduce power or take the chance of losing the starboard engine too.

A few minutes later, he frantically called that the temperature was on the red line. We were now down to about 50 feet above the water. Knowing I couldn't reduce my power, I told him there was a safety factor and to just tell me when it gets 20 degrees above the red line. The engine temperature must have stopped climbing because he never called back!

After about a half an hour which seemed like eight, we had used enough fuel to lighten the plane just enough to maintain our slim altitude and were even able to climb back a 100 feet or so.

A few minutes later, Rennell came into sight. This island is an old volcano that had been breached below sea level on the south side. The center of the old crater became a landlocked harbor with only one entrance. We were fortunate that the opening was straight ahead as we were approaching from the south—but because of the high crater walls around the high crater walls we were committed to land. There was no turning back and no chance ever to get airborne again.

Again I asked Hal if he wanted to land and he said, "No, you take it in," and so we came into the harbor on a swell, probably the softest landing I had ever made.

Now the question in all of our minds was "Have the Japanese occupied this island?" Well, as it turned out, it was only occupied by friendly natives. While it has been reported that we were there several days, actually it was less than 24 hours.

The natives were friendly and guided us to a safe place to drop anchor. When the tide went out the next morning we saw we had anchored in the exact spot where there were no coral heads that might have punctured our aluminum hull. The natives all wanted to inspect the plane as we anchored but we told them to wait until the sun comes up tomorrow. And so at sunrise, here come four or five dugouts full of men to inspect our "war plane." We let them come aboard through our rear blister—and out the front hatch—giving each a sharpened pencil. These were the only items missed when the crew jettisoned material to lighten the plane. The natives also brought us cooked taro and fruit. This was a friendly hour and they all went back to shore happy.

Before landing, we had radioed our position and a nearby destroyer just happened to be in the area. It came the next afternoon and hoisted the PBY up on its deck. The captain of the ship asked the pilot and a mechanic to stay on top of the wing where the sling was attached to guard against the wing banging against the ship's hull as the ship was rolling slightly. I and either Lee Hofheins or Redhage were volunteers.

That night while cruising back to Espirito Santos the escort destroyers were firing depth charges off and on all night because a Japanese submarine was reported in the area. All the ships crew which was not on duty were out on deck with their life jackets but I was so tired that when I found an empty bunk, I sacked out until the next morning.

Now the rest of the story—We all resumed patrol duty as soon as the engines were replaced except Ensign Denaree. He resigned his wings and was sent home. It was just too scary for him.

Around the first of November. I was one of four crews which received orders to San Diego to pick up new planes. Therefore, I was in San Diego when Lee Hofheins' plane was lost. The fact that the plane went down 50 miles from Oahu would indicate they were on routine patrol far from the war zone—but not out of danger.

LCDR Thomas Benton well remembers Rennell Island and a

time when a large number of Patrol Squadron 23 airmen came down with dysentery:

Slim Hallas and Art Hampy flew with me on my second tour to the Solomons. The Rennell Island incident happened when I was a co-pilot with Hal Lough. Hampy and Hallas came with me after I became PPC and we made a wonderful team! Canton Island was where most of the crews and officers who were flying daily patrols, came down with a parasite dysentery. That is, all except my crew and I.

The first afternoon after landing there, I took a stroll of all the facilities so that I would know where everything was in our assigned living and eating quarters. I found the fresh water plant where they converted sea water to "drinking" water. On closer inspection, I found a cap on the top of the storage tank open and when I looked in, I saw a dead cat floating in the water. I called the base officer in charge and he attempted to remove the cat but it fell apart so he screwed the cap back on and said he would have the medics add more chlorine. I told my crew not to drink any water so we were the only ones that didn't come down with the dysentery. We ended up flying all the rest of the patrols until we were relieved!

We picked up the radio news correspondent H.V. Kaltenborn off the beach on Bougainville island on Dec. 6, 1943. He had been with the Marines while they were occupying the island and he was all muddy and tired. In fact, so much so, that he sat down at the navigation table and went to sleep.

Captain Fleming, who was his escort, was concerned because we were not navigating. Or at least it seemed so, but by that time we had flown up and down "the slot" so often, we knew every landmark. We delivered him safely at Rendova after a bumpy take-off in the swells just off the beach.

Following are notes from Lt. Howard Dickerson's log book:

Conditions were extremely rough. There really was not an established port at Segond Channel in Espiritu Santo the first time they landed. Our Catalinas refueled off of rafts provided by the Army! Until the campaign officially started, home base was Noumea in New Caledonia.

Once the campaign started, home base was Espiritu Santo. The PBYs would forward deploy from there with the *Curtiss* and *Mackinac* to Santa Cruz and Mailaita just before any major action in order to search for the Japanese Fleet.

References in my Log Book note that bad weather conditions which could easily force the Catalinas to "fly over" the overcast. This made conditions extremely hazardous when it was time to come down to land. If

CHAPTER **7** *The Solomons* 63

navigation was off by only a mile or so, it would result in flying into the tops of the many volcanic peaks in the New Hebrides. This is probably what happened to "Snuffy" and crew.

Of major concern was the number of hours put on the engines and airframes of the PBYs during the early part of the campaign. Remember, the country had not yet been fully mobilized, conditions were sparse, the supply train shaky at best. I had at least one single engine failure down there, and a single-engine problem appears to be the contributing factor in the loss of Smith's PBY. I knew both Smith and Riepl, but not well ... but enough about the missions down there to bring closure with the families.

The log of Preston Thomas, AMM1/C, reads:

23 Aug 42: On patrol out of New Hebrides Island on Espirutu Santo.

24 May 43: Our squadron was again deployed to Espiritu Santo. Patrols were flown from the tenders there and at Vanikoro.

7 July 43: We flew out of Vanikoro and spent the night on a small seaplane tender, Chincoteague ... Jerry Corrigan. NAP 1/C, one other crewman and I slept on the plane. The PPC, first pilot and the rest of the crew slept on the tender. In the morning after their breakfast, the crew from the ship came to relieve us and take us to the ship to eat. The boat hadn't quite reached the ship when we heard what sounded like someone had thrown a hand full of gravel on a tin roof.

Then we saw 3 Japanese bombers in close formation flying so low we could see bombs leave their wings. The boat, before reaching us with our relief, immediately returned to the ship, taking our pilots with it. We raised the plane's anchor after starting the plane's engines and taxied around. Jerry and I discussed taking off to challenge the 3 Bettys, but thought better of it.

The ship had cut loose from its anchor and put to sea with our pilots aboard while the Japanese were making bombing runs. Fortunately, they couldn't bomb any better than the ship's gunners could shoot. We understood the ship had been on its shakedown cruise when it was ordered to the South Pacific. It was evident the gun crew had little or no training. They were missing their target by miles—literally!

A ship's crewman had jumped overboard from the fantail when the aviation fuel was ignited by a bomb. We taxied over and tried to pull him aboard the plane, but he had been burned and the skin on his hands had slid off in our hands. We managed to get him aboard, but couldn't give him a shot of morphine because the pilots had to keep it secure in their flight packet. He kept passing out while we applied wet towels to his burns. When conscious he would say how glad he was that he would be sent back to the States because of his injuries.

Another ship's boat that was in the water ran for the shore. By the time the ship returned, the tide had gone out and the boat was left high and dry. The crew was afraid to get out of the boat because there were so many coral snakes under the rock that the boat was sitting on. There they waited until their ship returned some time later. Probably quite thirsty, I've often wondered how long it took the tide to float them off the rocks. When the tender did return, they gave us back our pilots, the injured sailor was returned to the ship, we started engines, raised anchor and took off. The rest of the patrol was without incident. Needless to say the crew was happy to be back on their own tender.

At the end of August we moved to Halavo Bay on Tulagi Island in the Solomons. While at Halavo Bay, on a dumbo mission along the coast of Bouganville where a fighter had gone down, we were escorted by Marine F4Us and Army P38s. Unable to locate the downed pilot, but close enough to see the smoke on shore and small boats in the water. We witnessed "dog-fights" with Zeros. One P38 was hit, so he headed back to New Georgia—we later learned he crashed on his landing approach. We sure felt bad.

After our tours at Halavo Bay on Tulagi and Espiritu Santo, we headed back to Kaneohe. On the way we got into a typhoon that was so rough the pilots took turns flying manually because the auto pilot couldn't handle it. Navigation was so difficult that when we saw an island that gave shelter we landed. I broke out the raft for Lt. Hoagland and Lt.(jg) Ondrejcka to get ashore and find out where we were. The water was so shallow I jumped in to push them ashore. A lot of natives came out—swimming and in boats. I called for them to come and help push but they all turned and went back to shore. Some time later I realized what "push-push" meant to them. (There must have been some troops there before us!)

We did find that we were in Samoa. From there we were able to return to Kaneohe via Canton and Palmyra. After R&R at the Royal Hawaiian, we boarded a light carrier to San Diego. There was a big squadron farewell party in San Diego for the last gathering of VP-23. Some helped form VPB-23, the rest of us were reassigned to other parts of Naval Aviation.

Throughout my Navy career, VP-23 has always been home. It will always occupy a big place in my heart. I still miss those shipmates, some of whom have sailed off into the sunset—but I will always remember them.

A member of VP-23 when the squadron was reformed, Preston was transferred to PATSU on North Island. "Pres" and Ed Riepl had joined the

Navy together in Denver and went through their training in San Diego. Ed dated Preston's sister when the Thomas family was visiting in San Diego. He also knew Jim Pearson, with whom he "pooled" resources to buy an old Ford. And "Snuffy" Smith was the co-pilot of the first flight crew that AMM1/C Pres Thomas was assigned to.

Lt. Keith Guthrie remembers "bushwhacking" in the South Pacific:

I always considered myself a newspaperman on temporary duty in the Naval Air Corps. A hot pilot I was not! Probably Boardman Jones best puts that time period into focus in relating just how he ended up flying P-Boats: "I got a traffic ticket and went to city hall to pay my fine. Upon entering the building, I asked an official looking individual where to go to pay the violation. He motioned to a couple of lines, and so I lined up—in short time naturally. When I got to the head of the line, the young man asked me to raise my right hand and swear after him, which I thought was a bit odd..."

In my own case, I was busy running a weekly newspaper in East Texas when my final notice arrived from the draft board. Within a week, I had washed off the printer's ink, leased my newspaper and was shortly at Hensley Field in Dallas.

Weekends found would-be cadets "bushwhacking" in the jungles of Texas. Hurry, hurry, hurry was the watch-word upon arrival at Rodd Field, Corpus Christi, and after an equal number of ups and downs, I wound up at Cuddihy Field.

I had already discovered I had no desire to "wring out" a plane, so when they assigned me to PBY training squadron I was pleased. They looked durable!

In short order the Navy made a "gentleman" out of me with orders to San Diego. "Bushwhacking" in earnest started on the west coast. All good things usually come to an end—and I found myself lolling on a beach in Oahu on Christmas day in 1942.

"Bushwhacking" really got seriously underway with jaunts to sugar cane fields, museums, and Chinatown. Drinking pineapple juice out of a fountain was a unique experience for a country boy—as was a visit to a local fishmarket where fish eyes were a hot item.

At Midway Islands, "Gooney birds" were a constant source of amazement. I think these zany birds actually felt a kinship to Yoke-boat pilots. When they had trouble getting airborne on a still day, they seemed to enjoy being tossed into the air by "hot pilots."

I learned about celestial navigation from an old hand in the squadron. He put star navigation into a life-saving mode. Midway was a real experience with its coral beaches and Pearl and Hermes Reefs near by.

Actually, I also did some real "bushwhacking" at Midway Islands years later when I convinced the Navy (with the help of Sen. Lyndon Johnson) that a trip back to the bases where I had served during WWII would be good PR. My wife, a former Navy nurse, enjoyed the wonders of Midway also.

I was assigned to Lt. CMDR Brandley's crew, which was fortunate for me, since he was not inclined to question where I had been as long as I showed up for flight time. On the big ferry trip to the South Pacific we landed at Upolu. Since this was the burial place of Robert Louis Stevenson, one of my favorite authors, I immediately arranged for a visit to his grave. It fell through when the skipper discovered that it was questionable whether I would make the trip back in time for the flight to Espiritu Santo.

It also escaped the censors when, in a letter home, I bemoaned the fact that I did not get to visit the grave of "my favorite author" in Journeys through Bookland. My mother decided I was not in harm's way in Samoa. That was my last journey attempt to tell the folks back home where I was stationed.

Funa Futi offered little in the way of bushwhacking; however, I did manage to make it across the lagoon island where the natives lived, which was adjacent to the Navy's settlement. I got a big kick out of watching the natives tie their ankles together and make like a measuring worm to gain the top of the coconut palms. Since part of the squadron's mission was to map the Ellis chain, I enjoyed going ashore and seeing how these gentle people lived outside the Navy's influence. The bare breasted ladies in grass skirts were unique. We managed to take a Navy camera.

After arriving at Halavo Seaplane Base on Tulagi, Langhorn Washburne, Morris Hoverston and I began systematically exploring the surrounding jungle. Washburne claimed he was a dynamite expert, and we believed him until a charge almost got our "borrowed" boat out of the water. However, the menu was vastly improved when fresh fish was inserted in place of Spam at the officer and enlisted mess.

I've never seen such weird critters that the blasts brought up from the deep. We asked a native whether they were good to eat. He reached over and picked up the critter, and took a bite. Case closed.

A day-long row-boat trip and a trudge through the jungles brought us to a native village. Evidently they knew all about "sailors," because all we saw of the women were their backs disappearing into the jungle.

We were amazed at their church in the middle of the jungle. Later we managed to haggle for a stalk of bananas for $1. A trip deeper into the bush, at the direction of the native, brought us to the site of a downed Zero, but it had been visited by others and the choice logos had been removed.

Washburne did manage to con the Seabees into allowing him to borrow a barge and a winch that we used to bring up a Japanese float plane from Tulagi harbor where it had fallen the night of the attack on ships in the harbor at anchor. When we got ashore it caused such a crush of souvenir hunters that the skipper CO ordered the plane returned to the deep and put a ban on further relic seeking.

The tales of the Australian coast watchers were intriguing to the point that Hove and I asked for a visit to their base camp on Guadalcanal. Over hot Aussie beer (which almost gagged us) we listened as about ten of the former plantation owners told some of their tales.

One was told by a veteran Russell Islands plantation owner-turned-coast watcher. We took several Jap prisoners, but not wanting to slow us down, we turned our backs while our native guides quickly exterminated them with their long bush knives. At another time, they threw a pistol on the ground, and when the Jap prisoners made a dive for it, they were exterminated.

We had no love for the Japanese, so we saw nothing wrong in these tactics. We even went out of our way to see the sign that Admiral Bull Halsey put up on Guadalcanal that reads: "Kill the little yellow bastards!"

On another occasion, we even visited the Aussie headquarters and investigated the procedure to acquire the land for a coconut plantation. In order to qualify you had to be citizen of Australia. Any place we had spare time, we took off. The stop over tender at Vanikoro Island didn't offer too much in the way of sights ... however, Washburne and I managed to get a rubber boat and fishing gear on our layover day, and spent the time with a face mask diving among the coral reefs. We wondered what the huge fish that stayed nearby were up to ... until it dawned on us that they were sharks!

"Hove" had quite an experience in this bay. He was in a small boat between the shore and tender when a Jap bomber dropped a string of bombs. Hove, who had flunked his swimming test at San Diego, made it ashore so fast that the back of his shirt didn't get wet. Probably some of our best jaunts were while at the Espiritu Santo Harbor. We made the acquaintanceship of a French doctor who offered to take us on a wild hog hunt. Our party looked like a "safari" as we headed inward on the southern island. The beaters soon began their work and the wild hogs began to crash in all directions in the undergrowth. Borrowed army rifles made a lot of noise, but the hogs escaped unharmed. We returned to a huge tree that was also evidently home of a colony of large bats. This time our rifles managed to knock down one for inspection (wing span of at least fourteen to twenty inches). With the noon hour past, we were worried about getting chow time. Suddenly up on a trail came a dozen or more white clad natives bearing all sorts of baskets and boxes. Within minutes white tablecloths had been spread on the jungle floor and wine was served. To say the least we recovered from the surprise to partake in a sumptuous feast.

Still another time we borrowed a boat from our French friends and crossing the narrow harbor, tied our boats and proceeded to spend the rest of the day following jungle trails. We emerged from the other side to be greeted by a Seventh Day Adventist, who invited us into his mission/home to share his meager larder. What we really enjoyed was being allowed to eat our fill of oranges from trees around their home. The pastor asked for our birthdays so he could pray for us each year. Later we managed to liberate several pound boxes of black pepper (their no. 1 wish) to give our newfound friends. Our final meeting with our French friends came when Charlie G. (he was a plantation owner who had opened a restaurant in his home for service personnel) furnished us a guide for another pig hunt. This time we were successful and brought home a porker of sufficient size to barbecue for the entire squadron. Shortly after this barbecue hunt, the squadron got the orders to move out—to Hawaii. Our South Pacific tour of duty was over.

Report from Lt.(jg) Langhorn Washburn:

I was with VP-23 for a year and a half when George Garcia was skipper. We lived on the USS *Wright* at Espiritu-Santo and in the jungle at Tulagi. I still have large photos of the Jap Tower on Halavo Beach with PBYs on their beaching gear, being serviced.

Hoverston, Guthrie and I used to go into the jungles and hunt. We brought back wild boar—and dynamited fish inside the reef to feed the squadron.

I still remember bombing Nauru and tossing incendiaries out of the tunnel hatch. VP-23 43-44 were the golden years of action and comradeship. Sometimes in my dreams, I still push the throttle full forward and reach down to achieve "floats-up"!

Lt. Milton R. Cheverton's ('41-'44) first orders to active duty placed him aboard the USS *Wisconsin*, landing him in Pango Pango where he got some flight time in with a Marine squadron.

Sent back to Pearl aboard the USS *Indianapolis*, Milt was assigned some temporary duty during the Battle of Midway—and then was assigned to VP-23 in the South Pacific. In 1942 he was in

CHAPTER 7 *The Solomons*   69

the first tour which started in Nuomea, New Caledonia, then to Efate at Havana Harbor and Segund Channel at Espiritu Santo. He went on to Mia Maramaski Straits in Melata, Garasios Ndeni, and from there to Auckland, New Zealand.

A commendation from Nimitz reads: "On the night of 26-27 Oct '42 Ensign Milton Cheverton as a member of the crew of 23-P-13, and in the company of other PBYs, searched for and made a night contact on a Japanese Carrier and cruiser with torpedoes, bombs and guns hitting the bulls eye."

The commendation "further commends those crews for their complete and detailed reports of the enemy's position and composition." Milt was a PPC of his own plane, named "Pugnacious Polly" after his wife. Awarded the Distinguished Flying Cross, and recipient of several citations, Milt and his crew engaged the enemy at Bougainville and in another mission successfully landed on water under intense enemy fire to rescue a downed B-25 crew.

On November 24, 1943, Lieutenant Cheverton took off from Ondonga to attempt a rescue of the B-25 crew of the 70th Bombardment Squadron. Rendezvousing with P-40s from New Zealand, Milt set his course at fifty-feet altitude with air cover at 2,000 feet.

Approaching Ballale Island, he dropped two smoke flares and then made a water landing, picking up the six-man B-25 crew, three of whom were injured. Intense AA fire from all calibers and coastal gunfire was directed at the PBY in the air and on the water. Additional gunfire came from Kangu Hill and Kahili on Bougainville, with more coming from Nusava and Nusakoa Islands. One shell exploded less than fifteen yards in front of the Dumbo as it was taking off.

Naval dispatch sent word to Cheverton: "WELL DONE ON A COURAGEOUS DUMBO MISSION X HALSEY."

CMDR Thomas Benton ('42-'44) operated from seaplane tenders *Curtis*, *Mackinac* and two others, off Espiritu Santo, New Caledonia, Midway, Johnson, Canton, Tulagi, Rendova, and Vila. Among his special recollections: Picking up a downed PV crew from the Solomon Islands.

> I never heard anything about Lt. Truett, Ensign Conlin and crew that Clark, CAP Wiley ard I picked up off Choisel Island Oct. 17, 1943. Truett

and crew had survived a crash landing of a PV—and were rescued by a coastwatcher on the island. We picked them up on a stormy day—in fact, the weather was so bad that the P-38s assigned to give us fighter cover, turned back. We flew low and slow with poor visibility, because of the heavy rainfall—but made the dumbo pick-up O.K.

On September 15, 1943, Lt. William Geritz, VP-23 PBY pilot, and Capt. Bert Brown, skipper of the USS Destroyer *Saufley* (DD-465), took on a Jap sub (RO101) off the Solomon Islands, 10° 57' S., 161° 56' E.

Jim Sawruk, historian, notes: "It was the RO-101 commanded by LCDR Masataka Fujisawa that was sunk by the combined attack of DD and PBY at 10-57S 163-56E. 5. They used 2 Mk 29—650# depth bombs—of which the first one was a dud. All fifty of the submarine crew were lost with it."

DD Skipper Brown reported:

About 1100, 15 Sept. '43 near the Santa Cruz Islands (about halfway from Espirutu Santo) a freighter we were escorting signaled that a torpedo had just missed her. I told the two other ships we had been escorting to continue on to Espiritu Santo—and took the Saufley back to search for the submarine.

We soon located her and dropped a "15 depth-charge salvo"—which so disturbed the water that we could get no clear echoes from the sub and from previous experience, I knew it would be at least one hour before we could get good echoes.

The tropical waters are very different to work in. In addition to false echoes from the boils where depth charges were exploded, the reefs also give echoes ... and so do the temperature layers and current eddies.

Making a wide swing westward to cover a possibility that the sub was making a high speed run to escape, we found nothing. Returning to the sub's original position, we found that she was still close by. I believe she may have been damaged by our first depth charges.

We made another run over her—and dropped a pattern of 15 more depth charges. Circling the area, we stayed several miles from the sub to permit sound conditions to clear up.

By this time a Navy PBY Flying boat from Espiritu Santo joined us to help in the attack. We made two more depth charge attacks about an hour apart.

As we started in for the fifth attack, we saw the sub suddenly broach, dead ahead about a mile. She came up far enough to expose her hull as well as the conning tower. We read her number—RO 101. I or-

CHAPTER 7 *The Solomons*

dered the five inch guns to commence firing, turning the ship to bring all guns to bear. For a couple of minutes we poured heavy fire. I am sure we hit her many times.

The PBY then made a low level run and dropped a depth charge right on the sub. She went down slowly and soon we saw oil slicks and floating debris coming up.

We should have had full credit for the kill—but the PBY was given one half credit and the Saufley the other half.

The main result, however, was that there was one less Jap sub to harass our ships!

After the war we found that on 29 June 43, the RO-101 had reported the American invasion force moving into New Georgia. The Jap subs were often used as scouts.

Bos'un 2/C Al Eckel, crewman aboard the *Saufley*, gives the following account:

I remember the incident like it was yesterday. We were taking a transport from Guadalcanal to the New Hebrides, and the PBY reported the wake of two "fish" headed for the transport.

My battle station on the *Saufley* was the forward fire room, but they secured general quarters to the engineers, so I was topside and had a perfect view.

We forced the sub to the surface with depth charges, and when she surfaced it was a sight to behold. The conning tower and the bow came up at the same time. She was less than a mile away, we moved in closer and the captain ordered every gun to fire.

The PBY swooped down—and I swear it was less than 100 feet off the sub, and dropped a depth charge as the sub kinda rolled over, and sunk out of sight. There was a huge explosion under water, and that was the end of RO101.

Lt. William J. "Sabu" Geritz turned in this VP-23 Action Report of the attack on the surfacing submarine:

PBY-5 # 33 piloted by PPC Lt. Wm. J. Geritz, Ensign F.T. Ben and Ensign G.T. Hopkins. The aircrew were R.J. Redhage AMM1/C; C.E. Spencer ARM1/C; H.W. Isaacs AMM2/C; P.F. Mandrgoc AMM2/C; H.C. Kolb AOM2/C; and N.L. Robinson AMM2/C.

While flying on a circular course, Ensign Ben noticed an air bubble area form on our starboard beam and expand rapidly with large bubbles coming from the surface. When the disturbed area was at approximately 3 o'clock relative to the heading of the plane, the conning tower of the sub suddenly appeared in its center. The sub was canted approximately 45 degrees to port as it immerged so that the starboard side of the conning tower, superstructure deck, rail and hull were visible.

Ensign Ben reports that numerals he believed to be "54" were on the sub's conning tower. A flipper turn to the starboard was executed as soon as the sub was sighted and the run made on a bearing of approximately 120 degrees from the sub's bow. Depth charges were released manually by estimate, and both entered the water spaced about 50 ft. apart on the sub's starboard side just aft of the conning tower.

The starboard depth charge, which was dropped first, entered the water about 70 ft from the sub but failed to explode. The port depth charge entered the water about 20 ft from the sub and exploded, covering the visible portion of the water and hiding it from the view of the gunners in the waist blisters and from the crew of the other PBY which was in the immediate vicinity. When the water subsided, the sub was no longer visible.

While the bombing run was being made the port waist gunner Paul F. Mandgroc ARM2/C fired fifty rounds of his .50 caliber at the conning tower—and saw tracers from hits glance off. While the run was under way, and after the run was completed the DD #465 fired 20 MM, 50 caliber and heavier guns at the sub. We remained in the area 42 minutes after the attack, then returned to base leaving the other PBY and the Destroyer on station.

Lt.(jg) C. Langhorn E. Washburn ('43-'44) remembers flying with Skipper George "the Message" Garcia, and tossing out incendiaries from the tunnel hatch with CIC Rowlan over Nauru. He also remembers "living in jungle at Tulagi; picking up Marine General Vandergrift in Kula Lagoon... and watching 'Washing Machine Charlie' shot down over Guadalcanal."

Washburn returned home to Virginia, and to other achievements: operations manager for Hiller Helicopter Corp., assistant secretary of commerce under Presidents Nixon and Ford; and VP of Disney (International) EPCOT.

Washburn has served on many boards, including the Board of Eisenhower World Affairs Institute. A member of Edgarton Yacht Club, Metropolitan Club (Washington, D.C.), and the Union Club of New York, his hobbies include sailing, flying, and farming. Married to Judith, he's a dad of two and grandpappy to four.

Lt. Robert Elberg's ('43-'45) Flight Log reads:

> I flew six marines into Rekata Bay on Santa Isabel Island on Sept.

CHAPTER **7** *The Solomons* 73

12, 1943. We had information from the Coast Watcher that the Japs had left Rekata Bay, which was one of the larger sea plane bases. The Marines from Guadalcanal were sent over to Havalo to be transported to Rekata Bay to go ashore, hook up with the coast watcher and check out the base.

We also had six fighter planes to fly cover, which made us feel better not knowing what we would find. We had no problem landing and unloading the marines and the gear into two rubber boats. The only difficulty was after loading all the gear in the boats (big boxes, duffel bags, etc.) there was little room for the marines, let alone getting their paddles into the water.

I told the LT in charge to climb aboard and I'd crank up and blow them ashore. Boy, did they get a fast ride! No Jap could have picked them off at that speed.

I had a Mickey Mouse camera, which took pictures showing the type Zero observation single-float planes on the beach. I'm sure the guys in those boats will remember that fast prop wash ride to the beach.

One of my pictures showed the "Blondes of Vanakora" and their house. Vanakora is an island three hundred miles north of Espiritu Santo. We had a small sea plane tender there, which we used as an advanced base. My crew were as follows: Lt. Robert Elberg PPC; Ensign W. Boardman Jones, Jr., 1st Pilot; Howard Chamley 2nd Pilot; Rudy McClinton ARM 1/C; and Waldren ARM 2/C.

Lt. W. Boardman "Boardie" Jones, Jr., wrote the following "saga":

On October 15th, 1942, a group of us won our wings at graduation ceremonies at Corpus Christi, Texas. Or maybe it would be better to say we were "given" our wings to get us out of training!

Instructed to report to the CO, Transitional Training, Pacific Fleet San Diego after a 15-day delay for R&R, we were given a choice of 90 days in Alaska or a year in the Pacific. One guy chose the former and the rest of us were sent to San Francisco, and quickly put aboard ship to Pearl Harbor. Arriving November 28, we were promptly assigned to Patrol Squadrons VP-23 and VP-44. Obviously, I was assigned the former.

Now proud members of "THE FLEET," we paraded ourselves around Honolulu as if we personally had won the Battle of Midway! Shortly, we were assigned "patrol" out of Kaneohe and after the vast experience provided by two patrols—we flew off to Midway on December 30th.

New Year's Eve I found myself on a long search across the date line looking for some flyers who had ditched about half way to Wake—no luck—but in crossing the date line frequently, our crew had the pleasure of flying back and forth between years 1942 and 1943 several times!

We stayed on Midway until the end of February, flying short five-hour patrols almost every day. At this point our Plane Commanders in the squadron were all "veterans of Midway" and the early days of "the Solomons." One flight I took was with Lt. Francis "Murph" Murphy, who flew the "last man off Wake Island" just before the Japs landed. Another was Lt. Howard Ady, Jr.—the man who was first to "spot and track" the Jap Fleet coming into Midway in June of 1942.

While we were on Midway, I attempted my first landing of a PBY on a runway. I missed it by a good 20 yards a couple of times, so I was treated to a little "extra flight training." Most of our land time was spent watching the Gooney birds who were in the middle of their hatching season. These perfectly ridiculous birds though extremely awkward on land were superior flyers, and great fun to watch in their mating dances.

At the end of February, we returned to Kaneohe—where I was assigned to Ensign Bob Elberg and with whom I flew from then until February 1943. He is a great guy, a good flyer, and fun to be with. Anyway, in mid-March we left Kaneohe for Palmyra and Canton Islands, where we were stationed until the first week in May.

During our stay on Canton, we patrolled out toward Howland and Baker Islands fairly regularly, which was on the way to Jap-held Tarawa. Occasionally the Japs would send a night bomber to Canton to wake us up. We soon were arising preemptively about twenty minutes before the Jap Bomber arrived, quickly taking off in such planes as were working. We would fly them to a nearby island and circle until all clear. These experiences were colorful.

On one such night one of our crews took off and once aloft the "PPC" casually instructed the co-pilot: "It might be well to pull up a little higher." There was a silent pause, then a surprised answer as the co-pilot blurted out: "Aren't YOU flying the plane ... ?!!"

On another evening, we were circling a designated island—when we noticed that one of our compatriots flying on our wing had his forward cabin lights lit. We called to ask him to turn off the light, which he failed to do. Later on the ground, we questioned him as to why he had been so stubborn. His reply: "... but we never took off—my plane was grounded! Your night wingman must have been a Jap K navigation plane!"

We continued a heavy schedule of patrols until the end of April—when a goodly number, about six of our crews, were returned to Kaneohe and the Aiea hospital in Hawaii for recovery from acute dysentery! We later found out that it was caused by a dead cat found in a large communal canvas water bag.

None of the Canton flights were particularly eventful—except for one very early morning anti-submarine patrol which we flew. With approaching dawn, we spotted a light on the water. After we had passed it,

CHAPTER 7   *The Solomons*   75

we realized this was probably the sub we were searching for. Needless to say by the time we got turned around, there wasn't anything to bomb.

We returned to join the squadron toward the end of May as part of the group were preparing to leave for the Solomons ... or more particularly Espiritu Santo. Our "Canton group" started training in PBY-5s in preparation for joining the advanced party. We continued until the middle of June doing bounce drill, instrumental flights, bombing runs, and even a torpedo practice—until the Skipper felt we were highly qualified in all aspects of Patrol Bombers.

Arriving in Espiritu Santo after flying to Palmyra, Canton, and Suva, we took up quarters on the seaplane tender Chincoteague—which became our base. The forward group had gone on to Funafuti for patrol with the Skipper.

We continued alternating patrols out of Espiritu and Vanakoro (where Capt. Bligh found his first supplies after "the Mutiny"). The format was to leave Espiritu—fly out about 900 miles, and put in at Vanakoro which was about 400 miles north of Espiritu. The next day we would reverse the procedure and fly to our small tender about 400 miles—and then back again to Espiritu and the Officers Club or the Enlisted men's Club as the case might be.

About the end of August we were transferred to Halavo base on Tulagi—across from "Iron Bottom Sound" from Guadalcanal. A little excitement on the foregoing patrols: One day our crew flew out of some poor weather when we were startled to see three Battleships and their escorts off our Port wing. The ships weren't listed on our intelligence reports as being "ours"—so we ducked back into the weather to think a bit. We finally decided that since they hadn't shot at us—they must be ours—and continued on.

On another patrol, we practically collided with a Japanese "Betty" twin engine bomber heading straight for us. The pilot did a 180 degree turn almost as fast as we did and we didn't see "Betty" again!

Through September, October and November the squadron was working in different parts of the Solomons, namely Tulagi, Rendova, Ondega, etc. During this time a few selected incidents, which our crew experienced, may be of interest.

On November 12th, our crew, covered by fighters from Guadalcanal, flew into Rekata Bay on Santa Isabel to pick up an Australian Coast Watcher. We were the first American Plane to land in these waters, and the Australian turned out to be a most fascinating guy, my model of Michener's hero in "South Pacific." Anyway, we got him safely out.

On the 18th, six crews led by our Skipper Lt. Cdr Garcia, made a shot at bombing the Japanese held potash island of Nauru. The mission was so well planned that only "one plane" found the island even though it was a pretty good moonlit night. That single plane reported receiving quite a heavy bit of anti-aircraft fire—so it may have been a blessing that we had dropped our bombs in mid-ocean before returning to the base at daybreak.

Toward the end of November, our crew made a trip to Noumea for some needed repairs. Our personal spirits were also "repaired" by being among the lovely Colonial girls in the city, coupled with adequate quantities of alcoholic refreshment. The four days needed for those activities were indeed enough, as our exchequers were fully depleted.

On November 12th our crew, then stationed in Rendova, was called to fly into the Treasury Islands to pick up some personnel and fly them on to Empress Bay, a newly opened beachhead on Bougainville. To our surprise this turned out to be none other than Admiral "Bull" Halsey and some of his staff. Our landing in Bougainville waters is a tale so aptly told by PPC Bob Elberg in his memoirs. Pretty good fun.

Subsequently, we did a few "Black Cat" night patrols ... one of which caught us in range of a Jap fighter which pursued us rather too closely and for much too long a time. We tried to get close to Malaita Island—to see if that would give us cover from his radar if he had any, but without much success. Why he didn't fire on us, I don't know. In any event we got finally down to the water and eventually got rid of him shortly before daybreak.

Shortly after, the squadron regrouped at Espiritu Santo to await further orders. During this time our senior pilots trained the next level (of which I was one) in preparation for appointment as "Patrol Plane Commanders." My own certificate is dated January 5, 1944.

On January 7th we started home for Kaneohe. Our first stop was Suva, where the weather turned a little nasty. We made one false start and found ourselves heading into a typhoon. It was, to say the least, a bit rough—so we turned back to Suva. We spent the next two nights and days in Suva with the planes manned by part crews, and engines running to hold our place at anchor. We would change crews a couple of times a day until the storm apparently had blown over.

On the 10th we started out again and this time we flew on the trailing edge of the typhoon and made it to Wallis Island. This island turned out to have a number of natives with "Elephantitis"—which was a unique thing to view. None of the rest of us contacted this most unfortunate disease. From there, we made it back to Kaneohe, after crossing the date line, by the 12th of January. There we were put aboard a Jeep carrier out of Pearl, and in about seven days we were "back stateside" in San Diego. After a large squadron party (after which I found myself in a local jail) we disbanded and given a month's leave—with orders to return on March 2, 1944 to reform a new Squadron VP-23, in San Diego.

CHAPTER 7 *The Solomons*

Drink to the merry crews of VPB-23!

Adm. Frank Brandley (1942 skipper of VP-23 in the Solomons) later was CINC Naval Aviation Training Center. Walt Rapley, AVCM VPB-23 ('44-'45), who also served on the admiral's staff as assistant to LCDR Charles McCarthy (also a yokeboater), remembers a little recipe book entitled "Frying by the Seat of your Pans" and compiled by station personnel to which the ADM submitted a favorite egg nog recipe. Walt said he "thought the 'Malaria Cure' looked very effective. Other chemical formulas are an added bonus; they might be good—tho' I've never tried any of them. I'm a 'gin & tonic' man myself!"

Adm. Frank Brandley's "Very Best Egg Nog"

2 cups fine sugar   1 quart Cognac
10 eggs   3 quarts light cream
          1½ cups St. Croix or Jamaican Rum

Adm. Frank Brandley's "Get-even-with-your-friends Punch"

1 part Sauterne   1 part Brandy
2 parts Champagne

Pour over ice!

Capt. Malcolm Bonner's USN (Ret.) "Shanty"

1/2 ginger beer or ginger ale   1/2 beer

Serve with ice in a beer mug or highball glass. As good for beach parties as it is a miracle worker for the morning after the night before!

Junior Officer's "CURE for MALARIA"

Drop two cubes of ice in chilled highball glass. Add 1½ oz. commendable, ice cold gin, the juice of ¼ fresh lime (room temperature), 1 drop of extra-dry vermouth and a dash of orange bitters. Stir. Top up the glass with ice cold Schweppes tonic water. Add fruit and other debris only if required to remedy a Vitamin C deficiency or clear the bar top.

—Lt. James Pierce

Now get out the buttermilk!

8

The Lost Crew

ESPIRITU SANTO, AUGUST 1942

*Assigned the western segment of Sector Three—
never to return.*

Lt. Maurice "Snuffy" Smith departed for the Solomon Islands on July 13, 1942, in 23-P-15. Others in his crew were: Ens. Edward W. Riepl; Chief NAP Clifford Pindell; Plane Capt. William Osborne, AMM1/C; James Pearson, ARM1/C; Vernon Stolz, AMM2/C; William Pipes, ARM2/C; and Merlin Rich, ARM2/C.

On August 1 they arrived along with eight other PBYs and their crews, and their seaplane tender USS *Mackinac*, at an estuary between the islands of Malaitia and Marmasike—some fifty miles from Guadalcanal.

The VP-23 Catalinas would now be eighty miles from Tulagi, the vital seaplane base that was taken from the Australians by Japanese forces on May 3, 1942. The first major engagement for Guadalcanal was imminent and would require maximum effort from VP-23 crews.

Their mission: to spot all enemy activity, operating from Segond Channel on the southeast side of Espiritu in the New Hebrides Islands.

On August 6, 1942, the day before the Marines were to make their initial assault on Guadalcanal, Lt. Snuffy Smith and his crew climbed into their PBY, 23-P-15. Despite bad weather reports, distressing overcast, intermittent rain squalls, and generally stormy conditions, the crew took off.

CHAPTER **8** *The Lost Crew* 79

Assigned the western segment of Sector Three—they were never to return.

ooo

In December of 1994, over fifty years later, I was searching out former shipmates of VP-23 to bring them together for a first-time reunion and celebration of the fiftieth anniversary of the end of WWII.

In the same month, a WWII Navy plane that was reportedly found in the mountains of Espiritu Santo in the New Hebrides Islands (now the Republic of Vanatua) would reveal the fate of Lt. Snuffy Smith and the eight-man crew of 23-P-15.

The lost crew, missing since August 6, 1942, and discovered by loggers in the jungle mountains, was the only plane out of the nine PBYs sent on the mission that day that did not return.

The Navy was notified, and a DOD casualty assistance team was sent off to the crash site. However, it would take another five years to retrieve and sort the few remains that were left, search for families of the lost crewmen, complete subsequent DNA tests, and make positive identification before final burial arrangements would be decided upon.

ooo

The Crew of 23-P-15:

Patrol Plane Commander Lt. Maurice Seaver "Snuffy" Smith
Maurice Smith was born in Lodi, California, on August 24, 1912. In 1936 he joined the 184th Inf., California National Guard. He was discharged in 1938 to accept appointment as a Naval Aviation Cadet.

In February of 1941, upon winning his wings and receiving his commission, Ensign Smith was assigned to VP-25, later redesignated VP-23. He was promoted to lieutenant(jg) on November 1, 1941.

This report came from his hometown newspaper, *The Record* (Lodi, California):

Lt. Maurice S. Smith knew the airplane he was piloting on August

6, 1942 was running low on fuel. He and seven other Navy Air Corps crew members, however, felt they had a greater duty—to continue reporting the position of the Japanese Navy. Smith and his seven crewmates could have returned back to base for fuel, but instead stayed to finish their assignment. Fifty-seven years later Maurice Smith's and his crew's remains—have been found. (Jeff Hood, reporter.)

George E. Smith, of Stockton, California, a brother and the last survivor in a family of four boys, laments:

Maurice was a hero—I know he stayed with the Japanese fleet until he ran out of fuel, he knew it would happen! He was my favorite brother—and did many things for me—like giving me my first electric train, and teaching me how to drive a car. My dad was a farmer—and mom was busy with other things—so he was my favorite brother!

Surviving high school classmate and friend Bing Taylor, who graduated with Smith in 1929, reflected that he was one of three Union High School band members who perished in World War II.

The Smith family learned in 1943 that Maurice, a University of California at Berkeley graduate, was lost at sea and presumed dead. The next year, brother George Smith joined the Marines intent on wrangling his way to the South Pacific to learn more about his brother's fate. The war ended before he could finish his investigation.

George remembers that Maurice's medals arrived the day after Veteran's Day and included a medal for the Battle of Midway and the Purple Heart.

Lt. Maurice Smith was paid honors in 1999 at a sea burial near Pearl Harbor as requested, presided over by a Navy chaplain. He was also honored at the crew's group interment ceremony held later at Arlington National Cemetery.

Ens. Edward "Rip" Riepl was co-pilot in Snuffy Smith's crew.

Born 1918 in Herndon, Kansas, Ed grew up on a farm, graduated from Herndon High School in 1935, and attended McCook Community College. In February 1940 he enlisted in the Navy as an apprentice seaman.

After basic training at Naval Training Station San Diego, California, he was stationed at Pearl Harbor as an aviation machin-

CHAPTER **8** *The Lost Crew*   81

ist mate. In July 1941, Ed was accepted for flight school in Corpus Christi, Texas. While in Texas, the Japanese attacked Pearl Harbor, sending the United States into World War II.

In May of 1942, upon graduating from flight school, Edward was promoted to the rank of ensign, and after home leave he reported for further training. Instead, he was sent to Pearl Harbor, and from there to the South Pacific for assignment to VP-23. The young officer had been with the squadron about a week when, on August 6, 1942, the day before the allied invasion of the Solomon Islands, he took off with Lt. "Snuffy" Smith's crew. Their mission: a surveillance flight to scout for Japanese forces.

At approximately 1600 (4:00 P.M.) the crew made their final radio contact with base, reporting that the weather was bad. That was the last that was heard from 23-P-15.

It was some fifty years later, in May of 1994, that the Navy Department would notify Ed Riepl's brother, Jerry, in Cimarron, Kansas.

"Ironically, that was Ed's birthday," Jerry remembers, "...and I had the flag flying outside. I always fly the flag for his birthday." Jerry also served in the Navy, as a radar operator during World War II. He served aboard a destroyer that was used for surveillance.

Petty Officer William Osborne, ARM1/C

The five surviving brothers and sisters of William Osborne had long ago given up hope of ever giving their brother Bill a proper burial. Then, three years ago, the Navy called.

The Osbornes' local newspaper reports: "Fifty-seven years after Petty Officer William Osborne from Martinsville, Virginia was lost in a World War II plane crash, the Navy is bringing his remains back home to the United States! Thanks to DNA identification obtained with blood samples from two of his brothers."

Osborne's brother, Clifford, a retired instrument mechanic at DuPont in Martinsville, remembers: "I done gave him up a long time ago—but then about three years ago, the Navy called me and my brother, Harry Clifford, asking for blood samples."

Clifford and Harry Osborne, who still works in a paving business, went to the blood bank at Martinsville Hospital. They were instructed to have the blood sent to the Armed Forces DNA Identification Lab in Rockville, Maryland. There, investigators matched the blood samples with the deceased sailors' bone fragments.

"It was a good feeling to help bring 'Willie' back to the United States," Clifford said. "We've missed him for a long time."

Because of illness, Cliff wasn't able to make the trip to Arlington National Cemetery to bury his brother; however, Harry and brother Baxter Osborne, of Isle of Wight County, were able to attend.

"The Navy has been mighty good about it," Baxter said. "They've done everything they could. They're going to stay with me until they get the boy buried." (Tad Dickens)

James W. Pearson, AMM1/C

"The remains of James W. Pearson AMM1/C, an Alliance, Nebraska, sailor missing in action in World War II, have been recovered and identified. One of eight Navy crew members aboard a PBY-5 Catalina aircraft that crashed Aug. 6, 1942, in bad weather during a routine mission in the South Pacific, the Pentagon reports...

"Searches in 1942 failed to uncover any trace of Pearson's aircraft or crew. The crew's home base was New Caledonia, an island in the southwest Pacific.

"In 1994 relic hunters on the New Hebrides island of Espiritu Santo (now part of the Republic of Vanuatu) discovered the crash site.

"The Pentagon announcement had longtime residents of Alliance struggling to remember Pearson and his family. Bernie Girard, who runs a hardware store, said he vaguely recalled Pearson as someone who lived in town. Their circle of friends sometimes crossed paths.

"Like me, he was about 5-foot-8 and 150 pounds when he was around here, Girard said. Local historians noted that no relatives of Pearson's are known to live in the area. He was not a graduate of Alliance High School." (Article by David Hendee, *World Herald*, Alliance, Nebraska)

Vernon Stolz, ARM2/C Radioman

Ruth Steck, Vernon's sister, writes: "Vernon was 22 years old. Vern was with the USS *West Virginia* at Pearl Harbor just three weeks before the Japs bombed Pearl Harbor. He was at the Naval Air Station several miles away.

CHAPTER **8** *The Lost Crew*   83

"Thanks for letting us know of the reunion. Health prevents Fred and I from attending. Nor will my brother Earl Stolz and his wife. However, Earl's son Ray and his wife flew to Hawaii to escort the remains of our brother Vernon home.

"A service was held by his parents at the funeral parlor in Reesen, Michigan. A nice display was put up of Vernon's twenty-two years in pictures. On view were his accordion and guitar, art and poetry, medals, and other personal things returned from Hawaii.

"The other crewman from Michigan was Merlin Jack Rich from Davidson, Michigan. Merlin was also twenty-two years old."

William Pipes, ARM1/C

John Pipes remembers that his brother Bill, prior to joining the Navy, was a hard worker in high school. While in school he worked at restaurant drive-ins. William Pipes joined the Navy before the Pearl Harbor attack in December 1941. At the Naval Air Station 1, he was a radio operator and flew in the twin-engine amphibious flying boats (PBY-5), which scoured the land and sea for Japanese troops and ships. He was with Patrol Squadron VP-23 when the Japanese attacked Pearl Harbor, killing more than 2,800 Americans.

On August 6, 1942, Bill Pipes was patrolling the Pacific with seven other crew members in a PBY Catalina. After a routine radio report, no one ever heard from them again.

Bill Pipes' younger brother John remembers:

My brother Bill was fighting a war with an uncertain outcome in 1942, and wanted to insure that "his little brother" went to college some day.

A Pearl Harbor survivor, he'd tuck twenty dollars a month into letters back home, telling my mother to save it for "little John," for I was still safe in high school.

I recall when my brother sent me a wrist watch on my birthday, along with college money. He wrote that he got it from a hock shop. I was amazed my brother could afford a watch on a sailor's salary! I guess it's kind of late to be saying it, but he was probably my best friend.

After August 1943, the letters stopped. Like a sorry replacement—a telegram arrived around midnight one evening at our home in Lawton, OK. It was from the government and informed us that Navy Petty Officer

1/C William R. Pipes, 21, was reported missing in action in the South Pacific.

Bill's little brother, John Pipes, at an early age worked hard, too, delivering milk door to door. But as Bill wished, John did get his college degree at Norman (though it had to wait until he helped liberate Europe in 1944 and 1945). Later he attended Cameron College in Lawton and finished with a teaching degree at the University of Oklahoma—just as his brother wanted. His other Pipes brothers went on to serve their country, too. Bill would have been proud!

"I was able to give my brother back something, too," John said, and explained:

It was a blood sample at the Fort Sill hospital in 1995. The blood that tied we Pipes brothers to one another was final evidence for the U.S. Central Identification Laboratory in Hawaii. The Pentagon could confirm that it was William Pipes—and seven other Navy sailors who died when their Catalina patrol plane crashed on the island of Espiritu Santo.

John Pipes, who is now retired and lives with his wife Barbara outside of Lawton, Oklahoma, reflects that his family had always assumed that Bill had died in action: "We knew he was in the South Pacific and that things were really tough down there ... I just assumed he was dead when he didn't show up—certainly after a few months!"

In January of 1994, the U.S. Embassy in Papua, New Guinea, reported loggers had discovered the crash site of an American aircraft on Espiritu Santo, now part of the Republic of Vanuatu. In February of 1994, a U.S. team was sent to the site, taking custody of the bulk of the remains. Thus began a long journey home for the crew of 23-P-15.

The Navy buried Pipes with full honors in Hawaii, and he also was given honors at the crew's interment at Arlington National Cemetery.

The Arlington Funeral Procession

The Riepl family and representatives and families of all the crew of the 23-P-15 gathered on April 21, 2000, at Arlington National Cemetery to pay last honors. Two VP-23 squadron sur-

CHAPTER **8** *The Lost Crew*   85

vivors, Lt. Howard Dickerson and LCDR Preston Thomas, who also flew the day of that fateful mission, were also present, as were myself and kinfolk of VPB-23 LCDR Lewis C. Shepley, recently buried at Arlington.

Following the flag-draped casket, they filed slowly out of the old post chapel and organ postlude of the Navy Hymn—and into a gray wet misty spring morning at Arlington National Cemetery.

The silent kinfolk and comrades under black umbrellas had journeyed far. From California coast, Oklahoma, and Kansas plains, Virginia, and Michigan hills, they came to witness the final ceremonial proceedings taking place before them honoring a group interment of eight fellow Navy aircrew comrades missing in action since World War II—and whom at last were being laid to final rest.

Breaking the still silence at Arlington National Cemetery, crisp commands echoed through the assembled ranks of the large Navy compliment, smartly clad in white uniforms—officers and men, wearing leggings and web belts, raised swords and rifles to a presentation of arms.

Then as the Navy chaplain saluted the flag-draped casket, the Honor Guard with deliberate and marked precision, placed it onto the six-horse drawn caisson ... and the procession awaited a signal to step off. Attending attaches escorted families and comrades of the deceased to the honored position behind the caisson.

A sound of muffled drums marked cadence; the Navy band struck up a processional march; beribboned white-gloved young soldiers astride their horses, cap brims shadowing their eyes and chin-straps in place would begin the caisson's journey far along a winding way from chapel pathway into the garden of stone known as Arlington National Cemetery.

Through fields of green and patterned lines of marble stones, row upon row, hundreds upon hundreds, each with inscriptions of honor—and in endless multiples contrasted against an immaculately kept common green and large blooming shade trees.

Marching to the lonely tent shelter, military ranks took position to form a rectangular spot around the flag draped casket upon its stand. Contrasting the white uniformed sailors, darkly dressed mourners with black umbrellas walked slowly to the graveside.

In the quiet of the Arlington stone garden, sharp voice commands again broke silence, bringing the smartly dressed military detachment to presentation of arms. A smartly uniformed Chief of Navy Chaplain gave a final eulogy.

They marched—so very straight and tall—beside the flag-draped casket. With military precision and in slow practiced cadence, the president's guard marked the final distance of a long journey to bring home a fallen Navy aircrewman and a closure for the prayerful mourners in keeping a vigil of hope burning since first receiving missing in action notice.

For the group remains of a lost Navy aircrew of 54 years earlier, now carried in honor upon the caisson, it was a last segment of a long journey bringing them to final rest and a closure to families and comrades who had too long carried a pain carried by MIA.

The co-pilot flying with Lt. Snuffy Smith that day was Ens. Edward Riepl of Cimarron, Kansas, who was laid to final rest both in a separate ceremony at 1000 hours at Arlington National Cemetery and at 1300 hours when the eight crewmembers of 23-P-15 were given final honors at the group interment.

Lt. Howard Dickerson and LCDR Preston Thomas, shipmates of the lost crew—and representing all of the survivors of VP/VPB-23—presented wreaths at both gravesites, at long last paying tribute to their comrades and giving comfort to their comrades' families at a special reception arranged at the Ft. Myers Officers Club at Arlington.

A third wreath was also placed that day at the graveside of LCDR Lewis C. Shepley Jr., VPB-23 ('44-'45), who was given honors at Arlington December 26, 1999.

LCDR Howard Dickerson remembered the flight of 23-P-15:

As for conditions in the South Pacific, suffice to say that conditions were extremely rough! I knew both Smith and Riepl, but not well. We took off on the same day as Lt. "Snuffy" Smith. My diary continually notes the bad weather conditions which in the case of 23-P-15 could have easily forced the ill-fated crew to fly over the overcast.

This, of course, made conditions extremely hazardous when it was time to come down to land from a search sector. If navigation was off by only a mile or so, it could result in flying into the tops of many of the volcanic peaks of the New Hebrides. I believe this was probably what happened to Snuffy and crew.

Always conditions of our concern was the large number of hours put on the engines and airframes of the PBYs during the early part of the

CHAPTER **8** *The Lost Crew*

campaign. The country had not yet been fully mobilized, conditions were sparse, the supply train shaky at best.

I had experienced at least one single engine failure while I was down there, and a single-engine problem appears to be the contributing factor in the loss of Smith's PBY.

There was no established port at Segond Channel in Espiritu Santo. We refueled off of rafts provided by the Army. Home base was Noumea in New Caledonia, until the Guadalcanal campaign got started—and then we moved our home base to Espiritu Santo. The PBYs would forward deploy from there (Espiritu) with the *Curtiss* and *Mackinac* flying to Santa Cruz and Malaita just before any major action in order to search for the Japanese Fleet.

Helen Riepl reminisces:

Fifty-two years ago in August 1942, Jerry's oldest brother—Ensign Edward W. Riepl—was reported "missing in action" in the Pacific. He was a Navy co-pilot of a PBY Catalina which failed to return to the base on the opening day of the invasion of the Solomons.

Jerry's family received the news in May of 1994 that the wreckage of the plane had been found in the mountainous jungle region of the island Espiritu Santo in the Republic of Vanuatu (formerly the New Hebrides) northeast of Australia.

The wreckage was taken to the Identification Laboratory in Hawaii, and plans are being considered for the crew to be buried as a group in Arlington Cemetery in Washington, D.C. Attempts were made to locate the families of the crew. The Bureau of Personnel in Arlington, Va., first located our oldest son, John, in Kansas City. John happened to be named John Edward, in honor of his Uncle Ed ... but painful too—to learn and see the pictures of the wreckage and to know the plane had burned.

ABC-TV carried the story and sent John the footage of their live coverage. It is still amazing to learn that over 70,000 men are still missing from WWII—35,000 of them from the Navy!

In 1994 the *New York Times* ran an obituary for Walter Linn, prime minister of the Republic of Vanuatu (formerly New Hebrides). An Angelican priest who led the 83 Melanesian Islands and 172,000 people to nationhood, he governed the country for eleven years, stepping down in 1991.

Walter Linn was born on Pentecost, one of the larger islands then administered by England and France. In 1980 Father Linn was poised to become prime minister when a French-speaking planter by the name of Jimmy Stevens led 600 bowmen to take control of the island of Espiritu Santo. Stevens wanted to withdraw the island, which was to be proclaimed Vanuatu (which means eternal land).

Father Linn sought aid of the British who, over the objections of France, reluctantly sent 300 Royal Marines as peacekeepers to Espiritu Santo long enough for independence ceremonies to proceed on schedule. Father Linn then signed a defense pact with Papua New Guinea, and the British Marines quickly arrested Stevens, putting down the rebellion.

Though acknowledging the need for aid, he spurned any great leaps forward, declaring: "We have a lot of resources which we have not exploited but we are not so much in a hurry to exploit all of these. We have lived here many years before Britain and France came and we will continue to live here for many more years. Why should we use everything now?"

Father Linn supported independence for New Caledonia and was opposed to French nuclear testing in the Pacific.

In 1994 I received a brief note from his office in answer to my inquiry concerning the discovery of the 23-P-15 crash site.

Dear Sir,
Thank you for your letter. It is true that this news (discovery of the crash site) must be of great importance to your lost comrades. I have forwarded your letter to the appropriate ministry. I thank the people of America for the services rendered to the people of the Southwest Pacific, but more so for those Americans who served in Espiritu Santo. Regards from Vanuatu to them all.

> I have the honor to be Sir,
> Yours Sincerely,
> Friar Luke Titinsom DINAI
> Principal Private Secretary

Return to the Solomons
MAY 1943

> *"In private business, the new assignment might have been called the SOLOMON ISLANDS AIR TAXI & FREIGHT SERVICE. Its motto: 'To Any Island at Any Time.'"*

In May of 1943 twelve new PBYs arrived at Kaneohe from San Diego as replacement aircraft, and six of the crews ferrying the aircraft remained with the squadron as replacement crews. Training was begun in conjunction with operational patrols in Hawaiian waters.

In June the squadron was again deployed to the South Pacific, returning to its former base of operations at Espiritu Santo. A detachment was also deployed on the Island of Funafuti.

In August VP-23's base of operations relocated to NAS Halavo Island, Florida Islands—an advance base for attacks on the Ellice Islands and supporting actions for the planned attack on Tarawa. From this location the squadron would conduct special searches, convoy coverage, shipping patrols, "Dumbo" and resupply missions.

LCDR George E. "The Message" Garcia, USN, assumed command of VP-23, relieving Skipper Frank Brandley (who later would attain the rank of admiral).

The new skipper had retired from the Navy in 1939 because of deafness but had somehow managed a recall back to duty in 1942. After a year of shore duty, he was sent to Espiritu Santo and on August 25, 1943, the new CO and VP-23 left Espiritu Santo to operate from the Halavo seaplane base, in the Florida Islands, Solomons.

During this period, high priority mission for the squadron was in transporting and supplying "coastwatchers," an elite group reporting on enemy activities within their own perimeters. Periodic fly-ins to these remote outposts along shore inlets and bays became routine. Air-sea rescue missions were also significant, documenting some thirty-nine survivors picked up by VP-23 aircrews during this tour! After three and a half months the squadron was relieved by VP-14.

Lt. Francis Clifton recollects:

In early September 1943, all VP-23 crews were reunited at Halavo Bay on Florida Island in the Solomons. The ten or twelve patrols from Funafuti and Espiritu Santo were replaced by a special type of operation in the Solomons—particularly suited to VP-23's PBY-5 Catalina flying boats, known in the Navy as "P-Boats."

In private business, the new assignment might have been called the "SOLOMON ISLANDS AIR TAXI & FREIGHT SERVICE" and its motto: "To Any Island at Any Time."

I do not remember all the islands in the Solomons we went to—but it included nearly all the larger ones. Our assignments were routinely flown to drop off and/or pick up personnel, material and supplies—with a few "wait here's."

While we seldom went ashore, I remember a few "overnights" at Malaita, San Christobal, Ondonga, and a small island Rendova from which the PT Boats operated. Our passengers were either military or civilian—with a high priority to "Coastwatchers" and their supplies.

One of our Aircrews transported Admiral "Bull" Halsey as a passenger to Bougainville. Another carried Naval Command Intelligence personnel to Bougainville—for the purpose of interrogating captured Japanese soldiers. (The mission was doomed to near total failure—the Japs preference to die for their Emperor.)

I don't remember any "big names" that our crew took on—we never recorded the passenger list which at times numbered only three or four—to other times when we carried a plane load.

In the Solomons, the close proximity of nearby islands and familiar coastlines left little navigation to do, so therefore the Navigator became a "Chief Steward" or "Loadmaster," whichever the flight required. In our new "Taxi" business, we also had quite a bit of "Stand By" time—so to keep the meter running, we were even more "ready, willing 'n able" to meet all requests for any mission with very short notice.

CHAPTER 9 — Return to the Solomons

We would "stand by" at Halavo Bay, along with the PT Boats at their advanced base—and also for a F4U fighter squadron on Ondonga. Future president Lt.(jg) John F. Kennedy of PT-109 fame had already left his PT Boat squadron by this time, but a big name remaining was "Whizzer" White—an All American football player. Later, "Whizzer" became a Supreme Court Justice.

In addition to freight & quick taxi service, several downed air crew personnel were rescued from these stand-by locations.

My Patrol Plane Commander (PPC) was K.F. Richards, Jr., and my alternating co-pilot was Thomas Mulroy. (Tom and I took turns in the cockpit by flights, not hours.) "A flight" was from "take-off" to "return to base"—regardless of the duration of the flight. However, a new day meant the start of a new flight.

Sometime around the middle of October 1943, we were scheduled for a flight to Rennell Island, a couple hundred miles south of Guadalcanal. All crews hoped for such a mission because of the friendly Polynesian natives there. Unfortunately, we did not get to go ashore.

It was "my flight" in the cockpit—and while drifting on the water, waiting for the transfer of personnel and and supplies, I just happened to look down into the water outside the cockpit. There beneath the water's surface and only four feet from the hull, I spotted a large coral head! It narrowly passed between the hull and wingtip float—we had missed disaster by three or four feet! Needless to say, I headed for deeper water.

A week or so later, another crew was scheduled for Rennell. We told the PPC about our experience with the coral head and warned him about dangers in the coral reef waters of Rennell.

A few hours later an urgent message was received at the base: "SINKING AT RENNELL." It was from the same aircrew I had given warning to. The crew had fortunately managed to make it to the beach with the damaged plane. VP-23 rescue and salvage crews were sent to pick up the crew, and to save as much of the equipment and supplies as possible.

I do not know what happened to that VPB-23 P-boat hull left on the beach at Rennell in 1943—nor have I ever seen any mention of it in any PBY literature.

Lt. Dormas "Doc" Plank was born and raised (for the most part) in the small town of Walton, Indiana. He writes:

I had a normal childhood. In 1941, while only in my Junior year at Indiana U, I had to register for the draft—but the Board kindly deferred until the end of the semester.

My parents were in Enid, Oklahoma. Father was constructing a Federal Courthouse and Post Office there. I called my Draft Board in

Logansport, Indiana to get my draft status—and was advised I would be called in the next draft. I was a corporal in the ROTC at Indiana ... and rather than be drafted, I drove over to the Federal Building in St. Louis and enlisted in the Navy Air Corps.

The Rennell Island experience happened as a result of our skipper, LCDR George Garcia, who sent us there to check out a report of downed pilots. We landed in the lake—and to avoid drifting into shore, left the engines running. I went to the rear of the plane to talk to a native who had rowed out to see us.

While I was trying to understand him, we scraped some coral, which was difficult to see. It tore a hole in our hull. We began to take on water and used the bilge pump, but it didn't do any good. Though we could not tell the extent of damage, we knew the water was filling the plane rapidly to the point that we were afraid to take off. So we ran the plane on top of a reef. In the meantime, the radioman sent a message back to base that we were sinking and had to evacuate.

Our next concern was removing the guns and ammunition. The island chief who had a fair knowledge of English, helped us store all we could salvage in a hut and I assigned a guard to it.

The chief provided me and Ens. Dave Tenney quarters in his hut that he and his wife had vacated. The beds were mats on some kind of frame above the floor.

That night, possibly around midnight, his wife came in carrying a lantern looking for something. With my hand on my .45 hidden beneath my pillow, I laid still, watching her as she approached my bunk. She got something under my bunk and left. It was a scary few minutes.

The next morning, I went to the hut where the guns were stored and found a native boy who had already taken our automatic "Tommy Gun" apart—and was putting it back together! In talking to him he relayed that he had been with the Marines on Guadalcanal.

He also had one of our maps—and I asked if he knew where he was located. He pointed directly to his island. As the day progressed, natives from all over the island were gathering.

The Chief conveyed to me that his son had split open his thigh—and needed urgent medical attention. He pleaded with me to go up the hill to see the boy. When we got there, I remember the old Chief talking to his son in native tongue and the tears flowing down his cheeks. I could see the boy had a bad cut and needed help and said I would report to our skipper and request help from him.

When Lt. Cheverton was sent down to pick us up two days later, I relayed my story to our skipper, LCDR Garcia, and was surprised at his reaction as he told me we were fighting a war and couldn't be bothered with the natives. However, a few days after that, I saw the Chief walking

CHAPTER **9** *Return to the Solomons* 93

along our beach in khaki trousers and talked to him. The skipper, apparently with a change of mind, had sent another plane to Rennell to pick up the Chief and his son to bring them back to the hospital.

I was glad that the native boy got the medical attention he needed, but strangely the skipper never said anything about it to me.

Another mishap forced us back early from patrol one day due to a gas leak, and still another due to our plane captain being scalded with water when the pressure cooker exploded.

Five crews were sent to the Ellis Islands to patrol the sector when we took New Georgia Island. On our first patrol we ran "in and out" of rain squalls all day. That evening heading back, we realized we were lost.

Our navigator had taken a "sun sight" which indicated that we were right over the island ... No island in sight! We radioed Ellis Island to turn on the radio bearing, but got no answer. I then plotted a course from the sun sight location. Due to its getting late, I had the engines wide open—and we finally landed in the water at dusk.

Skipper Brandley met us on the dock to tell us he thought he had lost us—along with the only packet of confidential material which we had with us. In relaying our story to him, we found out that there was no one in the radio shack.

Needless to say, the skipper ordered a "24-hour watch" from then on!

We also found our compass was off a few degrees. We made the decision that thereafter one of us would be assigned to do the navigation, but there would be two of us checking him!

One night the Japs bombed Ellis Island all night long.

LCDR David B. Tenney was born in 1916 in Braintree, Maine. Dave's son, Brad, writes:

> In class one day at the University of Virginia, a professor asked with some concern just what my dad's group were doing there—reminding them that there was a war going on. He repeated the question again, asking just what were they going to do about it. With such intimidation, everyone in my dad's class that day was most likely "induced to sign up"—if not then, not too long after!
>
> And so, Dad first tried to sign on with the Army Air Force, but he failed his eye exam, so flight was out, but he had already "signed in." Promptly crossing the street to the Navy Recruitment office, and confirming that the results of his physical there were O.K. for Navy flight, he re-crossed the street and "finagled" an honorable discharge from the Army on 12/16/41 (convenience of the government) allowing his enlistment into the Navy.

He did his flight training in NAS Jacksonville, Florida, and flew training flights with LCDR George Garcia beginning in May of 1942 out of Kaneohe NAS. On May 26th, Dad headed to the forward area Espiritu Santo, with Garcia, the new Skipper to be.

Then he went on to Funafuti with Lt. Snedeker. During his second tour, he flew with Lt. Dormas "Doc" Plank and on a third tour he flew with Lt. Wallace Douglas.

SPAM, CRAM & SCRAM
by Art McQuiddy

(There are twenty-five smashing stanzas—here's three!)

There are P-Boat squadrons all over the sea
From 'Frisco to old Cathay;
But the squadron that's best, in the west and by test,
Is old 23 we'd say!

They'll take any old crate with a wing and a hull
And an outboard to give her a soul.
They'll take that old crate and away we'll go,
To fly the Goddamned patrol.

We've heroes in plenty and some known to fame,
Each one has a job in the van.
And we dive, fly and gun, 'way up in the sun,
On rations of beans, pork, and Spam.

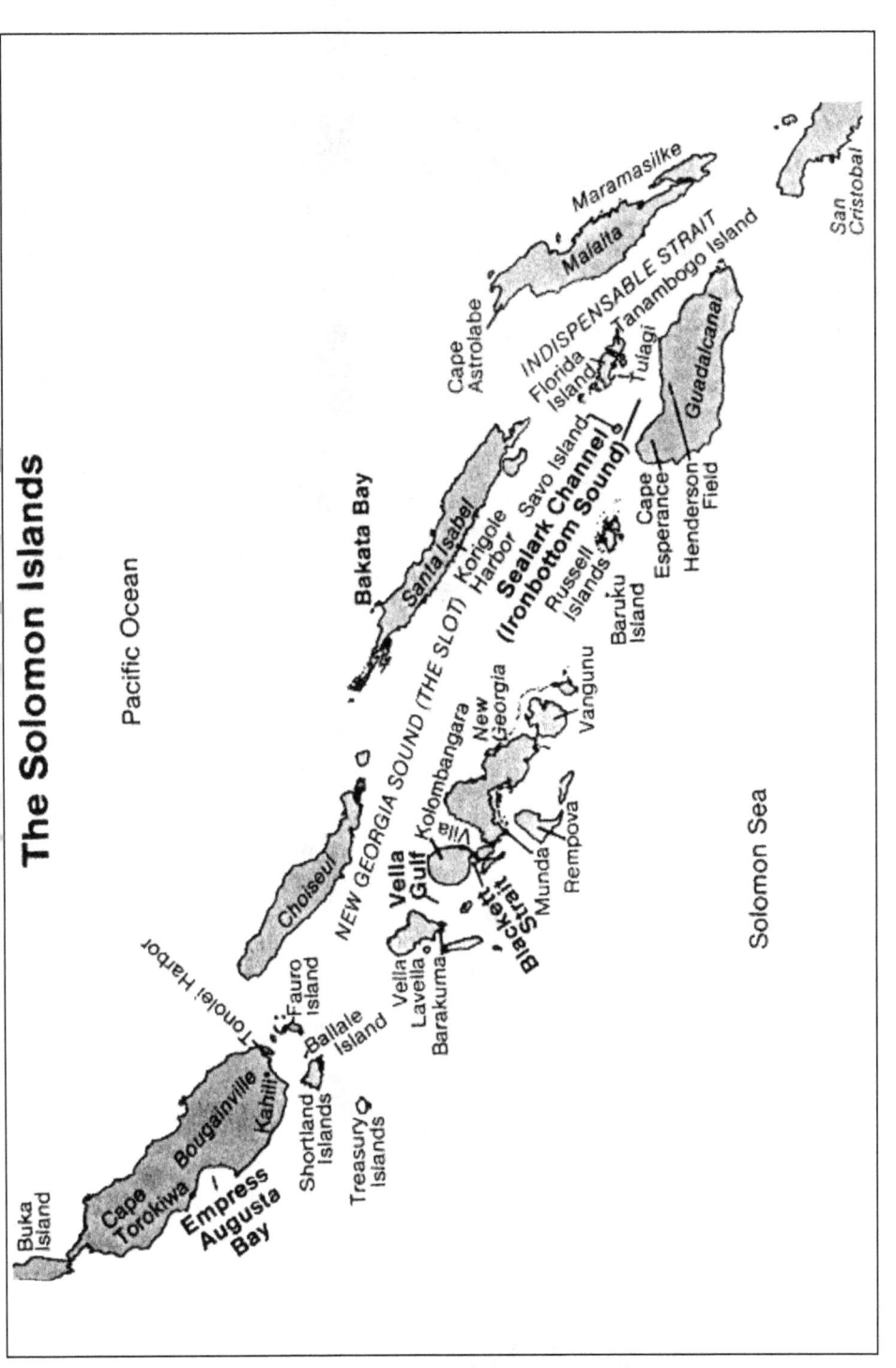

Pilots and Aircrewmen of *VP-23, Espiritu Santo.* (Official U.S. Navy photo; Collection of W. Decker)

(From top) *Night Stalker: Bow view of one of the squadron's "CATS" as it takes off from the harbor of a Pacific base for a night mission. Taking advantage of its slow and silent attributes, the PBY wrought havoc on Japanese ships.* (Don Klotz Collection)

Touch down! On the third bounce! VP-23 PBY-5 making a routine landing in the choppy waters of the South Pacific. (Don Klotz Collection)

Lt. Maurice Cheverton sitting at controls of PBY-5 "Pugnacious Polly," named for the woman he would marry. Hooked up to buoy offshore Espiritu Santo. Lt. Cheverton won the Distinguished Flying Cross and a "Well done" from Adm. "Bull" Halsey for rescuing a downed B-24 crew in enemy waters. (M. Cheverton Collection)

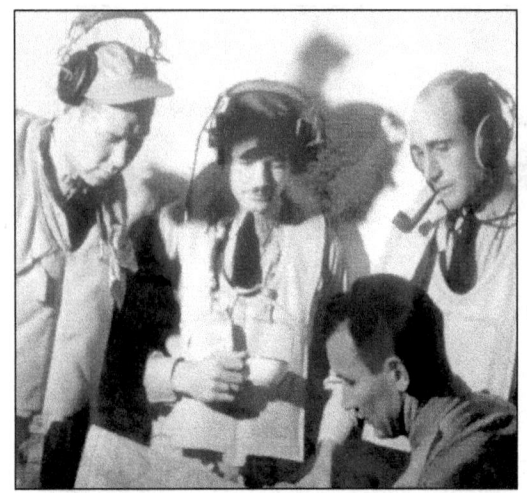

(From top) *VP-23 PBY pilots (L-R) Al Snedeker, Bill Geritz and Tom Benton get night briefing in the Solomons. All three pilots took part in the Battle of Guadalcanal.* (William Geritz Collection)

One of a six-plane detachment sent to NDeni, Santa Cruz Islands, in August 1942. (Hubbell Collection)

A blister view from one CAT to another. (Medeas Collection)

(Left) *Fishing for buoy to hook up to.* (P. Thomas Collection)

(Middle) *VP-23 PBY-5 at Espiritu Santo, back from night patrol.* (O'Quin Collection)

VP-23 pilots on Canton Island, 1943. (Back row, L-R) *A. Dunn, G. Goodlett, J. Young, A. R. Vaatvert, R. Hoagland, J. Abele, V. Flint, E. Leonard, T. Benton;* (front row) *B. Clark, A. McQuiddy, A. Snedeker, O. Owre, W. Geritz, C. Rich.* (Wm. Geritz Collection)

TICKET TO ARMISTICE

USE THIS TICKET, SAVE YOUR LIFE
YOU WILL BE KINDLY TREATED

Follow These Instructions:

1. Come towards our lines waving a white flag.
2. Strap your gun over your left shoulder muzzle down and pointed behind you.
3. Show this ticket to the sentry.
4. Any number of you may surrender with this one ticket.

JAPANESE ARMY HEADQUARTERS

投 降 票

此ノ票ヲ持ツモノハ投降者ナリ
投降者ヲ殺害スルヲ厳禁ス

大日本軍司令官

Sing your way to Peace pray for Peace

TRANSALATION OF JAPANESE CHARACTERS

--- SURRENDER TICKET ---
"THE BEARER(S) OF THIS TICKET HAS SURRENDERED.
IT IS STRICTLY FORBIDDEN TO KILL HIM (THEM)."
COMMANDER JAPANESE ARMY FORCES.

(Above) *Japanese surrender leaflet* (Cheverton Collection); (below left) *American surrender leaflet* (Craig Collection); (below right) *Lt. Hopkins and Geritz at Halavos.* (Geritz Collection)

(Top) *Crew of "Elmer's Tune":* L-R, top row: *Jack Moore, Ed Brown, Elmer Laughlin, Frank Leik, Bill Hughes;* kneeling: *Ed Lilian, James Hansom, Ed Hill. Taken in New Hebrides, May 28, 1943, with Brownie box camera by "Gunner" Tony McGee. We went on to Halavo Bay, Tulagi, during the Solomon Campaign.* (Laughlin Collection)

(Middle) *Top Brass on Canton. VP-23 Ensigns Goodlett, Rich, and Flint on Canton Island.* (Snedeker Collection)

(Below) *Lt. Ed Leonard and friends on Funafuti.* (Leonard Collection)

(Top left) *Up the down staircase! Jungle stairway leading down from Barracks Officers Quarters to airstrip on Tulagi.* (B. Geritz Collection)

(Top right) *Funafuti Ellis Island, 1943. Dave Tenney, Doc Plank, Bernie Joy, and Joe Huber.* (Huber Collection)

(Bottom) *Noumea, New Caledonia. L-R: Cox, Elberg, Snedeker, Leonard, Chamley.* (Snedeker Collection)

(Top) *VP-23 PBY flying over USS* Yorktown, *June 4, 1942, just hours before she was sunk by Japanese during Battle of Midway.* (J. Morrison Collection)

(Below) *Aircrewman McBride with babe in arms, Vanikoro, 1943.* (Douglas Collection)

Lt. Francis Clifton and Lt. Howard Chamley with native chief on Vanikoro, 1943. (F. Clifton Collection)

(Top) *VP23 Black Cat at Tulagi.* (Snedeker Collection)
(Below) *Crew of 15-P-23 reported missing in action, 1942. The wreckage was found in December 1995 by loggers in mountains of Espiritu Santo (now Republic of Vanatua).* (Snedeker Collection) *Missing in photos below: Clifford Pindell CAP and Merlin Rich ARM2/C.*

Lt. Maurice "Snuffy" Smith PPC of 23-P-15 MIA 1942   *Ens. Ed Riepl First Pilot*   *William Osborne* AMM1/C

Vernon Stolz AMM2/C   *William Pipes* ARM2/C   *Jim Pearson* AMM1/C

(Left) *Hula Guys at Funafuti Island, 1942—Lts. Morgan Saylor and Bill Geritz.* (Snedeker Collection)

(Right) LCDR Bebo *"The Message" Garcia, skipper of VP-23, Solomons 1943.* (Snedeker Collection)

(Below) *Life in the South Pacific, Lt. Cheverton.* (Cheverton Collection)

(Clockwise, starting above) *VP-23 Catalinas tucked in palm trees on Santa Cruz, hidden from enemy bombers. Standby crew in foreground.* (S. Jersey Collection)
South Pacific serenity (for the moment). (H. Aries Collection)
Jerry McBride on bow of PBY "Dare-Devil Dilbert." (Thomas Collection)
Sometimes they found us! Japanese Zero attacks in Solomons. (P. Williams Collection)

(Top) *"Mavis"—Japanese Kawanshi Navy H6KS flying boat was type shot down by Phil Williams and his crew flying patrol off Santa Cruz. The "Mavis" was used extensively by the Japanese in connecting far distant Pacific bases.* (Don Klotz Collection)

(Bottom) *L-R: Enemy slayers Rendal ARM1/C, CPO Phil Williams, and Pennock ARM1/C on liberty in Honolulu. Back from second tour of duty, Williams shot down Japanese float plane (like one pictured above) while on patrol. Pennock, in crew of NAP Gale Burkey, was in air fight with five Zeros.* (P. Williams Collection)

(Clockwise from top left) *Native village, Babelthaup Island.* (Douglas Collection)

On Wing—Lt. Chittengen, A. P. Brady, Chief Padaskowski, Sessions, and Mason, Canton Island. (Williams Collection)

USS Mackinac *Sea Plane Tender, which along with tenders USS* Curtiss *and USS* Chincoteague *serviced VP/VPB-23 PBYs in the South and Central Pacific.* (O'Quin Collection)

Ens. W. B. Jones, 1942. (Jones Collection)

Naval Aviators Certificate. Presented to W. Boardman Jones, Jr., at NAS, Corpus Christi, Texas, 1942. (W. B. Jones Collection)

VP/VPB-23

THIRD TOUR
1943-1945

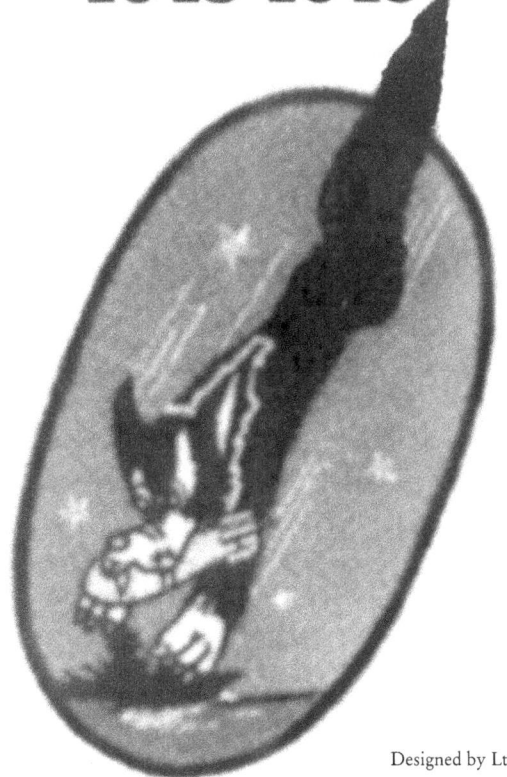

Designed by Lt. Art McQuiddy

Joining the Navy
JANUARY 18, 1943

"I pulled open my shirt and proudly showed everyone the purple iodine number on my chest."

In Chicago that December of '42, war had completely engulfed the nation. Most every window displayed a red-bordered flag on white centering either a blue star, which indicated a family member in the armed forces, or a gold star, which reflected the death of a relative killed in service. Those not in service were engaged in some kind of "war work" at assembly defense plants, working around-the-clock shifts.

Newspapers reported fierce desert battles in Tunisia and printed pictures of white-clad frozen corpses strewn on winter battlefields outside of Stalingrad. In the Pacific, Bataan and Corregidor had fallen, and the allies were desperately on the defense—but in May, at the "Battle of Midway," Japan's advance eastward was decisively halted.

The war in the Central Pacific was about to begin. In what would be a Task Group assignment essential in planning the invasion of Tarawa, twenty-four pilots and aircrew from U.S. Navy VP-23 were sent by tug boat from Pearl Harbor to Canton Island to fly patrol in six of the first "Black Cats" of the Navy.

I was in high school, and working after classes part-time as a Western Union messenger at Union Station. It was a hub of wartime activity crowded with uniformed personnel traveling home on leave or to far-off war fronts across the globe. As a messenger at the Union Station post, I wore a special patch on my uniform sleeve enabling me to board trains and take last-minute telegrams from passengers.

The big clock above the large circular counter hub where people crowded to get train information, the noise of the steam trains, the marble-columned facade waiting room and the Harvey House were backdrops to a wide panorama of human drama always on view. The scene constantly fascinated me. I remember an oversized jukebox with large screen in the outer waiting area leading into the main station. By depositing a small coin, a viewer could watch a short film of the Andrews Sisters singing "Any Bonds Today" or some other rallying patriotic hit.

I was later transferred to the main Western Union office in downtown Chicago to partake in a new venture the company had just initiated: the "singing telegram."

As messengers, we were making thirty cents an hour, but now we could earn a quarter extra per singing telegram (cost to the sender: $1.25). No talent was required. Birthday, anniversary, special occasion—all verses were sung to the tune of "Yankee Doodle Dandy." There was also the incentive of an extra tip. I volunteered and subsequently sang to light opera and movie star Nelson Eddy in his state room suite aboard the fabulous "20th Century Ltd." I also sang at gunpoint to a group of paunchy, bald-headed, unshaven gentlemen in tuxedoes, all looking like Al Capone and sitting in dark oak and red-carpeted opulence along a long table laden with silver candelabras and food. The gent who had answered the door and shown me in had jokingly pulled the gun on me, saying, "Buddy, this had better be good!" And on a more amusing occasion, I sang to a lady in a bathtub!

But there was a war on, and in early January of 1943, at age seventeen, I was determined to get into the fray. One day I took the leap and called Marine recruiters to question whether they'd take a 114-pound lightweight like me. A drill sergeant-like voice responded: "Eatta buncha bananas, drinka quartta milk, and get down here—on the double!" In a call to the Navy, I got a less demanding response: "Sure, come on down!"

I've often pondered a thought that "providence" was on the phone that day. But for the bananas I would have joined the

CHAPTER 10 Joining the Navy

Marines. Instead I journeyed down to the Navy recruiting office in the Municipal Courthouse to enlist.

A lot of other guys had the same idea that day, but it all went pretty fast. After a few questions and quick paperwork by a sailor on the other side of a desk, I was turned over to the doctors for a basic "stick-out-your-tongue, feel-behind-the-ears, and read-the-eye chart" medical exam. I stepped up to the scale, and without a hint of concern my examiner called out my weight: "114 pounds!"

Then I was hurried off to another line and another room, where we were told to strip down to the shorts. A commanding voice bellowed out: "Okay, now turn around and drop 'em. Bend over and grab your cheeks. Okay—now turn around!" A couple of doctor-looking guys came toward me. One felt my testicles and told me to cough; the other had an iodine swab and painted a number on my chest.

I then was pointed to the camera, where I proudly posed for a mug shot and was fingerprinted. I had passed my medical! They typed up my orders to report to Great Lakes Naval Training Station.

A few weeks before, and thousands of miles away, a detachment of VP-23 was on Canton Island in the Pacific. Chief AMM Pres Thomas remembers:

> We slept under mosquito nets. Not because there were mosquitoes, but because of the rats. One guy's hand had fallen out of the net one night and a rat had chewed on his knuckles. We got our drinking water from the evaporator taken from a ship that had gone aground on the island. It's no wonder because the island is so small that when flying, you can only see it when it's right below you.
>
> I had found an old harmonica in a waste basket that I repaired, and was able to furnish Christmas music for the crew. There were no radios, so that was all the Christmas music there was. I can play a lot carols!

Back in Chicago, after having enlisted in the Navy that day, I was sitting at the dinner table with my mother, three sisters, and brother, and could hardly contain myself. I remember the dialogue:

"Well, how was school today?" Mom asked.

"I've joined the Navy," was my reply.

"Did what?" came the reply.

"I joined the Navy!" I repeated.

My sisters laughed. "You're kidding!"

My brother sneered. "They must be pretty hard up if they'd take you."

Mom looked at me, teary-eyed. "I can't believe it."

I pulled open my shirt and proudly showed everyone the purple iodine number still on my chest.

The key, of course, was to get my parents' signature. My sister Gen's fiancé, Jim Roche, had been one of the first inductees into the Army in 1941. Jim was already in training at Fort Dix. My sister Anna Mae's beau, Bruce Aebischer, had joined the Marines and was in boot camp out on the West Coast.

Initial reluctance shown by my parents was met with my own vocal argument about joining the Navy with or without their signatures. I suppose my determination and the prevailing patriotic mood throughout the country brought the signatures of Mom and Dad to the enlistment papers that would send their seventeen-year-old son off to war.

A deeper reaction came from my elderly high school art teacher, Mrs. Booth, who, shaking her head, sighed sadly, exclaiming: "Oh, Donald, how foolish! You've so much talent. You belong right here in school!"

Mr. Berens, my mentor and English teacher, faculty advisor, and managing editor of our high school paper, was more sympathetic, but stressed how he would miss working with the best cartoonist on the *Austin Times* high school newspaper.

I was not unique. It was a time when many of the students had already dropped out of high school to join up.

When I notified the night dispatcher at Western Union that I was leaving to join the Navy, he wished me luck, and on a last telegram delivery, sent me out into the dark night to the farthest outreach on the edge of the city.

There were the classroom good-byes and the final family dinner party, and yet more last-minute sendoffs, before I finally joined a group of new enlistees at the recruitment office for the trip to Great Lakes Naval Training Station.

It was all big excitement for a young kid who had never been away from home.

ooo

CHAPTER 10 Joining the Navy

Thus began a series of new experiences, all performed at quick-time. Off came our "civvies" to mail back home. Then each of us was given a mattress bag and, clad only in Navy shorts, we proceeded in assembly-line fashion through a huge supply depot. "Sizes" were bellowed out from quartermasters from behind a counter, and as we single-filed it along, all sorts of items were flung into it.

Soon we donned our "uniform of the day"—a standard blue denim shirt, heavy denim dungarees, "boots" (laced-up khaki canvas leggings), and of course, two finger widths above the eyebrow and "squared-off," the distinctive Navy white round sailor's hat that we would wear throughout our eight-week training course.

Assigned a barracks, a company, and a chief petty officer, we were now lowly apprentice seamen or "Boots," ready to begin our indoctrination and crash course in learning basic rudimentary seamanship.

However, I would experience a couple of unexpected and unfortunate delays. The first, by way of a dental examination revealing thirteen cavities, would put me on "hold"—and in a dental chair for two days while a Navy "drill-master" filled them all. Second, I had volunteered for both submarine and aviation duty. Now I was to learn the new metal fillings in my mouth disqualified me from submarine duty because I'd act as a "transmitter" under water!

With dental work done, I was assigned a new "Boot" company, only to come down with "Cat Fever"—a common name for the Great Lakes "flu bug" to which so many new recruits succumbed.

Breaking out in a sweat and high fever, I was ordered to get my gear together and hightail to sick bay, a far distance across a parade ground and then through a maze of administration buildings.

"Gear" meant "full gear"—110 pounds of it! A canvas sea bag was packed with one's entire belongings, full uniform complement, blanket and hammock, all lashed together in a compact but ungainly mass. It was a hefty pack for a healthy sailor, let alone a sick one. And with records and smaller "ditty bag" to boot!

Wearing a heavy pea coat didn't help. Somehow, stopping often to rest, I managed and staggered into "sick bay." With records in hand, I was routinely checked in by two Navy corpsmen, was assigned a bunk, and left to myself. I took off my clothes and crawled into the sack.

Returning later to take my temperature, the medics seemed to realize the serious nature of my illness and began dousing me with alcohol to bring my temperature down. I was in bed about a week before I was able to report for duty.

Finally assigned to Boot Company 119, I was ready to get on with my training!

An "apprentice seaman," the lowest rank in the Navy, is taught the basics of hygiene and military manners throughout a rigorous eight-week training course. Reveille begins at 0400 in the morning and continues through taps at 2100—with little private time in between.

Contrary to the typical square-jawed shouting drillmaster, our commanding chief petty officer appeared on scene as a more fatherly figure. He was actually a schoolteacher who looked too old for the service, having joined up in one of those special categories allowing men so desperately needed to do their bit for their country. Nevertheless, we soon learned that he was the guy who laid down the rules—the guy you'd better not forget to salute, nor get on the wrong side of.

I remember the "wake-up call" of one non-complying shipmate who ignored reveille. Covers were whipped off and the mattress yanked from under the laggard and flipped to the floor. Then he was doused with a bucket of water and stepped upon. The "rebel" was ordered to clean up the mess on the double and report for duty.

The "Chief," always addressed as "Sir," was aided by a bo'sun mate attendant who could be as tough as any Marine drill sergeant and a couple of "appointed" apprentice seamen from the ranks to see to it that company orders were carried out. It was a no-nonsense environment.

On to quick-time: There were quick-lines for shots, quick-lines for chow, quick line-ups for morning calisthenics. "Fall in and count off!" were commands continually shouted out to bring instant responses. And a "double-time" order even quickened that pace!

"Now hear this" was an alert preceding an order and commanding the immediate attention of all hands. As "Boots" we would learn a whole new language: Reveille, aye-aye Sir, starboard, port, navy time, seabag, mail call, skivvies, smoking lamp, chow, mess hall, scuttlebutt, small stores, sick bay, square knots, ship-shape, square corners, lights out, and on and on.

I soon would regret joining the Navy in the midwinter of '43 at Great Lakes. No colder place ever existed! Knife-like winds swept in off the miserable lakes, going right through layers of thick clothing.

Oh, those very wintry early morning calisthenics! And that was in addition to the miseries of the Navy "duty-watch" system, which every sailor was called upon to do aside from normal duties for the rest of our Navy careers.

The hardest to stand was the "dogwatch" from midnight to 0400. What a jolt to be awakened in the middle of the night by a flashlight in the face, and a clipboard shoved at you to sign. God help you if you fell back to sleep. You scrambled out of the bunk, fumbling about in the dark lest you awake sleeping shipmates. Over the long johns came a heavy crew neck sweater, then the blue denim shirt, heavy dungarees, heavy socks, shoes, and laced-up canvas leggings. Just try lacing leggings in the dark! Next came the navy blue muffler, the heavy pea coat buttoned at the neck, with collar up and attached collar flap buttoned over the mouth for extra face protection. Then the watch cap was pulled down over the eyebrows. All this prep and still cold!

Upon relieving the guard, you put on your heavy woolen gloves—but only after he passed you a webbed belt which you hooked about your pea coat waist and from which hung a clumsy clipboard. On the clipboard was a long list of sentry rules, any one of which if broken would spell bad luck for the sentry charged. We also were passed a flashlight and a whistle that hung about the neck, and we might have had a club. I don't remember. No gun was entrusted to the "raw recruit" just yet.

The patrol area was, of course, outside around treeless barracks a couple of long blocks or more square. There were wide distances between barracks, so they were not very good windbreakers.

Watches were serious duty, and the petty officer and/or officer-on-duty were said to be adamant about delinquent guards.

I was programmed to be alert and ready for those jeep headlights that might come speeding toward us in the dark of night from varied directions. And I knew to break the silence of the night by barking out sentinel rules: "Halt! Advance and be recognized!" But the truth of the matter was that on those long, cold dogwatches at Great Lakes, it soon became apparent that no sane spy—much less the OOD—would be crazy enough to venture out in those frigid hours!

I covered my long, block-square areas of patrol on the run. Bundled up with limited vision, clipboard swinging from belt and bouncing on my butt, I was hardly a deterrent to anyone. I was a sentry duty on the run to get back as fast as I could to the hot laundry room inside the barracks, where I took refuge along with skivvies and sheets that were hung out to dry. Then, surveying my area from second-story windows and hissing radiators until guilt set in, I would venture back into the wind-chilled night, repeating the process several times until relieved. I can't remember ever being challenged. Heaven forbid a spy or saboteur infiltrating into the frozen landscape of the Great Lakes Naval Training Center!

A native Chicagoan, I had felt the cold and bitter winds along Lake Shore Drive many times, but never the cold like Great Lakes! It was on those watches that I would pray silently to be sent to a steaming hot jungle rather than some miserable cold Atlantic convoy duty or remote Aleutian outpost. Those guys deserved medals!

We were jumped out of our "sacks" at 0400 and were given brief time for toiletries and dressing. Then we scrambled outside for calisthenics, marched off to breakfast chow, and began a very busy schedule of demanding, character-building activities.

We learned how to roll up and "tie" all of our clothes—even our socks and skivvies—with little clothes ties and lay them out in proper order with the rest of our uniform for seabag inspection. And we learned to correctly repack all our duds back into the seabag. Also, we were taught how to make a "tight sack" (bed) with "square corners." The blanket and sheet were tucked so tightly that a coin could be bounced on top.

We had to stand at rigid attention, eyes always forward, and answered only when spoken to with a "Yes, sir" or "No, sir" or "AYE-AYE, SIR!" There was lots of discipline, lots of marching, lots of knot tying, basic seamanship and Navy doctrine, fleet ship identification and familiarity, communication, signal flags, and code. Additionally, an encyclopedic mass of nautical information was detailed in the *Bluejacket's Manual*—the sailor's Bible.

And, of course, calisthenics! Push-ups, sit-ups, knee-bends—you name it. All in the bitter cold dark morning hours!

Friday was "Field Day," the day every Boot prepared his company barracks for inspection. That meant cleaning and scrubbing and the "Great Lakes Shuffle." The wooden barrack decks were kept so clean that one could eat off of them. After moving all bunks and obstructions to the far end of the room, a line would be formed, shoulder to shoulder, from wall to wall. Each man was provided with pads of steel wool to put under his shoes. Proceeding forward, the line moved, shuffling the steel wool pads and thus cleaning the entire floor or deck. No spot was left untouched! The "Great Lakes Shuffle" very much resembled the legwork of cross-country skiers.

Then came the heavy machine waxers, and after a couple of coats with the brushes came the guys with rags now replacing the pads of steel wool, and we would again polish the floor spaces overlooked by the waxers. Windows received no less care and were polished to a sparkle.

"Head" duty required extreme attention, for it was where the inspection was keenest. This required using lots of soap powder and disinfectant, mopping, and polishing plumbing, faucets and mirrors.

White-gloved "Captain's Inspection" came the next morning. Everything had to be "4.0" or the company would lose some privilege. Every effort was aimed at coming out on top, earning your company extra liberty and the prized "Red Rooster"—a white flag with red rooster to distinguish your company as the best when marching from class to class that particular week.

Chow was a great daily vent for this sailor. I ate everything! Beans, grits, that "stuff" on a shingle (sort of hamburger stew on toast)—lots of starches. Signs everywhere read "Take all you want, but eat all you take!" I soon put weight on my 114-pound frame—upwards of 140 pounds!

Two incidents that happened while in boot camp have stayed in my memory. The first was when we were undergoing an assimilated high jump from ship deck height into the ocean below by climbing and jumping from a fifty-foot-high scaffolding. Forming a single line behind each other, we climbed the steep tower and, guided by an instructor on top, we were told to close our eyes, pinch our noses, and step off the platform for the big plunge.

The big, tough-looking guy in line before me (I don't recall his name, but we'll call him "Marty") was acting pretty cocksure as we climbed the scaffold ladder. He was full of jokes and wise comments. Once at the top, however, big Marty looked down and suddenly froze in place. The instructor pulled him over to the jump-off point, but Marty wanted no part of it and was already attempting to get back down. The long line behind sailors on the platform and on the ladder made that almost impossible.

The instructor ordered him to jump. Marty, now visibly shaken, was holding tightly onto a scaffold railing.

The Chief below, seeing the delay, shouted up an order: "Sailor, take the jump and get your butt down here!"

No such luck.

Then an officer called to the scene ordered: "This is an order! Jump, sailor, or face the consequences!"

Marty was sobbing by now. This hulk of a guy was shaking and crying! It took four guys to eventually and precariously half-lift and tightly maneuver Marty back down that scaffolding!

That was after the instructor had turned and quietly given me the nod to take the jump. I was scared, too, but what the hell? I pinched my nose, closed my eyes, and stepped off into the nothing.

Later we would do this drill with clothes on, hit the water, brush away simulated oil coming up to the surface, take off our trousers, tie the bottoms, and, sweeping them over our heads, capture enough air in the trouser legs to inflate them so we could float on the surface with our newly made life preservers!

I don't remember seeing Marty again. He probably was transferred to some job requiring shore duty only, but I've often thought about that jump and so many other things we're called upon to do in life requiring a certain mindset. Close your eyes, pinch your nose, and take the high jump. Like I did, writing this book! It's taken me over fifty years just to do that!

Now to my short stint as the "K.O. Kid." I was never a fighter, but you don't join the Navy without some idea that along the line you'll do a little boxing. The phys ed instructor at least gave each of us the opportunity to pick who we would get into the ring with. I looked about for a little guy, slight as I was, and picked a guy a bit smaller—one whom I thought I might have a fighting chance with.

CHAPTER 10   Joining the Navy

I was at least a head taller; he had broader shoulders. He wore a nice smile and seemed quiet as he agreed to go a few rounds in the ring with me. Shades of Jimmy Cagney.

I don't think I even had the time to lead with my left. The bell sounded, and we both came out of our respective corners. Dance around a bit maybe? A jab or two perhaps? No such time was afforded me. This little guy went straight for my jaw. Pow! Down I went—not out, mind you, but I was dazed and sprawled out on that canvas, and looking up! The referee, who was shaking his head and gesturing, confirmed the match was over for "Kid Klotz." He raised both our hands. We shook gloves and climbed out of the ring.

Can't remember another time I entered a "boxing ring" in the Navy, unless you count another knock-out punch given me in the islands after a comment I made about some newly fermented "kick-a-poo juice" we were indulging in.

Time went by so very fast at Great Lakes. There was a visitor's open house halfway through. Many commented that I had put on weight, and how good I looked in uniform. When boot camp was over, we were all pushing and shoving at the barracks bulletin board to scan lists of names to see if we got our choice of schools, who was getting sea duty, and where the drafts were being sent. Then came a two-week leave with orders to report to our new destination. As my hometown was in Chicago, I invited a few of my new shipmates to stop by on their way home. Some of them were from farms and other open spaces, and I suddenly felt a consciousness of my own surroundings in contrast to theirs. We paraded about in our pea coats and flat hats, looking like real sailors. After visiting a few neighborhood friends, we wished each other luck and they went on their way. I don't remember one of them! Nor would I meet up with them again.

I stopped by my old high school to see Mrs. Booth, my art teacher. She invited me to stand before the class while extolling me as one of her most accomplished art students with lots of talent and so much more potential and whom she wished had stayed in school. No query was made by her of my Navy career!

I also visited with Mr. Berens at the high school paper's office. Happy to see me, he showed me past issues of the paper where they were still using little cartoon spots that I had done. For a short time I strutted about the school hallways, enjoying the obvious attention and admiration of classmates, but the bell called them back to class and I soon returned home.

    Everyone was off working. Many of my friends were busy at school, war jobs, or had joined up. The family was preoccupied with their own interests. There was a prevailing feeling of a great change taking place. The talk was of rations, of sacrifice, and of their men in service. People spoke of quotas, victory bonds, a non-permanence and transitory existence. Everyone seemed on the move.

    It was soon time to board the train and get on with it.

Naval Air Technical Training Center
TENNESSEE

"Havin' trouble with the das 'n dits?—Go dance!"

At Great Lakes Naval Training Station, those of us with high enough grade marks were given a choice of Naval Training Schools. Those who didn't were sent to "sea duty." There were additionally two "extra pay" services that recruits could volunteer for: submarines and aviation duty. Those sent to a forward area would also qualify for "combat" pay. Not everyone jumped on these incentives offered by the Navy.

Having volunteered for both submarine and/or flying—and finding myself "dentally disqualified" for the deep below—I was now keen on naval aviation. In the summer of '43, I was already envisioning myself as a rear seat "radio-gunner" in a Navy SPD dive-bomber.

As training came to an end, it was a great feeling to see my name posted informing me that I had gotten my choice of schools. My new assignment orders were to report to Naval Air Technical Training School in Millington, Tennessee, for training as an aviation radioman.

It seemed strange, after having worked as a Western Union telegram messenger only a short time before, that I was once again passing through the massive facility and boarding a train at bustling Union Station in Chicago. Only this time I was in a Navy uniform, toting a seabag and hammock.

Our draft climbed aboard a hissing, cinder-smoking steam locomotive. It was the first and only "troop train" that I would experience during my three years in the Navy. Crowding inside, we found ourselves sitting on noticeably filthy green-velvet seats near broken, dirt-encrusted windows that nobody could see out of. Others were obliged to sit in the dirty aisle in a darkened, musty smelling unheated coach car!

It soon became apparent to the Navy officer in charge of our draft that this railroad car did not meet the health standards required by the Navy. We soon got orders to disembark and board another train, which, though not much better, gave us a good feeling that our Navy was looking out for us! I remember the many Army "cattle cars" we were to pass in the night that were no more than freight cars transporting Army troops packed in like cattle. I was glad to be in the Navy!

We were on our way—and I, to my very first out-of-state adventure!

ooo

Arriving at Memphis in the morning, we were put on a bus for the long ride out to the Naval Air Technical Training Center at Millington, Tennessee. Disembarking from the bus, we could see and hear the roar of airplanes overhead, competing with the commands shouted at us to form ranks.

A sky full of yellow bi-planes buzzed all about us like bees. We would soon call them "Yellow Perils," an appropriate nickname for the bi-wing two-seat trainer painted a very bright yellow. The "Perils" would be with us from that point on. Endlessly taking off, circling overhead, and landing at airstrips but a short distance away—and then doing it all over again! These were the AVCADS—new Navy aviation cadets undergoing primary flight training.

On "our" side of the vast facility was the Naval Air Technical Training Command, with its multitude of barracks and buildings, fenced in and guarded by Marines. This was home to Navy aircrewmen recruits in training: the aviation radiomen, ordnancemen, and mechanics of the Navy Air Force who would eventually join up with pilots and navigators in training to form a combat aircrew team to fly the aircraft of the fleet. There were also other trainees—from

CHAPTER 11 Naval Air Technical Training Center

allied nations and wearing respective uniforms of their countries—all in groups marching in military cadence to piped martial music. The music blared from a multitude of loudspeakers placed about uniformly on poles.

Music always seemed enhanced by the overhead roar of airplanes, to which we would hereafter be awakened. For early morning calisthenics, to march to class by, to drill by, eat chow by, double-time to, and otherwise, the music kept us in step and in fast tempo to, from, and through our many scheduled classes and activities.

We would also proudly march to the same music on parade ground with shouldered rifles. Drill instructors barked out staccato commands as they quick-stepped us through basic marching routines. We soon were molded into a cohesive and competitive platoon, doing our best to win and proudly carry in front the "Red Rooster"—the pennant that showed the others we were the best! We were Navy—we had arrived!

For the class of AR-6, Section F NATTC, the next eighteen-week "crash course" would be taught by determined Navy instructors with a dedicated resolve to make aviation radiomen out of us. More music! This time the dits and das of Morse code. With earphones and practice keys, we would listen and learn the code, the code, and more code along with "pounding the key," operating procedure, equipment knowledge and maintenance, general indoctrination to fleet, aviation and command structure, combat and life-saving measures, ordnance handling, plane identification, and maximum doses of calisthenics, obstacle course, duty watches, and barracks prep for field day!

The routine would, in fact, keep us so busy that we would become oblivious to the roaring "Yellow Perils" and often disconcerting crashes that brought sirens speeding to the aid of a pilot who didn't quite make it.

NATTC was also a training facility for Navy WAVES and women Marines, and some from the allied forces. They joined the other trainees marching to classes each day in platoon formation. Platoons were continually marching to and from, criss-crossing and quick-stepping, all intent on getting to the class on time.

The "Women Auxiliary Volunteer Emergency Service," or WAVES, were established in 1942, though their predecessors had served in World War I. By 1943 a good many were being trained in radio and mechanics at NATTC in Millington. So were women Marines. These stalwart enlistees initially attracted much attention from their sailor counterparts.

The WAVES duty uniform was a blue, one-piece coverall and floppy hat—not very flattering to most. And with GI undergarment, they marched with a sort of bounce that prompted many a sailor to turn for a look as a WAVE platoon marched by. There was always a new wise-guy on station who would make some remark in passing.

On one occasion we witnessed a WAVE platoon leader who had halted her platoon in midfield. Running back, she approached a male platoon of sailors whose platoon leader, sensing something had gone wrong, had also brought his group to a halt.

The WAVE ran right by him and into the formation of sailors—one of whom she took a swing at, landing him on the pavement. Running back to her platoon, she barked out: "Platoon, A-ten-shun! Quick-time... Fooorwaaard *maarch*!" and the group trotted on.

Our own platoon leader had called us to a halt to watch the action. We all started laughing but were immediately brought to attention and marched off on the double, leaving the surprised "wise-guy" rubbing his chin. We never knew what disciplinary action was taken, if any at all, but it conveyed a lesson: Never mess with a WAVE!

At the head of some selected platoons marching about was the coveted Red Rooster. This was evidence of "Captain's Inspection," held every Friday and called "Field Day," requiring more Herculean efforts from platoon members in cleaning barracks, the head, laying out for seabag inspection (outlay of uniform), and constant attention to making their bed or "sack." Never mind the serious studies and code-learning! Work began on Thursday nights and all hands partook. Decks had to be swabbed down, sanded, waxed, and polished. Winning that Red Rooster pennant meant an extra liberty in Memphis and prompted fierce competition.

For our platoon leader, "Cuccias," getting the Rooster was an obsession. He had us double-timing here and double-timing there, and on Field Day there was no end to his demand for perfection. I think he was priming for Officers Candidate School. Anyway, one day while double-quicking it across the drill field and heading back

CHAPTER **11**   *Naval Air Technical Training Center*   129

to the barracks after some gruesome physical endeavors on the obstacle course, I said "to heck with it" and dropped from the ranks to walk back to the barracks. Cuccias ordered me to get back in rank a couple of times, all to no avail, and the platoon left me behind. But it wasn't long before an OD on a motor scooter came up and put me on report. A month of extra duty taught me the negatives to rebellion and kept me on the double from then on.

In the classroom, there would be "sparks" who, having difficulty with "the code," were encouraged to get out and dance. I never became as proficient as I should have been—and suppose it was due to a lack of practiced rhythm required to send messages. Maybe this was why base celebrity "Clyde McCoy" (Musician 1st Class) and his band, who played most every Sunday afternoon, were so important. I was one of the shy lads who stood on the sidelines watching the swingers dance to Clyde's trombone and great dance band. While I marveled at the gifted sailors swinging the WAVES about, I could seldom drum up the courage to ask for a dance. The few times I did, the partner I chose did nothing to improve my rhythm in sending code. Most of the jitterbug music was too fast and required a carefree personality I had not yet developed. I don't know why they didn't give Clyde a commission—he was quite a well-known musician, both in and out of the service.

Though there was much to be said for the base activities available in off-hours, oh so sweet and savored was liberty when we got it! The highlight of Memphis memories was the fabulous and elegant Peabody Hotel, at which we always indulged ourselves in their famous Southern Fried Chicken Dinner: hot muffins, potatoes and gravy, and great coffee served from a silver coffee pot. In short, a dining experience served handsomely on fine china and silver, with an ambience of grandeur. Liberty brought a touch of class—the Peabody!

However we could not afford to sleep there. Sleeping was done at the YMCA—a huge gym floor crammed with closely placed canvas army cots, row upon row. But then, it was only for sleeping. Each had a mattress, pillow, folded sheet and blanket. The Y was our home away from home, and while not a deluxe hotel, it provided clean and cheap sleeping quarters. Once checked in, we took bearings as to relative positioning of our cots so as not to crawl in the wrong one upon return. Then it was a quick exit and a feeling of joy as we headed out on the town.

The young sailors always began their liberty in crispy-clean, overstarched, sparkling white uniforms. At liberty's end however, many sick and sorry "sinners" were "liberty dirty"! It was a "bring your own bottle in a brown paper bag, buy the ice 'n mixer" kinda town.

This was definitely the segregated South. Movies always had long waiting lines, and no one wanted to waste their liberty time waiting in line. On one liberty, my buddies and I were called over to the alley by a black boy. We followed him to the back entrance and up the steps through a door where we entered a balcony section. Giving him a small tip, we entered the darkened movie section and sat in a row of seats. As we accustomed our eyes to the dark, we felt conspicuous in our white uniforms. We then saw folks close to us giving a welcome smile and feeling no ill will as we watched the movie. After the movie, we were a bit anxious not to be seen by the Shore Patrol and quickly meshed ourselves into the white majority of strollers departing from the front of the theater.

My class appeared in the NATTC yearbook *Navy Log*, comprising class pictures, and those of commanding officers, instructors, and graduates. It also included a couple of cartoons I had submitted, with the following write-up:

Klotz, Donald Lewis—Age 18. "Don" hails from 4734 Hubbard Street, Chicago, Illinois. He flew the coop there Jan. 18, 1943 and trained with Co. 119, Great Lakes. Formerly a Correction Artist with the Curt-Teich Co., he likes to draw. The son of Mr. & Mrs. Harry Adams Klotz, he aspires to shoot down a Zero, and to become a cartoonist when he gets out of the Navy.

Commander A. R. Bueler, USN, NATTC, Memphis, Tennessee, wrote a special tribute:

Since the birth of Naval Aviation, the men who have shared in the heartache and glories of the Naval Air Force, by their devotion and skill, have rendered it supreme in the annals of warfare. Today there flies across the horizon again a gallant crew of men whose feats of valor and endurance will be indelibly written across the pages of history. We salute these men of Naval Aviation—The pilot who guides his craft unflinchingly into the blazing face of battle, the radioman who makes possible rapid and efficient communication, the ordnanceman entrusted with care of the armament, and the machinist mate whose job it is to "keep 'em flying!" To the men of this Naval service who have given their lives unselfishly for God and country, so we solemnly pledge that their sacrifice for the cause of civilization shall not have been in vain, To them in hallowed memory, we respectfully dedicate this class log.

I proudly sent off a copy of the NATTC's *Navy Log* to my mom with the following inscription: "Yes, mother dear, it is for you and all the lovely things you stand for that I am fighting for. May this war be over soon—and God grant us all Peace, Happiness and Prosperity for the rest of our lives and the generation to come. Your loving son, Don."

The war had hardly begun that summer of '43 for U.S. Navy Patrol Squadron 23, performing air-sea rescue, patrol, and bombing missions from Espiritu Santo and Funafuti in the Ellice Islands. Funafuti was a seaplane base for attacks on the Ellice Islands—and the squadron served as a support group for the planned attack on Tarawa.

During this time VP-23 carried out an attack and bombed Nauru Island, picked thirty-nine downed survivors from the deep, and was routinely supplied "coastwatchers" operating from behind the lines in Japanese-held territory.

The squadron, relieved by VP-24, was transferred from Espiritu Santo to Halavo Seaplane base, Florida Islands, in the Solomons after a stay of three and a half months. In August of 1943, Skipper Frank Brandley was relieved by LCDR George E. Garcia, USN.

That August I would graduate from NATTC Radio School as S1/C ARM, and proceed to NAGS (Naval Air Gunners School) at Hollywood, Florida. Upon completion of our training there, we would be assigned to an operational training unit for duty in a dive bomber, torpedo bomber, multi-engine plane, or other Navy aircraft squadron.

Naval Air Gunners School (NAGS)
HOLLYWOOD, FLORIDA

"By the sea ... By the sea!
Oh how happy we will be!"

I still hold fond memories of the four short weeks spent at Naval Air Gunners School in Hollywood, Florida. In contrast to the hot, flat, treeless and asphalted terrain, the sterile and stark barracks, and grueling curriculum at NATTC Millington, "Hollywood" was pure paradise! The Military Academy nestled among tall waving palm trees, exotic plants, and well-kept grass lawns was a picture book Citadel, with magnificent front facade and towers and roofs of red clay tiles. Blooming vines grew up the sides of the buildings, and the school was positioned just off the white sand beaches, complete with crashing surf!

In the 1940s, the academy was taken over by the Navy, and when the war broke out it was slightly altered for use as a United States Naval Air Gunners School.

The nearby Hollywood Beach Hotel was turned into a U.S. Naval Indoctrination and Training School, and the Hollywood Golf & Country Club became an entertainment and recreational center for U.S. servicemen.

What duty! Alas—it only lasted for four weeks! It was as if we were attending a prestigious private military school. We were billeted two to a room. Chow was served in a dining room and eaten at small tables. While the short time signaled a cram course in ordnance, our schedule was not so time consuming as to rule out some

CHAPTER 12 *Naval Air Gunners School (NAGS)*

fantastic liberty on fine beaches, and swimming in the frothy white surf and blue waters of the very cold Atlantic.

My good buddies—Don Obee, age nineteen, from Toledo, Ohio, and Dick "King" Newell, age eighteen, from Oakland, California, both shipmates who had been in my class at NATTC—had been assigned with my draft. "Obee" was a quiet sort of guy, serious, conscientious, but pleasant to be with, while "King" was personality plus. His love of a good time and enthusiasm for everything was contagious. Before boarding the bus to go into town on liberty, and all decked out in a spotlessly clean and pressed uniform, he would go into a little dance shuffle, singing: "By the sea, by the sea—Oh, how happy we will be!" He set the mood promising a good time, however tame it actually turned out to be.

For the young sailor who wanted to keep out of trouble, liberty usually meant going to the USO, a roller rink, town library, movie or sight-seeing of some sort. But just walking along the wonderful balmy Hollywood beach shore at night is a fine memory. Literally thousands of sand crabs would venture from their holes, providing a darkened and virtual "moving carpet" as they scurried out of pedestrians' way.

I can't remember standing any duty watches or "Field Day demands" at Hollywood. Or much drilling, either. I suppose because of the short time we would spend at the school, our time was prioritized to ordnance.

We did get called out once for a parade in Hollywood. But any glory was short-lived due to the short distance required for our Navy contingent to march through the small town's center. We did get a volley of cheers from residents, as we passed by with shouldered rifles, web belts, and canvas leggings. However, we were quickly marched to the bus and hustled back to the base—without either refreshment nor brief liberty.

At the gunner's school, we were introduced to an assortment of arms, but maximum time was programmed for learning the nomenclature, assembling, disassembling, cleaning and care of .30 and .50-caliber machine guns. The damned guns were never "user friendly" to me, and I was always fearful of getting a metal splinter in my hand when cleaning them, or worse—a bolt-switch plunger and spring assembly through my chest when removing the backplate. Or some other catastrophe, like a projectile explosion while firing or correcting a gun jam. I always laugh when I see these guys in the war movies pick up a .50 and, while holding it by the barrel and shooting from the hip, shoot down a Japanese Zero while getting off as much as a hundred rounds.

We also were given lots of written tests to ensure our knowledge of the nomenclature. We spent even more time with shotguns on the skeet range shooting clay pigeons from rotating clock positions. Oh, what bruised shoulders and sore chins initially received from the kick-back of that damned shotgun butt! We were continually warned about keeping our thumbs down, lest we lose an eye. The command still rings in my ears: "Load!" then "Pull!" and upon clay pigeon release, "Fire!" Instructors would shout: "Lead! ... "Lead!" ... and more "Lead!"

And we were introduced to "Jam-Handy"—simulated turret mock-ups of various Navy aircraft, including top, belly, side, and tail turrets. We would climb into the "turret," grab the controls, and in a darkened room work the movable turret and press the firing button at attacking planes coming fast and from all directions via screen projection. Sometimes the plane was "friendly," one target on which you had better not have pulled the trigger. The instructor stood by to score you. It was quite tricky and required very quick reflexes.

On the firing range we fired from varied turrets and from machine guns mounted on moving trucks, from which we shot at other moving targets. Actual flight gunnery training would have to await our next assignment to an operational training unit.

Less physical were classes in plane identification. We learned to spot Japanese "Bettys," "Zekes," "Emilys," "Kates," and our own planes, too. Many a plane was shot down by friendly fire.

Few of us wanted assignment to multi-engine planes nor even gave much thought to the prospect. Most wanted carrier duty in a dive bomber (SBD) or torpedo bomber (TBF) Squadron. Both aircraft won fame in sinking four Japanese carriers at the Battle of Midway. In the SBD rear seat position the gunner sat backwards and swung a pair of twin .30s about. In the TBF there were two gun positions, a top turret behind the pilot, and a belly tail-gun position.

Some of our instructors had seen combat with the fleet, and we listened with rapt attention to their war adventures. Any chance

CHAPTER 12 *Naval Air Gunners School (NAGS)*

we got to steer them off a prescribed class subject and on to their experiences, we'd do so.

As time went by, I soon realized that I wasn't the best shot. There was a little trick in learning which eye was the master eye, by closing one eye and pointing the respective finger to the target, then doing the same with the other eye. The eye that kept that finger on target was your master eye, which dictated how you held your gun. I was always scratching my head over this. I think my lighter weight, slight build, and non-calloused hands did not help. And the written tests complicated matters—I was not good at written exams!

I worried that I might actually be washed out and assigned sea duty! Anxieties increased as we came nearer to completion of the course, and after final exams we daily checked the bulletin board for the postings of our next assignment.

That day arrived. Drafts were posted—and I had made it. I was now a qualified naval air gunner! I was happy that I had passed the course and wasn't pegged for sea-duty, but I was sorry to learn that my good buddies and I would go separate ways. Don Obee was assigned to an SBD squadron and fleet assignment that headed him toward the West Coast; and affable "King" Newell was assigned to a TBF squadron, though he was not too happy with the prospect of being a belly gunner in the tail end of a torpedo bomber!

I was assigned to an operational training unit in Jacksonville, Florida, and would soon be flying in a twin-engine Navy amphibious flying boat known as a PBY.

13

Operational Training Unit (OTU-1)
JACKSONVILLE, FLORIDA

"Give the target plenty of lead..."

What's a PBY? I wasn't too happy on seeing my name on a draft heading for OTU-1 (operational training unit) in Jacksonville, Florida, to fly in PBYs. I had little idea of what a PBY was, though I must have been vaguely aware that such a plane existed. At previous training stations, SBDs and TBFs were on display to admire or climb about in. These were the Navy's "glory" planes, and along with fighters, the "hot-shots" of the Navy. Especially after the Battle of Midway!

While we learned about varied transmitters and radio receivers, I don't remember any instruction on equipment in the radio compartment of a PBY. Maybe that's because I had just assumed I would be a radio gunner in a Navy dive-bomber or TBF squadron. A "PBY" sounded like pretty dull duty, and I wanted action!

So be it. I had my assignment, and most important, the opportunity to get up in the wild blue yonder and fly as a Navy combat aircrewman!

Jacksonville Naval Air Station was a large seaplane base where pilots, navigators, aviation mechanics, ordnancemen, and radiomen were brought together as aircrews to train in operational training units.

On first arrival at the base we all headed down to the hangar

CHAPTER **13** *Operational Training Unit (OTU-1)*

area and seaplane ramps to see the PBYs landing and taking off from water and the hub-bub of activity making it all happen. It brought on a sudden urge to climb aboard one of the magnificent flying boats!

Not so fast, though. We would first learn that privilege would only come by way of the "beach crew." The beach crew at any time of the year was no great duty, but in the late fall/early winter, when we arrived, there were few clear, sunny days.

These were old PBY-5s that we would learn to launch and recover. (The amphibious PBY-5As were being sent out to the fleet.) The wheelless PBY-5 had to be towed down to the ramp and placed in the water. After removal of attached wheels it then would taxi out for takeoff. Upon landing, it would taxi up to the ramp, and again wheels were attached by the beach crews, enabling it to be hauled up the ramp by a line attached to a tractor on shore. Both feats required the handling of two very cumbersome, heavy landing wheels, and a pair of tail wheels. The tires were big enough that they would float, but it was an effort requiring several people on each side of the plane, and tractors with long lines to haul them into place down and/or up the ramp.

It was a good beach crew that could launch a plane in less than five minutes. Recovery would take somewhat longer because of the need to make a slower approach, and it was, to say the least, a bit awkward getting a plane turned around so that it went back up tail first.

Beach crews could wear a pair of swimming trunks in summer, but in the very cold winter water crewmen needed a heavy, one-piece waterproof canvas suit that zipped up to the neck replete with heavy rubber boots. It had to fit tight and snug around the neck, for if you slipped off the ramp, you'd be in deep water—which would very likely fill your suit with water and sink you!

Talk about a Woody Allen movie! Grappling and maneuvering those big rubber-tired wheels bobbing about in water with a mule-like tendency to shy away from wherever you wanted them to go, and then getting the darned wheel mounts attached with pinions to the side of the plane, was a challenge you really anticipated by fearless young lads seeking to fly in a Navy PBY!

After a while, though, we would feel a sense of great pride in the swiftness and teamwork mastered in "beach the craft." But how we envied the pilots and aircrews inside those flying boats. As we worked about, outside the "amphibs," we found ourselves falling in love with the PBY, affectionately called a "Catalina."

How could an airman not love the PBY? Designed by Macklin Laddon, under the visionary Rueben Fleet of Consolidated Aircraft in 1928, it was first designated the XPY-1: "X" for experimental, "P" for patrol, "Y" for Consolidated (as the letter "C" had already been given to Curtis Aviation). The first prototype was modified over various design stages. Upon the outbreak of World War II, the PBY-5 had earned its role in the Navy fleet, soon to be followed by the PBY-5A. The "B" was added behind "P" for "patrol" to accent its versatility as a "bomber," the "A" for "amphibious."

The sleek, all-metal, twin-engine amphibian PBY-5A, with a 63-foot-10-inch-long flying boat hull, was equipped with retractable tricycle-type landing gear and powered by two Pratt and Whitney engines. The 104-foot wingspan was braced by four struts, two from each side, extending under the surface of the wing. The stern portion of the hull tapered to a point, sweeping up vertically to form a dorsal fin. Rudder and elevator were also metal frames, fabric-covered.

Main panel and leading edge structures of the wing incorporated ducts for the heat anti-icing system, deriving its heat from engine exhaust. The wing also incorporated the engine narcelles, fuel and oil tanks, and two retractable auxiliary floats and their operating mechanism.

The hull was divided into five watertight compartments, separated by four main bulkheads equipped with watertight doors. The bomber's compartment was in the bow forward the pilot's compartment and extending aft to the first watertight bulkhead.

The radio and navigation compartment was aft of the pilot's compartment: radio and radar equipment on the starboard side and navigator table on the port side. The engineer's station comprised the superstructure, which supported the wing, and immediately below was the galley compartment containing stove, food locker, and auxiliary power unit—narrower because of the indentations to accommodate the landing wheel wells.

Crew quarters aft of the galley compartments were equipped with four pull-down bunks, and directly aft were the distinctively designed teardrop port and starboard blisters, and tunnel hatch or tail compartment.

CHAPTER **13**   *Operational Training Unit (OTU-1)*   139

Armament consisted of single or twin .30-caliber machine guns in the bow; two .50-calibre machine guns (one starboard; one port) in blister positions; and a single .30-caliber machine gun in the tail. The PBY had variable bomb load potential: two to four 1000-pound demolition bombs; four 500-pound demolition bombs; eight 325-pound demolition bombs; twelve 100-pound demolition bombs or two torpedoes. As the war progressed, various combinations were contrived by the ingenuity of P-boat pilots! One pilot even installed four .50s in the bow nose!

The time at OTU-1 in Jacksonville went by very fast. During our brief stint in the beach crew, we were given more ground courses, more code, and more watches, but were soon flying as aircrews! The winter cold and damp fog in Jacksonville required thick leather lambskin-lined flying jackets, sometimes with bulky pants and padded lambskin flying boots. Add the yellow Mae Wests and leather helmet with goggles, and we were beginning to feel a lot like Navy aircrewmen! Parachutes were stowed on the plane, but our training was minimal and the fact that we were amphibious and flew close to the water gave us a somewhat cavalier attitude toward their use.

We went up on all sorts of training flights: landing and take-off, navigational, gunnery, etc. I remember one particular gunnery flight, when I first crawled between pilots and up into the bow gun position.

The bow gun is on a hydraulic turret, or electrically controlled gun mount. In this obsolete PBY-2 trainer, the .30 is locked in position, requiring the gunner to pull a ring to allow movement of the .30-caliber on circular track. Before firing, the gun must first be loaded with a linked belt of ammunition from the ammo cans stashed on the catwalk beside you, and then with bolt cocked the gunner awaits command from the pilot. Standing in the open bow, with wind whipping about your face, is the first challenge. (Helmet and goggles do more to hinder vision in this case.) The gunner's job now is to site the target and swing the gun while grasping a hand-held mike to facilitate communications with the pilot. The WWI bombers had much in common with this old bird.

"Give the target plenty of lead," we were told time and again at gunnery school. The target was a twenty-foot-long white cloth sleeve on a wire pulled by a tow plane (another PBY). The overall exercise was most frustrating.

In my bow-gun indoctrination, I thought I heard the pilot give me the command to fire. Not wanting to lose my target, I pulled the trigger. *Rat-tat-tat... Rat-tat-tat... Rat-tat-tat*! went my gun. This was the fun part. I was shooting away merrily, giving the target plenty of lead. The plane suddenly banked and veered steeply and swiftly away from the target.

"Stop firing, goddammit!" I heard the pilot yell. "You want to shoot down one of our planes?"

Actually, I was surprised when the target was brought down, and the number of hits I had scored was recorded!

On another gunnery flight my position was on the tail gun. This gun had to be an afterthought, put in out of desperation. It was surely a blind spot and most vulnerable to an attacking plane.

Crawling back with little space to maneuver, I opened up the tunnel hatch, making sure I was harnessed in to prevent falling out of the plane. Unlocking the .30-caliber secured to the side bulkhead, loading and cocking, I swung it over and out of the open tail hatch.

Visibility? Zero! Any target had to be directly below before a gunner could see anything to fire at. In gunnery practice, it helped to first hang out—upside down from the hatch—and looking about for the "target." Even if we were lucky enough to catch a glimpse, it required swift, acrobatic skill to get back inside and on gun position for that "split-action pull of the trigger" required before the target whipped on by!

The idea was to give it all you had in the hair-breadth second you had to hit anything. It took luck, not marksmanship, to hit something with the tail gun! The tail hatch was much more suited for dropping empty beer cans at night over Japanese positions—or paper bags of waste (which was done with some accuracy).

The .50s in the port or starboard blisters were the best bet, with special mount and chest brace to help in holding the gun steady. It was the tracers which were crucial in finding your target. Together with a little weight, a firm wrestler's grip, and stance—and a couple of strong arms. Once that trigger was pulled on the .50, a little guy like me would bounce all about. Bless providence that I never had to fire in combat, excepting an island strafing we once did. And even at that, there seemed no visible target. All I hit was incoming waves.

CHAPTER 13 *Operational Training Unit (OTU-1)*

Toward the end of our training period in OTU-1, our crew flew to Banana River Naval Air Station, deep in the Florida Keys. On the edge of the Everglades—this was the tropics! Lush and densely green. The base was almost hidden by trees and the climate hot and humid. We were there in preparation for a Pacific posting, and would see the bigger and more contemporary PBMs.

Taxiing up to the docks in the inland waterways, we felt like a crew from "PT-109." We kibitzed back and forth with other crews and slept that night in tropical huts. In the early morning light next day we took off and headed back to Jacksonville.

Upon finishing OTU training, I would be given another leave—and another treat: Travel orders routing me to San Diego via a "one-man draft" through Chicago! With a leave thrown in to boot! Just me! I was only a first-class seaman, and this was unexpected travel style. I wondered if there had been a mistake made, but not for long. I basked in every moment. It was a grand trip from Jacksonville up to Chicago, and it was great to be home again.

All the family was eager to hear about my radio and gunnery training, and particularly my flying adventures in a PBY. I could now wear my aviation radioman's rating on one sleeve and my aerial gunner's badge on the other. There was some anxiety and worry apparent with Mom and Dad wondering when and where I would be sent in the Pacific. But both my sisters were now out on the West Coast, and I was looking forward to seeing them. My leave went by very quickly.

I boarded the posh Santa Fe Super Chief—in first-class Pullman style, no less. This was "dinner in the diner, nothin' could be finer!" Choice of any entree, silver service, and bed made up by a congenial Pullman porter. And there was the option to relax in the club car.

I left Chicago from the Illinois-Central Station to continue my first-time travel across the great United States—its little towns, many train depots, farms, prairies, desert canyons, and high mountains. In California, our train actually went through lush orange groves so laden and close that one could pick the fruit off a tree! At last the Pacific Ocean—and San Diego, where we would report into Fleet Air Wing Fourteen, and await further assignment to one of many squadrons forming.

I will never forget seeing San Diego Bay and its massive Navy anchorage area, and feeling so small amidst the gray mass of tall fleet ships. The aircraft carrier USS *Ben Franklin* was in port, and the very sight of it rekindled a desire to somehow work a transfer to one of its dive bomber squadrons.

However, a query to the yeoman receiving my orders brought a quick negative response: I was not transferable. That was to my good fortune, for the *Franklin* was later hit by a kamikaze off Ulithi. I would witness the explosion from ashore and later fly over the ship as it was heading back to Pearl with a huge gaping hole in its hull.

14

A New VP-23
(1944)

"...overwhelmed with a great sense of pride, and a feeling that I was now truly part of the Navy's Pacific Fleet."

In 1944, Admiral Nimitz began his thrust eastward up the Central Pacific, making it the Navy's war—a war fought across more than 3,000 miles of blue water dotted with small, heavily defended islands. Some of these islands had to be seized as advanced bases in preparation of the next step forward.

In February 1944, Kwajalein Island was taken by the Marine's Fourth Division and GIs of the Seventh Division. At sixty-five miles long, it was the largest atoll in the world.

Lt. Arthur McQuiddy VP-23, after a Solomon Islands tour, was among the following pilots transferred back to the States to re-form a new VP-23 for a third tour to the Pacific and fight the final battles of the war. Phillips, S. M. Dunn, P. L. Gibson, and McQuiddy were assigned to an operational training unit at NAS North Island from October 20 until VP-23 (soon to be redesignated VPB-23) was organized. McQuiddy said, "Why we were picked, I do not know!"

On March 1, 1944, at NAS, North Island, San Diego, U.S. Navy Patrol Bombing Squadron (VPB-23) was re-formed under the command of LCDR William M. "Bill" Stevens.

A 1937 Naval Academy graduate, Commander Stevens first served with the fleet and won his wings in April of 1943 after flight training at NAS, Pensacola. Going on to advanced training at NAS, Jacksonville, and additional months as an instructor in PBYs, Commander Stevens reported to Fleet Air Wing Fourteen in San Diego, where he was assigned the task of re-forming VP-23.

Commander Stevens would "welcome aboard" the squadron's first fifty-eight officers and thirty enlisted men. However, with no planes yet assigned, its operations were limited to ground instruction of personnel. The newly re-formed squadron comprised a nucleus of some 25% of former VP-23 pilots and aircrewmen.

VPB-23's squadron complement was filled by April of '44, and shortly afterward fifteen PBY-5As, painted black, were delivered. Interesting to note are reports that show 3,200 rounds of .50-caliber ammunition would be expended in training. And by May, a total of 15,381 hours would be flown by the squadron in flight training operations—an average flight time of 90.4 hours per combat team!

Capt. Robin Larson remembered:

While serving with VP-23 in the Solomons, I was ordered back to the States with an ear infection—and grounded for a month or so. I then became executive officer of the Operational Training Unit of COMFAIR Wing 14 at San Diego.

Skipper LCDR William Stevens (Naval Academy '37) was forming a new VP-23 (redesignated VPB-23) at North Island and asked me to be its executive officer.

I was honored to accept and looked forward to flying the new PBY-5As (the amphibious type).

PPC Lt. W. Boardman Jones, Jr., said:

After a month of leave (Feb. '44) selected officers from the previous VP-23 tour, and now back from leave, reported to San Diego to re-form the squadron. Because of bad weather in the eastern half of the country, most of us were at least two days late. The yeoman who handled the paperwork was very vehement in pointing out our tardiness, invoking our response: "Court martial us and send us home—or get on with it!" And so, we proceeded with the reformation of VPB-23.

Originally informed that a "Lt. Commander Young" was to be our "new skipper," a group of us who had been under his direction on Canton a year earlier decided that this was a bad idea, and proceeded to go to a higher authority.

CHAPTER **14** *A New VP-23* 145

As diplomatic as we could be on the subject, we let it be known to the higher authority that we would not—repeat, not—go overseas under this officer's leadership, and were willing to stand court-martial if necessary, to escape such an assignment. We shortly got word that "Bill" Stevens would be our next skipper. Happiness reigned.

Thus during the first few days of March, we got organized and on March 7th started our training with our first flight—this time as Black Cats (PBYs painted black). During the next few months, we "solidified" our crews and did a lot of training. The flights were up and down the coast of Santa Barbara—night flights to train the pilots and radar men, bombing attacks, torpedo runs, navigation flights, etc. This involved about 250 hours of training and it must have been pretty good, because we all survived.

I clearly remember traveling to VP-23. Arriving January of '44 on a one-man draft from Jacksonville, Florida, to San Diego, California, and reporting into OTU, COMFAIR Wing Fourteen for further assignment, couldn't have made me happier.

Only a year in the Navy, and I had already traveled a good portion of the United States. The super deluxe Santa Fe Chief train had delivered me to one of the great Navy harbors on the West Coast.

I was absolutely in awe standing on the docks of San Diego Bay, seeing the massive and mighty armada of sleek battleship gray and camouflaged Navy ships, masts and command structures soaring above and bristling with armament. Tugs tooted and puffed about doing their work. Captains' gigs and LSTs scurried in all directions transporting personnel and supplies from ship to ship. Docksides were crowded with cranes and crewmen loading or unloading ships, and sailors and marines boarding troop transports or ships bound for the Pacific. Suddenly, I was looking upwards past a great gray curving wall in front of me, and feeling a towering island superstructure. The aircraft carrier USS *Ben Franklin* was in port.

Looking at the clusters of cruisers, destroyers, and subs nestled together—and across the bay to a beehive of planes taking off or landing at North Island Air Station—I was overwhelmed with a great sense of pride, and a feeling that I was now truly part of the Navy's Pacific Fleet.

At North Island I was assigned to FAW-14 OTU for additional operational training and instruction pending assignment to one of several PBY squadrons. Billeted with other aviation radiomen, we were issued distinctive leather fur-collared flight jackets worn only by Navy pilots and aircrewmen. That jacket would have an immediate effect of "bonding" us together as an elite group and giving us a sense of deep pride and comradeship that we would take with us for the rest of our days.

Although we had already experienced some "rivet-popping" in prior OTU training, we were to experience more of the same as new pilots awaiting assignment, and practiced both day and night at "touch and go" water landings.

As a consequence, many of the accompanying aircrewmen experienced air-sickness, especially the radiomen who were enclosed and positioned sideways in the radio compartment of the PBY. We took to carrying paper bags in our back pockets for obvious purposes. At the barracks, my aircrew comrades discussed this particularly common ailment.

"It's just like sea-sickness—it'll go away," said my good friend Harry Blenco.

But for another shipmate, Harvey Poenack, that would not happen. His air-sickness continued and was so severe that the scheduling officer at FAW-14 Command decided to try him out in other aircraft.

We all sort of envied Harvey's tryouts; that is, flying in the different planes. But Harvey continued to get air-sick. Strangely, after several flights, it appeared the only plane that Harvey didn't get sick on was the SB2/C "Hell-diver." Harvey was not happy with the antidote, and soberly pondered a forthcoming transfer to a carrier "Hell-diver" squadron.

When his papers arrived one day, Harvey let out a joyous yell. Months before, he had applied for aviation cadet training. The papers he received were not a transfer to a carrier squadron but instead informed him that he had been accepted for flight training. His orders were to report to Pensacola, Florida.

We saw Harvey off shortly after. My own air-sickness would continue for another month or two. However, I was not offered a "Harvey" option, and slowly acclimated to flying in a radio compartment of a PBY, as did my other buddies. We would soon be talking about our new squadron assignments.

Sometime in April of '44, I was assigned with many of my buddies in OTU to Patrol Squadron 23.

CHAPTER 14   A New VP-23

While training with the squadron at North Island, I called on the base's news publication, *The North Islander*, and submitted my first cartoons.

The managing editor was Bob "Windy" Winn—a grand guy, a native of California, and real pro. The publication's staff was terrific, and I found myself spending a good deal of time at the newspaper's office when not flying or going to training classes.

Soon I was set up in my little corner of the office and my cartoons were appearing regularly. I was even given a credit line. Editor "Windy" wanted to put me on the staff permanently and offered to get me a transfer. With Bill Mauldin in mind and a thought of bringing a "Willy & Joe" counterpart to the Pacific warfront, I pondered the offer but then respectfully declined, expressing my desire to stay with my squadron and what might have been a foolish eagerness to get out to the "forward area" and into "action."

My picture and bio appeared in the issue of *The North Islander* for which I had illustrated the cover:

> Don Klotz is one of the *Islander*'s most popular "blood & guts" cartoonists (most of 'em are classified as such)—but turns the tables by offering his charcoal sketch of this month's cover. From now on Don will be sending us cartoons from the South Pacific, however, because he's just shoved off. Middle name: Ferdinand (oh, not that!) Don hails from the Windy City, where as a youth he once heard a policeman say over a slain body: "They shot his guts out!"—and to Klotz, then a tiny youth, it made an impression on his art ever since. The cover sketch, however (a lovesick swabbie sitting on a bucket with mop in hand, reading a letter from his girl at home), shows his other side.
>
> He's modest, likable and may some day be one of the top notchers, for he's possessed with a natural sense of humor.

Though I continued to submit cartoons to *The North Islander*, a hectic squadron flying schedule commanded my time, and my talents would not be called upon again until a certain sighting was made by my pilot, Lt. W. Boardman Jones, while on patrol one day in the South Pacific.

ooo

In May 1944, with the prospect of moving out, we were given

a short leave—time enough to make it to Chicago, I thought. It turned into a hectic railroad trip home. This time no deluxe, expense-paid travel ticket. It was economy coach, and with little money to spend I hopped off the train in Albuquerque, New Mexico, to get some free chow at the USO. When I came back, my train had departed without me—gear and all!

Fortunately, a kind mother working at the USO canteen, with her own son in the Navy, put me up for the night, and I caught the train the next morning. That coach was no Santa Fe. I made it home for only a day or two, before heading back again.

PPC Lt. W. Boardman Jones was a red-haired, freckle-faced, Ivy League college sort of guy from St. Louis, Missouri. A quiet sort of guy with a wonderful sense of dry humor, "Jonesy" had flown with VP-23 in the Solomons and after a home leave was assigned the task of re-forming what might be also called a "quiet" crew. Jones had picked himself a group where there were no hot-shots, cut-ups, or bully buffs. All were like himself, essentially businesslike and quietly genteel. His first pilot was Lt.(jg) "Bill" Rider from Ennis, Texas, the first new pilot to report into 23. He was a quiet, good-looking, amiable fellow with accompanying Texan drawl. Bill wore his khaki uniform in a casual way, with blousy hat jauntily cocked and angled over his left eye, sleeves rolled up, and pistol hanging from the hip. He was well-liked by all crew members. Ens. Harold Hearon was navigator: curly-headed, thin, a bit taller than the other two pilots. Hearon, a Texan, too, came from the enlisted ranks. Quiet, projecting a military bearing and an eagerness to please, he was a loner who kept a respectable distance between himself and the rest of the crew. Capt. Fred "Freddie" Zaugg, AMM1/C, was a no-nonsense sort of guy from Pittsburgh, Pennsylvania. "Freddie" was the "mother hen" of crew #9—thoroughly competent and an authority figure that kept all crew members on their toes, while taking on more than his share of duties.

Second mechanic was Frank "Whitey" White, AMM2/C: a good-looking, lean, white-blond Texan with a pompadour. Quiet, very amiable, and a skilled mechanic, he inspired confidence and conveyed savvy empathy to his job and crewmates. On radio there was First Radioman William "Boo" Booher, ARM1/C, a preacher's son from Whittier, California. "Boo" was an "old man" at twenty-two, having been out on the previous tour of duty. Among other younger members of the squadron, "Boo" was the old vet, a skilled and competent "Sparks" whose manner inspired confidence in all of the crew. As S1/C (ARM), I was the lowest ranking and one of the youngest members of the squadron. A "less quiet" member, I drew portraits of my squadron shipmates. Robert C. Day, AOM1/C, was advanced to chief and left the crew soon after Midway. Chief Day was replaced by Art Hernandez, AOM1/C from Arcadia, California. He joined the crew at Eniwetok. Bob Watson, AOM3/C, was the crew's second ordnanceman and a scrappy little feister, who carried on a constant and challenging dialogue on any and all subjects with any member of the "quiet" crew who would take him on. Unfortunately, with a bad complexion and a susceptibility to "jungle rot," once in the tropics Watson was otherwise preoccupied and covered with a purple medicine. In a capsule, this was Lt. W. Boardman "Jonesy" Jones' crew.

Lt. Francis H. Clifton recalled the start of the re-forming of VP-23:

> I reported to the Commander Fleet Air Wing Fourteen "San Diego" on 29 of February '44. On March 7th I began training flights to re-form Squadron VP-23. Our brief training period on water was at Salton Sea, a desert lake, 100 miles of San Diego with an elevation of 235 feet below sea level. Hollywood has used the dunes for many years in shooting desert scenes. ("Beau Geste," no doubt!) The lake water has such a concentration of salt that on take-off a great salt trail would remain on the surface of the lake. The hardness of the water made landings sound as if we were landing on concrete with our wheels up! Returning to North Island, we continued training night and day throughout April, May. The type of flights flown and noted in my log book are: Familiarization, Night Training, Ferry, Instruments, Torpedo, Bombing, Night Search, Night Navigation, Camera Gunnery Tactics—and finally a night simulated Trans-Pacific flight of 11.4 hours on the night of June 14, 1944.

In April our new squadron began flying a heavy training schedule, including both day and night flights. As radiomen, we were kept so busy on the "circuit"—taking or sending messages, and operating other equipment—that we soon became accustomed to the "big bounce" and rivet-popping training flights, pre-empting the "rough ride" we would get from whichever pilot was at the controls.

The night flights where we flew in low over San Diego, looking down at the crowded streets below, provided a great view from the air. And likewise, when on liberty looking upwards and waving to our flying crews above, I took particular pride in pointing our planes out to my sister Anna Mae. Alas, she was soon to return home as her husband, Bruce, had been shipped out with the 4th Marine Division. He soon would be fighting on beachheads of Tarawa, Kwajalein, and Eniwetok, and go on to Iwo Jima.

Our day flights were flown daily over Marines circling in their amphibs offshore from their training base in Coronado. Looking down into the waters below, we soon became sharply aware of the massive activity going on all about us, which accented our own anxieties that we would also soon be heading out in support of some new island invasion.

I remember one night on the crowded street of downtown Broadway, before seeing my sister off on the train heading back to Chicago. Finding a quiet place where we could sit and chat was impossible. I could not have had a farewell drink with her if I wanted one, for I wasn't twenty-one, the legal age to do so. Besides, the bars were too loud and noisy. The long lines at coffee shop counters along the way ruled out any quiet retreat where we could talk. We finally found a squeeze-in, stand-up place at the counter for our last farewell cup of coffee.

San Diego's overcrowded facilities and heavy presence of Shore Patrol encouraged a weekly exodus to LA. Sailors and Marines looking for a little space, and some "better liberty," routinely lined up to hitch a ride on scenic 101—the highway leading to Los Angeles.

Once off base we would hightail along the highway to join the long line of sailors, all intent on getting to Los Angeles—fast! Trekking as far out along the highway and away from Navy base as possible, we would weigh the best vantage point to catching a ride, before thumbing our way to LA.

I don't ever remember going by bus or train. If lucky enough to quickly get a ride, this was by far the faster way—at least in going. And most always it was free, or a token amount was given to the driver for gas. Getting back was another story!

Route 101 was a beautiful stretch of oceanside towns, cliffside surf, endless orange groves, vast vineyards, purple mountains, tall

CHAPTER **14**   *A New VP-23*   151

oil fields—topography so varied, I sometimes think that it was the challenge and attraction of the picturesque highway that was the true motive for hitching it to LA.

Los Angeles offered a friendlier environment, with less presence of the Shore Patrol and more to see and do. The Hollywood Canteen was of course a big drawing card, and the prospect of seeing a movie star or two always a hopeful possibility.

I remember thumbing it to LA with crewmate and good buddy Frank "Whitey" White. A good-looking, not too tall, lean Texan, "Whitey" had blond, almost white hair, which he was always taking the comb to. He had a quiet, worldwise, low-key kind of personality, making him instantly likeable and a good friend. He seemed to have his feet on the ground and was in the know about everything. Arriving in LA, we found our way over to Whitey's favorite bar. I was very impressed when the bartender called out a "Hi, Whitey!" and proceeded to pour us both a shot of whiskey, without even asking for our ID! With elbow on the bar, one shoe on the brass foot railing, and puffing on a Lucky Strike, I truly felt like an old salt. Usually after deciding on a place to meet for the return trek back to San Diego, Whitey would amble off to see his girlfriend, and I would go on to my own pursuits.

VPB-23 Third Tour in the Pacific would take me to the following islands: Hawaii, Midway, Eniwetok, Saipan, Guam, Ulithi, and Pelelui.

15

Destination: Kaneohe

"Finally, on the eve of June 20, 1944, loaded with external wing tanks, personal effects, about three cases of booze and lots of hope, we headed for the war."
—Lt. W. B. Jones

The first VPB-23 flight of six planes led by our squadron commander, LCDR "Bill" Stevens, took off June 20, 1944, for the long flight to NAS Kaneohe TH. By June 25, the last flight group of planes arrived at NAS Kaneohe, in Hawaii. The squadron would spend a month in training at Kaneohe, and another two weeks patrolling out of Midway before moving to its forward base at Eniwetok in the Marshall Islands.

The following aircrews of VPB-23 took off under the command of Stevens. Lieutenants (jg) Dave Tenney, Frank Ben, Howard Chaney, W. Boardman Jones, Jr., Oscar Owre, and A. R. McQuiddy.

Lt. W. Boardman Jones, Jr., remembers that flight:

As it turned out, it was from North Island, California, to NAS Kaneohe, TH, with a stopover at Hilo, TH.

Finally on the eve of June 20th, loaded with external wing tanks, personal effects, about three cases of booze and lots of hope, we headed for the war. 20.8 hours later, and low on fuel, we landed at Hilo instead of Kaneohe. Since it was a Wednesday, and aware there was a party going on at the "OC," we hastily refueled and two hours later landed at Kaneohe—slightly tired.

My memory of that experience is that our crew had made sim-

CHAPTER 15 Destination: Kaneohe

ulated Trans-Pacific flights on June 11 and 12, and finally in the early evening of June 20, loaded with external wing tanks (175 gallons of fuel), our personal effects, and anxieties, we headed for the war.

Frank "Whitey" White, our second mechanic, and I had been on liberty in Los Angeles, and thumbing our way back to San Diego took longer than expected. We almost missed it. Upon arriving at the hangar at dusk, we were confronted by an angry, red-faced operations officer who, after threatening court-martial and other penalties, put us in a jeep and raced us out to our plane. It was the last on the tarmac, waiting to take off.

We grabbed on to the ladder as the plane was revving up for takeoff, and in flight suits hastily pulled over our dress blues, joined the rest of the crew. They were all grinning and shaking their heads disapprovingly, but with empathy, for we were off to the war. Nor did we get any "flak" from our skipper, Lt. "Boardie" Jones.

The plane roared down the runway, and though heavily laden with auxiliary gas tanks on the wings and a heavy load of personal gear it took off with ease and soon climbed upwards above the clouds where the lucky ones on blister watch watched the moonlight make patterns on the billowy white clouds below.

We then began alternating our watches, in the blister and at the radio from which periodic coded messages were sent and received. In the semi-darkness but for a map light, the navigator peered over his map with a pair of dividers, jotting down notes, taking sightings, and calibrating our way over the vast ocean. It gave me no comfort when our navigator was reminded that the bright star he was taking a reading on was our tail light!

Hot coffee was brought to us by our plane captain, "Freddie" Zaugg, AMM1/C, and an occasional word or two over the intercom broke the silence. Otherwise it was the steady drone and vibrations of the two engines that kept us alert.

A coolness in the night air gave us an appreciation for the leather flight jackets we wore, and we pulled the fur collars about our necks. While there were four bunks to catch a cat-nap in when not on watch, on this particular flight there was little inclination to do so as we pondered what was ahead.

Lt. W. B. Jones remembers:

A little over twenty hours later, short on fuel and our final destination, we landed at the lovely island of Hilo in Hawaii. As our pilots were aware of a planned arrival party at the Officers Club in Kaneohe, we hastily refueled. Two hours later, though slightly weary, the pilots arrived for their big celebration. I don't remember any celebration awaiting the enlisted crews—other than barrack and bunk assignment.

Lt. Francis Clifton, PPC, of another crew gives his recollection of the Pacific crossing:

In the late afternoon 12 June '44, we departed San Diego in PBY5A #46476 with fourteen men and their personal gear on board—destination Kaneohe Bay, on the Island of Oahu, in the Territory of Hawaii. A distance of approximately 2,200 miles, all over a vast Pacific Ocean! And attached under the wings, two disposable auxiliary gasoline tanks, each with a capacity of 150 gallons, gave our PBY a total capacity of approximately 1,750 gallons of gas for the trans-Pacific flight. It was to be a long, taxing, and uneventful flight of 20.8 hours!

The Naval Air Station at Kaneohe was located on the southern island end of Oahu nestled in a valley between mountains and an expanse of Pacific Ocean. It was as the movies portrayed it, and what I imagined the Hawaiian Islands to be—lush foliage with tall swaying coconut trees, green expanses of lawn and tropical palms, and flowering plants everywhere. The Pali mountains and majestic Diamond Head towering above white sand beaches with foaming incoming surf riding huge waves on a brilliant blue-green ocean. This was truly an island paradise!

That is, until a closer observation brought sudden awareness of Navy ships, island fortifications, gun emplacements, barbed wire, tanks, weaponry, and busy activity of thousands of Army, Marines, and Navy coming from or going to forward areas.

In contrast to the bright sea island colors, dark harbor tones of "battleship gray" and "olive drab," and a conspicuously white hospital ship with huge red cross on its hull, provided the palette of colors of war in 1944.

VPB-23 lost no time in settling in. Our new planes, painted a distinctive though conspicuously flat black, gave us a sort of "celebrity status" that brought comment and questions wherever we went.

CHAPTER 15   Destination: Kaneohe

Then came the day we assembled in the hangar area. There, spread out on the deck before us, was a large array of battle gear, providing instant speculation that we were being transferred to the Marines Corps!

Along with olive green steel helmet and liner, a Smith & Wesson P-38 pistol with ammo and leather shoulder holster, a pair of scuffed "Boondockers" (the Marine combat shoe), Navy issue combat knife, a machete, mosquito netting, pith helmets, olive-green trousers and shirts, fatigue jacket, poncho, olive green flight suit, mess kit and canteen with web belt, first aid kit, sunglasses in aluminum case—and extra large green parachute bag to hold it all—came a darker realization of purpose!

While the squadron would soon move from Kaneohe, we did get a few liberties. Like San Diego, Honolulu had been completely taken over by the military, and there were few people who were not in uniform. But Liberty was best enjoyed by taking the wild "bus ride" across the "Pali" to get to Honolulu! The ride to town on rickety old buses driven by native Hawaiians in brightly colored shirts and no sense of fear—on a narrow, winding, curving road with bare allowance for any passing car, and going straight up at a 45 degree angle, or straight down, always on a treacherous looking outer edge, with little visible roadbed to give any sense of safety.

Looking out the bus window it was a sheer drop straight down! Nor was it a smooth ride. Our drivers seemed to enjoy driving with bouncing and brake-racing speed. Passengers rode into town grasping hats and gripping their seats. It was a ride to remember!

The adrenaline was pumping as we departed the bus in Honolulu—into the mass of uniformed personnel crowding their way shoulder to shoulder in a contained strip of cheap souvenir shops... Competing for the military dollar were crowded sidewalk beer bars, tattoo parlors, restaurants, movie theaters and whorehouses with block-long standing lines of eager sailors and marines trying to get in.

Of course sight-seeing was a major attraction. The Iolani Palace where once reigned King Kalahua—but now office of the military governor—and the Aloha Tower, the elegant "Royal Hawaiian Hotel," with its pineapple juice fountain in the hotel lobby. Pineapple juice was freely served there by the hotel staff in little white paper cups. As "non-residents" we never got beyond the lobby, but did wander about the grounds and gardens leading to beautiful Waikiki Beach with its far off "Diamond Head" panoramic setting—and sun-drenched Hawaiian surfers so effortlessly riding the massive and repetitive white-capped waves.

The Royal Hawaiian Hotel was taken over by the Navy at the start of the war to serve as special R&R (rest and relaxation) for battle-weary submariners, and plane crews back from the Pacific in need of a brief respite from the bloody war.

Whether it was limited liberty, logistics, or some inward reluctance to view the wrecked and sunken hulls along "Battleship Row" at Pearl Harbor, I never ventured to the site ... nor do I remember flying over the sunken ships. We were allowed little stay in Oahu and soon were off to Midway. Priorities allowed little time for reflection, and we were all anxious to get on with the war.

16

A Return to Midway

By June 25, 1944, the last VPB-23 flight group arrived at its destination ...

In June of 1941, the tiny island base, only six miles in diameter, was the pivotal point of one of the greatest battles fought in naval history.

On June 30, 1944, in accordance with verbal orders from Commander Fleet Air Wing Two, nine combat teams and six planes of VPB-23 were transferred to Naval Operating Base Midway Island for the purpose of making routine flights.

Headed by Skipper LCDR "Bill" Stevens, XO Lt. Robin "Bob" Larson's crew consisted of Lieutenants(jg) Charles Frantz, "Bobo" Phillips, Bill Decker, Howard Chamley, Frank Diehl, Frank Ben, Whit Barnhill, and A. R. McQuiddy.

The log book of Radioman William "Boo" Booher, ARM2/C, in Lt.(jg) W. Boardman Jones' crew, records the 9.6 hour-flight from Kaneohe to Midway on July 30, 1944. The assigned crews flew patrols from Midway August 2 through August 16, 1944.

I was in Jones' crew, which arrived on Eastern Island July 30, 1944. This was a return for some of the vets of old VP-23, who had taken part in the Battle of Midway. It was a first for me and most of our crew.

So this was Midway! Barren, hot, sun-bleached, a brilliant white coral—an eye-squinting piece of island. One could imagine the terror of enemy planes shielded by the blinding sun, strafing swift and low over the tiny island. As with the Marines in the earlier battle, our uniform of the day was a pith helmet and shorts.

It was a very flat little island atoll with scrubby vegetation and a natural bird sanctuary that made it a "Gooney-bird" haven.

The "Gooneys" (Laysan Albatross) are fascinating birds. Those of us on the island would dance with them, talk to them, feed them. Those units stationed on the islands more permanently sometimes got too carried away, and were labeled "rock-happy."

But watching the "dumb" birds was obsessive. It appeared that they sometimes thought they were airplanes. They would continually run beside our planes on takeoff as we'd taxi down the runway. Running like hell and wildly flapping their wings, they would get airborne, then suddenly look downward and stop everything—resulting, of course, in a crash landing. Then they'd get up and do it all over again!

Midway living quarters were something else. Aircrews were assigned billeting in deep-dug high mounds of coral—revetments—which also provided ground protection for the squadron's planes. It was a strange hole-in-the-ground mole-like typography.

Inside, the dugouts provided a cool escape from the hot blazing sun, but did not offer much more. Bunks were placed under and between huge wooden beams holding up the rock. There were six to eight of us in each revetment. I remember Fred Zaugg, Bob Watson, Chief Day, Frank White, Gamblin, Carbine, Perry... and the rats! We'd sleep with blankets over us, because the critters would come down from the beams at night and scurry over us.

For kicks, someone thought of rigging a heavy wooden ammo box upside down, propped up by a stick with a string, and with bait inside. Then we'd lie in our bunks and wait for a rat to come down and take the bait. The "trap springer" would then pull the string to trap the rat. Now, once trapped in the wooden ammo case, the idea was to "zap it" with our P-38s, taking aim from our bunks, no less! Well, that didn't set well with our ranking petty officer, Chief Day, who had no wish to get caught in the crossfire.

After the first volley, Chief Day blew his top, telling us to knock it off or we'd all wind up in the brig. I don't think we hit the rat, because by morning it had chewed its way out of the crate. So much for rats.

CHAPTER 16 *A Return to Midway*

Some fifty-three years later, a Midway tourist pamphlet about the bird sanctuary informed: "Rats introduced in the early 1940s, to decimate a 'bad bird' specie called 'Bonin Petrel,' which was preying on the eggs of other birds..." Which accounts for the sharing of our underground quarters with those miserable rodents! The pamphlet said the birds are back. Today it seems that the rats—like the Navy—are gone!

The nights on Midway were star-filled and beautiful. On that flat little atoll it seemed we were living in a cathedral of stars—all so very big and bright. My buddy "Whitey," a second mechanic in our crew, and I would sit out many a night until the wee hours. Lighting up cigarettes, we pondered our fate and talked of those we loved back home, sometimes of philosophy, and at other times what we were going to do when we got out.

The ground was dark with nestling birds cooing night noises, and we could hear the gentle surf surrounding us. They were warm nights with cool breezes. If you sat very still, it seemed as if we were the only guys on the island. The war seemed so remote—so very far away.

Other nights were a bit bizarre. Some of the farm boys from down south after a wee too much beer ration would tell of killing chickens on the farm and how with a snap of the wrist they could kill a chicken. Then came the bets. Too many of the little Gooneys were killed in the same way that night by the drunken sailors.

Charles C. "Chuck" Chollet, AOM 2/C '44-'45, had a very special recollection of an incident on Midway. While Chollet was stationed in the blister during a takeoff, a Gooney bird suddenly came crashing through the blister, causing him severe facial lacerations. The pilot circled back, and upon landing, Aircrewman Chollet was taken by jeep to the base dispensary, where he was patched up by a corpsman, and immediately returned to duty. Chuck was given neither sick leave nor a Purple Heart!

Aircrewman Charles C. Chollet went on to fly Anti-sub, Scouting, Dumbo, Search and Rescue, Emergency, and Torpedo missions (FIDO) out of the Marshalls, Marianas, Palaus, Hawaii, and Eniwetok.

PPC Lt. W. Boardman Jones remembered:

On October 30th, 1944, our crew flying out of Midway was assigned a Wake Island Patrol. A couple of Seabees had asked to go along, offering steaks for my crew as an incentive. (It should be noted that the "Seabees," Navy Construction Battalion, comprised a large "provisional" force on the island, and were the guys to look to for in acquiring most anything.) The vision of fresh meat brought a spontaneous affirmative from my crew.

Upon arriving over Wake and circling at a respectable distance, one of the Seabees commented on how great it would be if the Japs attempted to shoot us down—so he could tell his girlfriend he had been under enemy fire. Happy to oblige, I went in close enough to awaken the islanders.

Midway was a bypassed island, and the beleaguered and half starved Jap garrison was very frugal with their ammunition. However, the Jap gunners did manage to get a round or two off at us before I climbed up and into safer range.

Fortunately, as I had counted upon, their aim was far off—and our Seabee "providers" experienced the joy of being "under fire."

However, my choice of daring did not gain any greater confidence among the crew for their patrol plane commander. The steaks, in retrospect, were truly enjoyed.

The closest I ever came to being a "combat artist" was during a patrol out of Midway one day. We came across a strange sight floating in the water. It almost looked like half of a submerged pilot house off some ship. We were without camera, and our patrol plane commander, Lt. W. Boardman Jones, called out on the intercom: "Klotz, report to the blister ... I'll circle about, and you draw this damn thing."

I felt my true calling had arrived. A Navy combat artist!

As other crewmembers looked on admiringly, I scurried from the radio compartment aft to the blister, sitting down in the gunner's place who was presently on watch. As Mr. Jones then swooped in closer, banking the plane to give me a better view, I opened my mighty sketchbook, surveyed the scene, and began to draw. I am sure I was not the only crewman aboard that PBY who suspected an enemy "trick" to lure us closer, before concealed enemy guns would shoot us down.

Directing the pilot as we circled about the object to make just one more pass, allowing me to finish the job, was to be my only "command" performance in the Navy! Lieutenant Jones then wisely suggested I draw a Gooney bird upon the drawn object to indicate its relative size.

CHAPTER **16** *A Return to Midway* 161

Mission accomplished and without incident, we proceeded on our patrol. Upon landing, Lieutenant Jones presented my "combat aircrew artist's" sketch along with his verbal report to our squadron intelligence officer. He would later write in his memoirs: "The result of our finding was charted on the sector map as a possible 'navigational hazard.'" We got no medals for our effort!

On August 5, 1944, Lt.(jg) Dave Tenney and crew while out on patrol spotted and escorted a lost PT boat out of a Midway maze of coral reefs. It seems that the PT boat had "gone fishing" and could not find its way out.

Some half century later, my neighbor in Wilton, Connecticut, Carolyn Larsen, returned from a snorkeling tour at Midway. She reported that the battleground is now a bird sanctuary and a place where tourists fish and snorklers play—the birds finally won out! She and her husband Tom had gone to Hawaii several times to dive, but that year signed up for a Midway tour.

The U.S. Fish and Wildlife Service allows only 100 visitors on the island at any time. Several buildings and fortifications from Midway's military past are still standing. Designated as National Historic Landmarks, among the sixty-three WWII sites considered eligible are a cable station, powerhouse, command post, which was shelled by a Japanese destroyer, ammunition storage huts, gun emplacements, and yes—those damned underground revetments!

Carolyn and Tom also saw sailors from two Japanese Navy ships whose crews had came to pay respects to the men lost on aircraft carriers *Kaga*, *Soryu*, *Akagi*, and *Hiryu*—all sunk by our planes in the Battle of Midway. The USS *Yorktown* and USS *DD Haman* were also sent to the bottom in nearby waters. The videotape that Carolyn and Tom brought back includes some magnificent underwater shots taken by their diving team—of rusted barge remains and a WWII Navy Corsair with myriad brightly colored fish swimming about. (More than 250 species call the atoll's lagoon home.)

And the Gooneys prevailed! Their favorite nesting place is the runway on Sand Island.

After our tour on Midway, our crew returned to Kaneohe, but soon we were off again—island hopping to Palmyra, Tarawa, Kwajalein, and to a new forward area base on Eniwetok in the Marshalls, where the fleet was again gathering for a new invasion.

17

Eniwetok
FEBRUARY 16, 1944

> *Operation "Catchpole" was taken by U.S. Marines on February 16, 1944, eleven days after landing on Kwajalein—at a cost of 339 Americans killed or missing and 2,677 Japanese killed.*

For the primitive Micronesians who called Eniwetok atoll "the land between the East and the West," it had been a place of call and refreshment in their long canoe voyages. In the Pacific War, the atoll, with its deep-water lagoon, afforded a much different place of call and refreshment. The natives, numbering fewer than a hundred, had been removed to another island, and Eniwetok was now a forward staging area—a depot of endless supply and crowded habitat of men bringing the Navy's mighty task forces and supply ships another 575 miles closer to Tokyo.

Today, Eniwetok in the Marshall Islands is no longer accessible. Nor is it a welcome place for the traveler. Target sites for U.S. nuclear testing from 1945 to 1958 now include "Kwaj," a site of fierce fighting in WWII, as a target and tracking center for missiles test-fired from Vandenberg Air Force Base in Santa Barbara, California. Kwajalein is the world's largest atoll, and while a Guam-Honolulu "island hopping" flight does land there, only authorized personnel can get off (unless special permission is received from Washington or Majuro).

On August 20, 1944, the first five planes of VPB-23 left for Eniwetok, a vitally important forward staging area for the Pacific Fleet. By August 31, the fifteen-plane "Black Cat" squadron had completed its move. At Eniwetok August 20 through December 3, 1944, were the following crews of Squadron Skipper LCDR William M. Stevens: Lieutenants Robin Larson, Oscar T. Owre, Thomas J. McKeon, Charles W. Wilson, Charles S. Frantz, David B. Tenney; Lieutenants(jg) W. Boardman Jones, Jr., William Barnhill, Donald K. Guthrie, Clyde B. Phillips, Albert M. Crocker, G.W. Clark, Frank T. Ben, Willis M. Decker, Franklin P. Diehl, Howard C. Chamley, Francis H. Clifton, and Arthur R. McQuiddy.

Operating under the command of Group One, Fleet Air Wing Two, Eniwetok became the new HQ for Patrol Bombing Squadron 23. The squadron was already making daily reconnaissance patrols over enemy-held Ponape Island, Wake Island, and in searches lying west of Eniwetok. In addition, VPB-23 planes had already participated in sixteen anti-submarine patrols, as well as six "Dumbo" and other miscellaneous strike missions.

Lt. W. Boardman Jones, Jr., recalled:

On August 16, 1944, after our "tour of duty" on Midway, our crew returned to home base on Kaneohe, but on August 21st, were soon off again to a forward area—island hopping via Palmyra, Canton, Tarawa, Kwajalein, and a final destination to Eniwetok Atoll in the Marshall Islands on the 28th. (Jones' crew would operate out of Eniwetok from August 30 to December 5, 1944.)

We started patrolling shortly after arrival in an arc of about 240 degrees from base to about 320 degrees. Operating under the command of Group One, Fleet Air Wing Two, VPB-23 engaged in daily reconnaissance patrols to enemy-held Ponape and Wake Islands, as well as anti-submarine patrols, "Dumbo," and other miscellaneous flights directed by Commander Task Group 59.3 We continued these patrols during October and November.

The main Pacific Fleet was using Eniwetok as an assembly point to the invasion of the Philippines, so there was plenty of action in the lagoons. Our patrol missions took on greater significance in assuring command that the Japs didn't get too close without warning on our part. The fleet was also busy working over Truk and also Saipan, Guam, and other enemy held islands in preparation for later invasions to come.

My brother-in-law, Cpl. Bruce Aebischer, a 4th Division Marine, had left San Diego a couple of months before us. We would often fly over him and his buddies crouched in the amphibs operating offshore and circling endlessly about in the waters below. It is ironic that the 4th Marine Division would fight desperate battles and secure so many of the island airstrips from which our squadron would operate—yet being so close, I was never able to make contact with my brother-in-law.

As we island-hopped our way to Eniwetok, we landed on barren little Tarawa, shell scarred coral, palm stumps, burned out pillboxes, twisted metal and other litter of war. I could only imagine the unbelievable horror and hell wrought by any concentration of force fighting on an island so small.

On our approach to Eniwetok, we flew over the mass armada of ships in an endless perimeter below, and I got a first feeling of finally being out where things were happening. Looking out from blister I became aware of Admiral Halsey's famous Task Force 58 spread out below, gathering for a further push westward.

Eniwetok, another battle-scarred island where much of the same kind of devastation as Tarawa had been cleared away and replaced by a mass of tents, Quonset huts and supply depots, was to be our home for the next three months!

The tents we were billeted in had previously been erected by Seabees along with latrines and open showers. We slept four men to a tent on collapsible army cots rigged with mosquito netting to give protective cover. Empty ammo crates, oil drums, and canvas water bags were put to innovative uses to serve as rainwater catchers, showers, and counters outside the tents. Holes cut in wooden boards for helmet insert provided wash basins. "Heads" (latrines), usually "eight-holers" enclosed in open tents with mosquito netting for airing, were placed a distance away. Desalinated water held in large oil or wood drums erected on wood scaffolding provided "showers in the raw," and large canvas bags with inserted spigots provided drinking water.

If lucky enough to get assigned a tent where foresighted occupants had erected their own oil drum to catch rainwater, you had a fresh water bonus—depending on rainfall. Chow was served in a mess tent or in some areas a Quonset hut which provided a bit more comfortable eating facility for the "C" rations ladled on daily basis.

The squadron, in spite of a heavy flying schedule, quickly adapted to their new tent town habitat. Signs appeared in front of tents with names like "Dew Drop Inn" and "The Sack Rats" outside of coral-lined entrances and portable metal runway "walkways"

CHAPTER 17 Eniwetok

neatly laid out. In each five- to six-man tent there was someone who was constantly foraging to make their habitat more livable.

Eniwetok was a sliver of an island—long and skinny. One could walk across its flat, almost treeless, white coral surface in ten minutes, or travel its perimeter in an hour and a half. The pillboxes, fought over so ferociously, were still forbidding.

Surrounded by blue green waters, the island offered a safe lagoon and anchorage for Admiral Mitchner's forward staging area, and offered, as well, some good swimming, shell hunting, and sometimes a war souvenir, though others had picked the area fairly clean.

Swimming was great once you got beyond the shallow waters, sharp coral ocean bottom, dodged the man o' wars, and swam out into the deeper waters. Of course, there was always an alert for a shark or barracuda.

I remember swimming on one occasion when the "beachmaster" blew the warning to clear the area and be alerted that a barracuda was prowling about. Not for long, however. The beachmaster and his crew were soon in the waters barracuda hunting. Gunshots sounded the end of the intruder, and we went back into the water.

Shells—there were endless varieties—became big business with some of our squadron-mates who made rings, necklaces and all kinds of ornamentation out of them to trade with the pilots for dollars or whiskey.

Shell hunting required only a little box with a piece of glass at the bottom, and/or a pair of goggles and a good pair of sandals made by cutting up shoes, to search the coral bottom for shells. Brown and white speckled ones, gray pearly ones, or snake-eyes, a kind of shell that when prepared and polished and set in a silver ring was a prized possession.

The trick was to bury the shells for a while to let the ants eat them. Then stuff with cotton and craft thin wire fasteners to make necklace or bracelet, and presto—they're ready for gift or trade.

Movies were always the big event at any island base. Most movie areas were somewhat spontaneous and primitive—outdoor arenas with large movie screen, where a few coconut tree trunks provided some seating or in many cases necessitated bringing your own indispensible "helmet" to sit on. And of course your poncho, for the unpredictable but spontaneous rain.

I can remember a couple of "celebrity-spotting" occasions while on Eniwetok. Our planes were parked in scattered areas along the airstrip. One day as I was watching a MATS DC-3 taxiing in after landing, I looked up at the cockpit window to see the pilot with his head and arm leaning out the window. Then I recognized movie star Tyrone Powers—square-jawed, tanned face, squinting and looking so casual. It was like a scene in one of his movies—but this time for real! I don't remember if we even exchanged glances, but it made my day!

Then there was film star Henry Fonda, who was on the islands at the same time as VPB-23, and in fact, hung out with our pilots. Lts. (jg) Joe Huber and Art McQuiddy both remember him singing with their VP-23 "barbershop" group.

Fonda had enlisted the Navy in '42 as an ordinary seaman, and served a year aboard a destroyer as a quartermaster and signalman, before the brass made him an officer. They put him in Air Combat Intelligence, gave him a two-week crash course in Anti-sub warfare, and as a Lt.(jg), he was assigned to Vice Adm. Hoover's staff, which served under Adm. Nimitz's Pacific Command. In February of 1944 he was sent to Kwajalein and assigned as ACI to the USS Curtis—and would soon be "singing with the boys of '23" at Eniwetok, Saipan, and Guam.

On Saipan, Lt.(jg) Fonda plotted movement and search patterns for submarines. PBYs of VPB-23 would converge on these areas. One such plotting resulted in the sinking of a Japanese sub.

Then there's the Skipper's celebrity flight, when VPB-23 was ordered to transport USO Bob Hope's comedian Jerry Colonna, Carole Landis, and the Andrews Sisters to another island for a USO show. Of course, the skipper's crew—always "first in battle"—got the assignment, and there was a lot of talk in the squadron of the fancy preparations. Silk parachutes to make comfy bunks for the girls, and scenting the area with perfume and the likes.

We all suspected the Skipper as being somewhat of a cavalier, and this was accented on the morning of the takeoff when we all lined the runway to see the curvaceous ladies being helped up the ladder and into the blister.

With a grin and a smile, the skipper looked out at us, gave a wink, a "thumbs-up" and, revving up the engines, made a quick hot pilot's takeoff. We all let out a big cheer for the skipper's team!

CHAPTER **17** *Eniwetok*   167

Eniwetok was a forward area where, without orders from the CO mandating dress code, the uniform was "casual to nonconformity." Squadron crews quickly adopted their own comfort level by cutting shoes up to make sandals; tearing off trouser legs to make shorts; or, when not flying, walking about in skivvies—or no clothes at all!

This was brought to a halt by the arrival of a hospital ship with nurses aboard. Officers soon were escorting the ladies about in jeeps, including along shorepoints in the enlisted areas. It was soon decided that it was neither fit nor proper for women to drive through a spectacle of enlisted men "romping about in the bare."

Lt. Fran Clifton remembers:

> On Eniwetok, the officers lived in Quonset huts. About 15-20 men per hut. The only shower water was waste water—from the Navy 24 Photo Squadron. Food was bad all the way, morning, noon and night! All I remember was the C-Ration "hash" which seemed the main bill of fare for all meals. I believe the officers and men ate in the same hut, officers at one end and enlisted men at the other.
>
> The Officer's Club was about a mile down the road from the living area. I remember a small bar with many outside "beachfront" tables. Lt. Bill Clark's folks sent him a bunch of Roy Crane's "Buzz Sawyer" comic strips, about the adventures of a Navy Dive Bomber Pilot and his rear gunner named "Sweeny." One day while on Eniwetok, Bill got some of the strips out and said, "Look, Buzz is walking down the road out there on the way to the Officer's Club!"
>
> Indeed it was a very recognizable scene, and cartoonist Roy Crane (the cartoon strip's creator) had been there (or someone had furnished a photo of the road) and he had drawn in Buzz walking along it.

As a senior in high school in Birmingham, Alabama, Elbert B. Craig registered with Local Board 18 requesting deferment to graduate in June 1943. With his request granted, he was inducted in the service of his choice on January 18, 1943, along with eight or ten of his high school classmates.

Gunner E.B. Craig had this memory:

> I reported for duty on June 25, 1943, and was sent to Boot Camp at Great Lakes, Ill. From there, I was selected to attend Aviation Ordnance School NATTC (AOM) at Norman, Oklahoma. Graduating after fourteen weeks, I was sent to Naval Air Gunners School, Purcell, Oklahoma. I

qualified by hitting the required number of clay pigeons, shooting trap and skeet. Then went on to another two-week stint at Radar Operators School.

Some of the Gunnery School was tough—especially the long march every Monday morning in cold weather wearing bathing trunks and sneakers, to purge our bodies of the 3.2 beer absorbed over the weekends!

Having earned my AOM3/C rating, I was offered Air Bombers School training at North Island, San Diego, California. The school was very interesting—four weeks ground training and five weeks flying, which I had done before. Clarence Cardoza, AOM1/C AB, was the instructor, and Chuck Chollet, AOM2/C, and Art Hernandez, AOM2/C AB, were in the same class. All of us would be assigned to VPB-23.

After graduation, I met "Salty" AMM1/C O.H. Gottsch and asked his advice about Navy Bombing Squadrons. He told me of his tours "down south" with a PBY squadron and stated emphatically the best chance of returning was to be selected for a PBY Squadron. I took "Salty's" advice and was accepted into VPB-23 for what would be its third and last tour of duty in the South Pacific (1944-1945).

After several practice gunnery and bombing flights out of North Island, we boarded a Jeep carrier for Ford Island, T.H. And that is the path I took to become a "Combat Aircrewman" in the best damned squadron in the Navy!

My crew was: PPC Lt. Tom McKeon; 1st Pilot Lt.(jg) W. A Schneberger; and navigator, Ens. Ralph A. Kottner. Others remembered are: 1st Mech. Joseph F. Maney, AMM2/C; Radioman Gene A. Brock, ARM3/C; 2nd Mech. Glen E. Middaugh, AMM3/C; and Ordnanceman Charles M. Wesley, AOM2/C.

Among special recollections is "sneaking" a Merchant Marine sailor on to one of our ten to dawn flghts—and dropping a 5 pound can of spam to natives on flight over Ponape.

One of the most humorous occasions: On Eniwetok one day while on plane watch, I was cleaning our machine guns. Our plane was parked across from Marine gun emplacements along the landing strip—dug-in pits with sandbags and covered by a big tarp, the machine guns pointing toward the landing strip.

An F6F fighter off a carrier was landing when its left wheel collapsed, sending it skidding toward one of the Marine gun emplacements. In one side of the emplacement came the F6F, and simultaneously, out the other side like a bat-out-of-hell, came the Marines.

No one was hurt, but it sure scared the hell out of that fighter pilot and those Marine gunners!

And how could I forget manning the PBY bow nose turret on a reconnaissance over Yap ... the wind whipping in my face as I was pointing our pilot to the cannon fire coming up at us from the Jap ground forces below.

Another recollection was while on plane-watch off Tanapag Harbor in Saipan and watching the Jap "Bettys" overhead making night runs on the B-29s. It felt like "all hell was breaking loose" when the AA's opened up from the hundreds of ships in the harbor.

What a sight! The 5 inchers & 90 mm's lighting up the ships as they fired ... searchlights sighting out Jap bombers ... and steel shell fragments falling into the waters around the plane!

On a patrol out of Eniwetok flying to Jap-held Ponape, we exercised our machine guns, as was the customary practice, to see if all was in working order. In my assigned bow gunner's position, I fired the twin .30's. Charlie Wesley, our 1st Ordnanceman, positioned in the starboard blister, fired his .50-caliber.

After firing a good many rounds, Charlie closed the blister and returned the gun to the tie-down position. In doing so, however, he forgot to clear the last round from the chamber—and as a result, the round left in the chamber fired off.

Winging two smoke bombs positioned nearby, the projectile continued out the bottom of the plane through the tunnel hatch. Running back to the blister, I "unstopped" the two smoke bombs, and as Wesley opened the blister, I threw them out.

A bit shook up already, Charlie received a stiff reprimand from the PPC—and after landing had to report the damage to Patsu, who, after shaking their heads, patched up the bulkhead and .50 caliber hole in the bottom of the plane.

Thereafter "Gunner" Charlie Wesley, AOM2/C, made certain he "cleared the chamber" after any firing!

Humor was abundant in my memories. On one reconnaissance over Wake Island, my log book records 26 Nov 44, I was flying with Lt.(jg) W. Boardman Jones & crew.

A "Bird" Colonel was on this flight to observe activity on Wake. About three hours into the patrol after a "wake-up call," the Colonel climbed down from the sack, and came into the blister area we normally occupied while on patrol—asking where the facility was to relieve himself. We casually pointed to the tail and told him to go through the aft bulkhead, not thinking that we should "check him out" as to just where the facility was ... and how to use it.

After about five minutes, a red-faced Marine Colonel stormed past us through the blister area and up towards the cockpit. Lt. Jones immediately came on the intercom and tersely "chewed us out."

Seems the Colonel, unaware of the plane's "paperbag" commode facility, had instead opened the tunnel hatch from where the tail gun was swung out—and proceeded to do "his business"! Some trick, but even worse was his not not knowing that objects would fly back in!

Needless to say, it wasn't the ground action nor AA fire from Wake that the Colonel would remember that day. Such incidents broke the monotony of otherwise long and uneventful patrol.

Elbert B. Craig, AOM2/C, went on to win the Air Medal, Asia Pacific Medal with two battle stars, American Defense Medal, and WWII Victory Medal.

Cosmetic Surgery on Eniwetok

The accessibility of modern medical miracles to our motley assembly of aircrews at Eniwetok became apparent when one of our aircrewmen, Elmer "Murph" Pasquariello, ARM2/C (a radioman), decided that Eniwetok was the time and place for a little medical rehab. With the absence of women and some time to spare, Murph decided to undergo a bit of aesthetic plastic surgery at Navy expense.

Having a very large hooked nose, Murph first reported to the island sick bay for a little "nose reshaping" and soon happily returned back to duty black and blue and all bandaged up—but soon would heal and display a smaller straightened nose, and a handsomer Murph. Then Murph decided to get circumcised! After all, it was on the Navy. Again, off went Murph to the dispensary, this time returning with a very sore and fully bandaged penis.

Now at certain risk, Murph had not given thought of the hazing he would receive from crewmates. He walked into the enlisted men's tent area half naked with his "privates" bandaged. His crewmates went to every length to conjecture pornographic pictures and/or stories guaranteed to get Murph excited. How he suffered.

Murph did not pursue any further surgical "freebies" after that. Nor did he inspire any others in the squadron to line up for surgical rehab.

On patrol over Wake Island, August 29, 1944, Ordnanceman Clarence Cardoza, AOM2/C, was on bow turret watch.

Our Patrol Plane commander Lt.(jg) Willis "Pop" Decker told us to man our stations. As we got in closer to the island, I stuck my head out the nose bow with my helmet on and my guns ready. Looking down, I

CHAPTER 17 Eniwetok

saw something going across the bridge, between the two islands. It was a man on a bicycle. Then I saw a flash and picked up the mike to tell "Pop" that the man below was "signaling to us with a mirror," but to my surprise the flash turned out to be a gun firing at us!

At that very moment, there was an explosion to our starboard side. I heard a click, which was a piece of flack hitting our tower. Instantly "Pop" veered off to our port side and we got the hell out of there. We had ventured a little too close!

We had arrived at Eniwetok but five days earlier—this was our crew's first war experience!

On September 7, 1944, on our way back from patrol, I looked up from the port blister and saw smoke coming from the port engine. PPC "Pop" Decker immediately surveyed the problem and feathered that engine. Then he told me to get up in the bow, as we had to start "unloading" because we could not maintain altitude. Everyone was at their stations tossing all guns and ammunition overboard. Pop jettisoned the bombs and whatever else we had that would help maintain flight.

We had an extra passenger aboard, and Pop jokingly told the photographer, if we had to dump anything else, he was going to be the next thing to go. The photographer was scared. We were out four and a half hours when all this happened. It took us six and a half hours to get back. Two cats flown by Lieutenants Francis Clifton and Franklin Diehl came off their sectors to fly us in.

Pop asked the crew over the intercom: "What do you want to do, boys ... try to make it to the nearest atoll (don't remember the name) ... or ditch?"

If we had landed on water, we could have been picked up by Clifton and/or Diehl. We told Pop that we would stick with him and try making it back to Eniwetok.

As we approached Eniwetok, three Marine Corsairs came out to fly us in. Clifton and Diel then went on in and landed. As we made our approach, Pop started the port engine to see if it would run long enough to make the landing with two engines. No luck!

So, shutting it off, we went in with only one. Then the starboard engine coughed—and quit just as our wheels touched down on the airstrip, leaving us engineless as the plane rolled to a stop.

We came out of that plane like rats abandoning a sinking ship. They had to pull the plane off with the mule tractor so that other planes could land.

On September 15, 1944, Lt.(jg) Whitcomb R. Barnhill and his crew sighted the conning tower of a submarine in an unrestricted area from a distance of two miles. Lieutenant Barnhill made the attack on the submarine but without obtaining evidence of serious damage.

Though a second sighting of the submarine was made during this operation by Lt.(jg) C. S. Frantz, the plane's distance from the submarine terminated the "Hunter-Killer" operation.

During October, the squadron continued operations from Eniwetok under command of Brig. Gen. L. E. Woods, USMC Shore-based Air Force Task Force Group.

When not flying, some aircrewmen of VPB-23 were thinking of ways to supplement their ration of two beers a week. Of island "stills," none produced more lethal "kicka-poo-juice" than this squadron's "Black Cat" brewers.

An observer, Chief Clayton Dewhirst, ACMM, describes a fifteen-gallon jug as containing

> a diluted battery acid, life-threatening nectar, homemade extremely mean alcohol! The enterprise, I suspect, involved a VPB-23 radioman, Don Klotz, S1/C ARM 44-45, and associates, who set up a still in an empty tent and began brewing a large jug filled with dehydrated potatoes, rice, raisins, canned peaches, pears, yeast, and a few coconuts—not to mention a little antifreeze "starter" syphoned off a plane. The resulting "mixture" began fermenting immediately and perked along for days, attracting flies by the thousands.
>
> Now the brewers, aware that their kicka-poo-juice was valuable, scheduled guard duty on a 24-hour basis. There followed an occasional tasting, and an awful lot of discussion as to the flavor and the strength of this nectar.
>
> On the day it (the fermentation) quit working, there was much excitement as the interested parties gathered around to do the sampling. There was no known alcoholic content!
>
> After an evening of partying, Radioman Klotz, the smallest crewman in the outfit, decided he could whip anyone and all. He found a taker, the biggest guy in the outfit—I can't remember his name—and having flight duty that night I didn't see the match, but one look at Klotz the next day convinced me he hadn't won! To my knowledge there was never another kick-a-poo juice bash in VPB-23.

I am still pondering and searching out the facts in what really happened that night with only fragmentary bits of memory of the events.

As an innocent outsider with no knowledge of stills, or the

CHAPTER **17** *Eniwetok* 173

making of such beverages, I was drawn into the kick-a-poo intrigue by associates whose names I cannot remember. If there are readers out there who can shed further light on this story, please, let's hear it. I vaguely remember talk of a still, and an innovative "Rube Goldberg" contraption made of narrow-gauge bendable aircraft piping and other aircraft anti-freeze components, a red anti-freeze fluid with high alcohol content.

It seemed everyone in the squadron was aware of the brew, sworn to secrecy and standing protective guard over the tent. I cannot deny I wasn't looking forward to the big day.

The day did arrive, and receiving a healthy ration in my canteen cup, I remember sitting on a coconut stump next to one of the brewmakers and taking one or two big swallows. Not wishing to be perceived as a novice, I well remember smacking my lips and commenting to someone: "Not bad, but it's still a little green."

The voice next to me drawled out slowly: "What did you say?"

"Not bad," I repeated, expressing an expert-like opinion, "but it's still a little green."

POW! The lights went out!

I remember nothing. Many stories persist. Some say the blow lifted me up and sent me sliding across a long table. Others remember taking me to my tent. I know I returned, looking for the guy who hit me. I think I had driven a weapons carrier through a row of tents.

Others reacted to the kick-a-poo juice that night on Eniwetok by going after one of the cooks with their pistols (the food on the island was truly awful). Our guns were confiscated the next day (but shortly returned).

Still, names like Gamblin, Maupin, Carmichael, and Kimbrough (the undertaker) come to mind, and I wonder where my own crew was—Day, White, Owens, Zaugg, Booher.

There's really no documentation of this "kick-a-poo" story. Dewey and I are in agreement on one fact: There was never another "kick-a-poo juice" party in VPB-23!

Chief Dewhirst's log lists a few comments that say much about his tour of duty.

(Sept. '44) Lt. Wilson says he got 255 knots out of a PBY!
(Dec. '44) Even used bailing wire on the Cowl flaps.

(Apr. '45) On 4/6 flight with Lt. Wilson the brakes locked starboard upon landing—putting our plane in palm trees!

On 4/10 A flight with Lt. Chamley: Engine went out. We threw everything over the side. (Guns, all our gear—anything we could get loose—we even had two cases of beer we were saving! We went down on Tinian. They weren't about to let us out of the plane. Such were the tight security measures for the Atomic Bomb!

Photos were hard to come by in the islands as cameras were forbidden—obviously for security reasons. However, shedding light on photos that did come into aircrewmen hands, Dewey remembers: "On Eniwetok I took pictures, developing them in a foxhole in the ground. I had helped an Army Air Force Photography Squadron move, and in turn they gave me all the supplies I needed."

Clayton Dewhirst was honorably discharged from service in 1945 with two Air Medals to his credit, among a host of others.

ooo

On January 6 Lt.(jg) W.B. Jones Jr., USNR, directed a search for possible survivors of a B-29 which had ditched on January 3 a few miles west of Auatahan Island after a bombing attack on Japan. In early morning his co-pilot, Ens. H. T. Hearon, noticing sun reflection from a mirror, sighted a lone survivor in a life raft. An hour later, the USS *Grayson* responded to a call from Jones and "homed in" to make a successful rescue of survivor Sgt. Harold J. Smith of the 871st Squadron, 497th Group, 273 Bomber Wing. The *Grayson* had only the day before rescued four survivors of the same plane.

On January 11, Lt.(jg) Willis "Pop" Decker was flying a strike escort mission when he sighted and "attacked" a submerging enemy submarine five miles northeast of Yap. Though he was without bombs, low on fuel, and flying with only part of his crew, Pop alerted the submarine patrol in the area and initiated a search. The efforts of Lieutenant Decker and his crew resulted in a kill by a DD twelve days later.

During his tour of duty on Eniwetok between August 29 and December 4, Ens. Wallace "Doug" Douglas played voyageur in the Eniwetok Lagoon:

Ensign W. "Bill" Snedeker and I discovered and decided to refur-

CHAPTER 17 Eniwetok

bish an abandoned sailboat that was left near our Quonset hut. Countless fleet supply ships dropped anchor regularly in the lagoon and here was the answer by which we could get out to those ships and forage up a few goodies.

Salvaging a couple of tail-wheels from a scrapped TBF to use for "beaching the boat" (much like the beaching gear for a PBY), we proceeded building our "dreamboat." We talked the seabees into building us a steel "centerboard" and fashioned a sail made from meal sacks.

Then on one fine day, Bill Snedeker and I cast off on a "maiden" voyage in our refurbished sailboat. However, as our boat was very sluggish, we cancelled our initial plan, and instead settled on sailing to one of the coral sandbars to "look for shells."

We beached the boat, but because of the soft sand, we could not pull the craft entirely out of the water. Later, upon launching our boat laden with booty, and much to our dismay, we found that the surf had caused a chafing to the hull's bottom and the coarse sand had so torn the fragile fabric that we could no longer sail the craft back to port.

Thus we ended up in the shallow water, with the prospect of having to push or pull the boat back to our quarters. Fortunately, a long boat from one of the ships came along, and we persuaded them to tow us back. All we could give them was a bottle of wine!

Stuart "Chippy" Miller, former radioman in VPB-23 ('44-'45), just happened to see a PBY bumper while shopping in Florida earlier this past year. It belonged to "J. J." Smith, another radioman and VPB-23 vet ('44-'45), and so one more squadron vet was brought in! Catching up on the news after some fifty-two years, Chippy was soon talking with me about Eniwetok and Peleliu days.

Chippy was first radioman in Lt. O. T. Owre's crew and also was a close buddy of William "Boo" Booher, a first radioman in Lt. W. Boardman "Boardie" Jones, Jr.'s, crew. I flew as Boo's second radioman. Though only some twenty-four years of age, Chippy—a Pearl Harbor survivor—and "Boo" were both vets of a prior tour, and therefore looked upon as the "old men" of the squadron. We'd sit around our tents at Eniwetok, drinking our ration of beer, and listen while they swapped South Pacific tales—giving their sage advice on every subject.

Chippy was a quiet sort of guy with deep-set, tired-looking eyes and a wonderful soft way of talking. He had a low, soft, raspy chuckle, and a gravelly voice that came from too much smoking. A very likable guy.

I can't remember ever seeing him in proper uniform. He was always in a motley array of garments, torn and faded green shorts, scuffed sandals, faded out-of-shape Navy blue ball cap, and puffing a cigarette loosely held in the corner of his mouth. But he gave us "kids" a feeling of confidence and dependability, like we could count on him to pull us through if things got rough.

In our visit, I found that Chippy had lost touch with Boo a short while after service, but spoke of Boo's divorce, then death, some years ago. Chippy had enjoyed a long marriage before his wife passed away, and later married Romayne (whose own husband, a friend of Chippy's, had also passed away). With no children of his own, he became a stepfather to three sons. They moved from Maine to Florida some years ago.

He spoke of major medical problems over the years. As a heavy smoker, he had developed emphysema and was on a breathing apparatus. One August, Chippy and his wife stopped by to visit us in Wilton, Connecticut. It was as if we had just got off the islands. We recognized each other immediately and soon were swapping Pacific tales, continuing on over a wonderful and extended lunch. Chippy had brought his old flight log book, and flipped through pages guiding me back through dates and times almost forgotten.

And then he handed it to me and told me to keep it, adding that I might find something in it to use for the squadron's history.

We kept on talking, the four of us, on through late afternoon, as though we had been together as old friends all through the years. We posed for pictures, with arms around each other.

Chippy left with squadron hat, a shirt and jacket, and a determination to attend VP/VPB-23's big second reunion. Upon returning to Florida, however, Chippy called to say he regrettably would not be able to attend. He had talked to Clyde Reedy about reunion activities and felt the trip would require him to be away too long from his breathing apparatus. Shortly after the reunion, sometime in September, Romayne called to say that Chippy had passed away, apparently from a heart attack.

She conveyed Chippy's great joy and appreciation of our visit, and finally making contact with his old squadron. "He spoke of it as one of the happiest moments in his life," she writes. "He was looking forward to getting more involved and making other contacts with squadron mates. He was going to join PHSA (Pearl Harbor Survivors Association) too!"

I'm happy Stuart "Chippy" Miller, ARM1/C, and his wife Romayne found us before his last patrol. God bess you, Chippy! Floats up!

18 Saipan–Tinian

U.S. troops landed on Saipan June 15, 1944; Saipan secured July 9, 1944. U.S.: 3,000 killed and 3,000 casualties. Japanese: 50,000 casualties.

Tinian captured July 24, 1944.

1st atom bomb dropped by Enola Gay *August 6, 1945.*

04 Dec 44—VPB-23 to forward area—moves HQ to Saipan.

07 Dec 44—Fifteen low-flying "Bettys" strafed the bivouac areas a half hour later, 13 more Jap planes came in at medium altitude and destroyed three B-29s; major damage to three more and minor damage to twenty.

23 Dec 44—Bogies at low altitude damaged parked B-29s and also hit a Quonset hut at Tanapag, killing many Marines.

26 Dec 44—25 planes at high altitude destroyed one B-29; considerable runway damage at Isley, East and Kobler Fields.

02 Jan 45—A twin-engine plane came in at 0355 and dropped bombs on Isley Field, destroying one B-29 and damaging three others.

16 Apr 45—Enemy air action over Saipan: There continued a number of unsuccessful raids, but the intruders were destroyed by AA and/or our fighter planes before reaching the island.

—From *The Global Twentieth* by Chester Marshall

Lt. W. B. Jones, VPB-23, recalled Saipan:

On December 5, 1944, we set out for Saipan arriving in late afternoon at Isley Field #2. That night we had a visit from a couple of Japanese

CHAPTER **18** *Saipan–Tinian* 179

bombers, presumably from Iwo Jima. No damage. We then moved to Tanapag Harbor, where we undertook search missions for B-29s forced to ditch in the drink between Iwo and Saipan.

The idea of working off the water sounded great, but when we tried to take a PBY5A off loaded with fuel and 500 lb bombs, it was too close to clear the reef at the upwind end of the take-off area. We would clear only with the throttles pushed to the limit and about five inches beyond.

Again on January 31st, despite high winds and visibility approaching zero, and with Ens. Bill Rider as co-pilot, we spotted two TBM pilots in a raft who had ditched between Guam and Ulithi. Working in conjunction with DD USS *Bailey* we homed in on the vessel to make the rescue. Their names were Lt. Charles Taylor and Lt. J. E. Nafstad.

During the month of February '45, the troops were getting ready for the invasion of Iwo Jima. The main carrier force was based at Ulithi atoll. Our crew together with others moved between Saipan, Agana and Orote fields on Guam, Ulithi and Peleliu. The latter was slightly dangerous because the island hadn't been completely secured. These were mostly short strike missions, but we did locate a couple of TBF pilots gone down in the drink, and circling overhead, saw that they were safely put aboard a nearby ship.

On February 28th, my orders came to return home and Bill Rider took over as Plane Commander.

Lt. W. Boardman Jones, Jr., returned to St. Louis and his bride Becky, added two daughters to the family roster, went on to a distinguished career in business and community leadership, gathering laurels along the way too numerous to mention, and lived happily ever after with four grandchildren—Luke and Ted, Charlie and Rebecca—and a good set of golf clubs!

From November '44 through January '45, the "Dumbos of VPB-23" continued base operations from one of those anchorages at NAB Tanapag Harbor, Saipan, operating as part of Task Unit 94.4.2 (air-sea rescue unit). Other detachments had been established at Agana Field on Guam; Isley Field on Saipan; Falalop Island, Ulithi; and Peleliu Islands.

Two combat teams at Eniwetok were brought forward to Saipan leaving two ground officers and an enlisted man in charge of squadron equipment at Eniwetok.

Operations logged in forty-seven searches for downed air crews, fifty-three "dumbo escorts" on air strikes, and eleven ferry escorts. Over 42,640 square miles of ocean was searched resulting in the rescue of four downed aircrewmen. In all, squadron planes made 175 flights during the month for a total of 764 hours, an average of 42.4 hours for each combat team.

Even though Saipan had been declared "secured" at the time the first PBYs from 23 landed at Isley Field, scattered Japanese troop remnants were still hiding in the hills, and Japanese bombers from Iwo Jima were carrying out raids on the B-29s operating from Saipan and Tinian.

I remember standing guard on our plane one night while anchored in Tanapag Harbor. The crew had gone ashore for the night. We had heard all sorts of scuttlebutt about the enemy coming down from the hills and swimming out to toss grenades into the seaplanes. At least one PBM was reported to have been destroyed. The idea of a desperate Japanese soldier in loin cloth, knife in teeth, and grenade in hand, swimming up to my PBY, was most disconcerting (to put it mildly) and assured no sleep on my watch!

As waves continually slapped against the hull of the bobbing aircraft, every imagined noise sent me scurrying fore and aft, climbing topside to the wing or racing to the bow pistol in hand on constant vigilance. Never a night had seemed so black and wrought with danger. Then I heard an engine and saw a boat coming alongside. Two silhouetted figures climbed aboard, one shouting: "Goddamnit, Klotz, put that f——g gun away!"

The Central Pacific was the Navy's war—a series of bloody and costly amphibious operations, involving eleven divisions (six Marine, five Army) massive supply operations and Navy carrier forces. With seizure of Saipan, Guam and Tinian, the Navy now provided the B-29s with vital bases needed to hit the Japanese homeland. The operations also provided the anchorages needed by Admiral Nimitz to finish off the Imperial Navy and Merchant Marine.

Stationed at the new B-29 base at Isley Field, Saipan, in December 1944 were VPB-23 aircrews: Phillips, Scholze, Bentley, McQuiddy, Reeves, Smith. Robert "Moose" Van Matre, AMM3/C ('44-'45), served in Lt. Art McQuiddy's crew and recollected:

> I didn't know I had signed on for a six year enlistment in the Navy—until I got to the end of my tour in the Pacific, and they started letting men out on the point system! What a rude awakening, when the yeoman told

me I wasn't getting out until 1948! I decided to stay in ... and did, for 27 years!

"Moose" commented on a VPB-23 plane loss at Ngatic:

It wasn't all that I lost on the plane at Ngatic. I had traded one of the natives that came out to the plane—an old pipe and some tobacco wrapped in a handkerchief—for a grass skirt and hat.

Axel E. Matsen, AMM2/C, and I developed film in a Jap dug out on Eniwetok. I think he was from Minnesota, he got his supplies from VB-5 there on the island.

I'm proud to have been in Mr. McQuiddy's, Smith's and Reeves' crew. I was a poor uneducated country boy, but their flying and navigation got me through the war.

I remember when we buzzed a Coast Guard or Navy dress parade on Catalina Island just before we trans packed—and I remember the setter pup we took with us.

Other memories: The "fighter take-off" that Lt. McQuiddy made on Eniwetok which didn't work. Nose wheel up and then a quick nose wheel down—skidding to the very end of the runway!

... And the Japs coming down from Babelthaup and Peleliu to do sabotage. Picking up Marine pilots at Babelthaup, one in a lagoon, one in the open sea. A lot of rivets popped on the open sea. Pilots picked up were Lts. Rath & Smith. I remember the first time I got shot at ... by AA at Wake Island Peacock Point.

While stationed at NAS Hutchinson, KS, I met my wife Lois and we were married in 1946 (50 years next January!). We have one son and three grandchildren. Enough of my rambling ... just writing this brings back memories.

Robert H. "Moose" Van Matre is recipient of: Air Medal with two gold stars; Good Conduct with one silver, one bronze star; WWII Victory Medal; American Campaign; Asiatic Pacific with two bronze stars; China Service, extended; National Defense with one bronze star; Armed Forces Expeditionary/Korea; VietNam Service with three stars, Meritorious Unit Commendation Ribbon; Republic of VietNam Campaign 1960 Device; and Combat Aircrewman wings with three stars.

Lt. Keith Guthrie wrote of a "bushwhacking" sortie he went on with his crew on Saipan:

Hostilities were over when we landed on Saipan, but the hundreds of caves where the Japs holed up during their fanatic defense were easy to find, especially with a seasoned Marine as a guide.

The first cave, replete with the rotten remains of the defenders strewn in and out of the cave, was a bit much, but after a few others we became accustomed to the raw facts. One of the gunners from my plane crew gave me a start as we prepared to leave a particularly gruesome cave, littered with bodies of men, women and children. I suddenly became aware of his bragging about how a Japanese grenade worked—needless to say the subject was closed and the souvenir returned to its resting place.

I remember the caves on Saipan. Our squadron's Quonset area was for some strange reason built in a valley adjoining those high forboding hills, where only a short time before, ferocious battles raged to route the enemy out of hundreds of caves dug deep into the hillsides and mountain crevices. Though the island had been declared "secure," there were still many Japanese hiding out in some of those caves and the heavy vegetation surrounding them. Marines went on daily patrols to root them out.

Knowing this, viewers were quite anxious about sitting on coconut logs while watching a movie positioned below those cave-pocked hills. We were always expecting some of the "Banzais" to come screaming down at us.

A number of daytime forages in search of "souvenirs" had already been made by our crews. On one such "day off" from flying, I joined a small group of shipmates for a hike up into the hills. Strapping on our P-38s and forsaking a Marine escort, we set out as cocky as could be, quickly covering the brush leading from our Quonset area to the foothills and rapidly ascending the slopes, making as much noise as we could. This was to warn anyone roaming about and send them back into hiding.

Soon we entered the darkened, battle-scarred area and peered about ghostly stumps of trees and brush and blackened caves filled with rotting bones and helmeted skulls of the defenders. Sometimes the remnants took on an appearance of a partly clothed skeleton. Our chatter had ceased with the sight of such human carnage, and the realization that, in fact, we were walking on the dead.

Then we came to a small clearing suited for a campsite—and saw a teapot neatly hanging over a smoldering fire.

"Geezus!" someone whispered. "Let's get the hell outta here!"

CHAPTER 18 Saipan–Tinian

And we took off, losing all sense of bravado, down the hill—half running, half jumping, sometimes falling and then getting up again and praying no enemy was following or waiting to ambush us. We ran down that hill as we never had run before.

Poor Marines we would have made, I thought. Afterwards, when asked about our adventure by buddies back in the Quonsets, there was a common sober note in the telling of our story. I did not venture back into those hills again.

Souvenirs of war were never on my priority list, though there were many still to be had. But I had neither appetite nor money to barter for trophies of the dead. The Marines and CBs made periodic appearances in our squadron area looking for buyers of Japanese rifles, helmets, samurai swords, battle flags, and personal items like pictures of family or sweethearts taken off the fallen. There were the counterfeits, too. Many a bullet-ridden, blood-spattered Rising Sun battle flag pawned off to a sailor was simply the work of an innovative entrepreneur. Something about the faces of those Marines, though. They had seen death.

On Saipan, we had been warned about "booby traps," and there was little about that I was tempted to pick up. On one of the islands, I picked up a little piece of splintered wood signage small enough to tuck away. Never did find out what it said. Other war wreckage and debris lying about was either too big or unfit to carry.

After of our first landings in Tanapag Harbor and aside from the initial enemy air activity over Saipan and Tinian, the squadron's HQ move to Saipan soon resulted in better quarters, better food, and an improved flight schedule that provided a breather day off—valued leisure time to write, go "bush-whacking," or otherwise put our time to other interests. I began sketching portraits of buddies—though I somehow couldn't bring myself to charge for my talents. Once shipmates found out it was for "free," I had a long waiting line. I had also enrolled in an armed forces mail study course in psychology and, of course, spent a great deal of time writing letters. With no steady girlfriend, I wrote to many, increasing my "mail flow" in any way I could.

One day, I was lucky enough to get some quiet time at the Quonset. I say "quiet" for I remember "quiet" as a luxury seldom enjoyed in a Quonset. I was relishing the unusual silence and lack of commotion and deeply preoccupied in writing a letter home.

It was then that I became aware of a dull scraping sound. Someone was at work at something. I went back to my letter, but the strange and sporadic noise attracted my attention once more. A bit irritated that someone was intruding on my quiet time, I got up from my cot and walked over to where the noise was coming from—a corner of the Quonset. There, hunched over and deeply involved in his own chore, was a fellow crewman who had also been on a sojourn up into the hills—and had brought back a Jap skull. He was scraping the dried skin off of it. Squatting there in his shorts, barefoot and bare chested so intent on his work, the crewcut young airman gave me a wide grin. "Look what I got me ... I'm gonna scrape this mother-f—— clean!"

I went back to my letter-writing.

ooo

The crew of LCDR William Stevens, "CO" of VPB-23, was: "XO" Lt. Robin Larson, Ens. George A. Hecker and Ens. Leslie H. Crook; Neil Dicken, AMM1/C, Dysart, Iowa; "J.B." Earnest, AMM3/C, a teacher in Muleshoe, Texas; Chief "Red" White, ACRM; Ray Chenowith, ARM2/C, Portland, Oregon; Roy A. Miller, AOM2/C, air bomber from Portland, Oregon; and Harold Moehlman, AOM2/C air gunner from Indiana.

"Gunner" Moehlman shared this memory: "Our skipper volunteered us for almost anything, especially transporting USO entertainers—of the opposite sex!"

On a more serious side, Moehlman remembered:

> Our crew, with Lt. Robin Larson flying as PPC, volunteered to pick up an Army Sgt. who shot himself in the leg with a .45 pistol aboard a ship off Eniwetok.
> Taking off from Isley Field on Saipan, we had no difficulty in locating the AKA Kenmore and making a successful open sea landing on rough water ... however, after bringing the injured man aboard, we proceeded to take off in the same rough sea and in doing so, tore a pontoon off a wing and a hole in bow. We were forced to ditch the plane and board ship for rescue.

Watching the rescue attempt from aboard the ship was crewmember Clyde Bennett, S-3, who wrote:

CHAPTER 18 Saipan–Tinian

I was there! I was on board the AKA *Kenmore* as the S-3 to the Troop Commander. It was my job to investigate the accident involving the PBY and Lt. Larson.

We had left Eniwetok Lagoon the previous day headed for Anguar in the Palau Islands. On board was an Aircraft Control Tower unit headed for duty at the B-24 base on Anguar. One of the non-coms from the unit was in the troop mess in the evening after departure, cleaning his several fire arms. (That control unit was armed like a movie commando outfit.) He had just finished cleaning his .45 and placed it on the mess table beside him, thinking it was "safetyfide."

Along came another soldier, who later claimed he was afraid of guns. He pushed the .45 away but in the process it somehow went off and hit the first soldier in the left leg, breaking the thigh bone. There were two young doctors aboard but they had no X-ray equipment or other facility too repair such a complicated break. Nor was there any such equipment in the convoy. The decision was made to call a "dumbo" since the doctors thought it important that their man receive attention as soon as possible. The ship's captain agreed and the call was made.

The next morning dawned bright and windy. We had been aboard that bucket for 60 days and this was the first rough day we had had at sea. The PBY flown by Lt. Larson showed up in midmorning. There was considerable conversation between ship and plane as to whether a landing should be attempted. Finally, it was decided that the *Kenmore* would try to lay a wake smooth enough for a landing. (That was a joke, because we were on one of Mr. Kaiser's Liberty ships with a flank speed of 10 knots. Try smoothing 4-5 foot seas in that rig.)

Larson's concern was to get the injured man out even if it meant endangering his own ship. Consequently, in one of the most courageous acts I saw in the entire war, he landed. It was a rough but successful one. The plane was in one piece.

The injured man was put in a wired tension splint, wrapped in blankets and life preservers and strapped into a basket type stretcher. This was loaded into a LCVP and lowered over the side for a trip to the PBY. A couple of crewmen stripped and got into a rubber life raft which was streamed out to meet the LCVP. The transfer of the patient was made from the LCVP to the raft and eventually into the side gun bay of the plane. The LCVP stood by.

Larson started his take off run going roughly parallel to the ship. The sea was so rough it was difficult to make any speed. As he slowly gathered speed, he began to take on water over the fuselage and, in fact, over the engines. From the ship it looked like he was going to get airborne, but a wave seemed to throw the plane into the air before it had flying speed. The port wing began to dip and the outer float caught the water. The plane cartwheeled and stopped belly down but sinking.

Through our field glasses we counted people coming out of the plane into the water. Then we saw them all go back into the plane. After this, one body was heaved out followed by the same number of men who got out of the plane in the first place. We learned later that the aircraft commander Larson was the last man out, and checking, found the patient was still on the plane. All were ordered back in to get the injured man out. Another class act.

Meanwhile, the LCVP was speeding back to pick people up from out of the sea. They got them all and brought them back to the *Kenmore*. All were wet and two naked as jaybirds. There was no shortage of clothes volunteered by all hands. Lt. Larson even had his choice of several sets of Army captain's bars. All were welcome additions to our Palau bound group.

I am not all quite sure whether the PBY crew welcomed their new mode of transport. The injured man did well and was air lifted to Hawaii, eventually returning to duty. The wrecked plane did not immediately sink and since we did not want to leave it for possible discovery by the Japs, it was sunk by gunfire from the ship.

Adventure for the PBY crew did not stop there. They shared the Typhoon of November '44 with us, anchored in Korro passage with 30,000 Japs on Babelthaup, the closest land. There we saw the demise of a number of PBMs and PBYs torn loose from their moorings and washed out to sea by the storm.

I have often wondered what happened to PPC Lt. Robin Larson and his crew. My friend former USN Lt.(jg) Francis Clifton showed me an article in the VP/VPB-23 newsletter, "Black Cat Log." All memories came flooding back and I felt I had to write about them. And so Lt. Robin Larson, wherever you are—here's to you. You were a hell of a man and you led a great bunch of real men even if you were in the Navy—a brown shoe at that.

I forwarded Bennett's recollections to Robin Larson, and he responded:

Thank you very much for forwarding the article on my attempted rescue of the man from the AKA *Kenmore*. It has bothered me for many, many years that I failed and felt that I had let the Navy down, as well as our CO of VPB-23, LCDR William M. Stevens USN.

The article was kind to me and I appreciated it very much. I would also like to thank the gentleman who wrote the article . . .

CHAPTER 18 Saipan–Tinian

In my reply I included Clyde Bennett's address and wrote:

> Your action and courage in spite of the ill-fated consequences that followed is indeed to be commended. Unfortunately, too many acts of courage and valor in war did not end with ultimate success. These deeds were performed in highest tradition, by brave men and women of our armed services who put their own lives on the line in an effort to save others.
>
> The testimony of Clyde Bennett gives credence and pays honor to you and your crew for your meritorious rescue attempt. It is unfortunate that your concerns have not been alleviated in a shorter span of time. Indeed you and your crew acted in the highest traditions of the Navy and had Cmdr. Stevens received S-3 Bennett's eyewitness report he would have agreed.

Clayton Dewhirst, CAMM ('42-'45), was, along with me, one of the last to go home. He was relieved in late 1945 and sent back for discharge in San Diego. He wrote a humorous note about his last days in service:

> As we were being processed at the Discharge Center, they gathered our group for a final urine sample, handing out paper cups and directing us to the "head."
>
> Having previously relieved myself and unable to comply, I passed my cup to a fellow shipmate and asked him to put in "a little" in for me. Would you believe it—turned out the guy had sugar diabetes! Getting out took a little more time than I figured, and I had to do some fast talking before it was all straightened out!

ooo

Max Ricketts, Cmdr. USN (Ret.) served as last CO of Patrol Bombing Squadron VPB-23 ('45-'46) before the squadron was decomissioned in 1946. He contacted me some fifty years later, after seeing a reunion announcement in the latest issue of *Proceedings*.

"Hey, that's my squadron!" he said in a phone call, then asked, "Who are YOU?"

The "YOU" Skipper Ricketts was questioning was me, Don Klotz, an aircrew radioman rarely to be seen around squadron HQ on Saipan in 1945. While I was sure he didn't remember me, I informed him that I did have his signature on my orders back to the States.

Joining the Navy as an apprentice seaman in October of 1933, Max Ricketts served aboard the USS *California* and USS *Sirius* before earning his AMM3/C rating at FAB Pearl Harbor. Then, after advancing to AMM2/C and a tour aboard the USS *Ranger*, he went on to flight training at Pensacola.

As AMM2/C (NAP), Max was with VP-23 at Pearl Harbor from January 1940 to June 1941, surviving the Japanese attack on December 7. NAP Ricketts then went on to South Pacific duty with VP-11, returning to serve as instructor in VPB-2, Jacksonville, Florida. Transferring to VH-5 in Alameda, and then to VPB-101, he returned to the Pacific, and assumed command of VPB-23 in '45

Flying patrol and search and rescue missions out of Saipan, Guam, Peleliu, and Iwo Jima, Ricketts and his crew took part in the USS *Indianapolis* rescue operation.

In 1958 he retired, ending his twenty-six-year career in the Navy. Max and his wife, Josephine, live in Lexington Park, Maryland, and are the parents of four children.

In August of '45 on Saipan and throughout the other islands where they were dispatched, war-weary crews of VPB-23, who had been out in the Pacific for almost eighteen months, were beginning to "count their points" and yearn for home.

One of those war-weary aircrewmen, Elbert B. Craig, wrote his brothers:

Dear Robert & Ted:
This is another day and I'm sure down-hearted—Had good hopes of going home soon, but the situation don't look so good now. The plan calls for those crews to be replaced each month sending men back with the most time overseas first.

Well, there were only three Air Bombers with overseas time and they have already returned, so I thought I might be in about the third replacement, but the chances are slim now because the married men are putting up a fuss to go.

I am in my third crew now, and it appears I'm to be used to replace a married fellow in another crew. Well, things might change—I hope so. A single fellow has feelings too, and besides changing crews isn't so good for pilots—or the crew either.

I'm hoping crews aren't broken up from now on. This squadron has done some crazy things but since we have a new Executive Officer, all problems should be solved.

CHAPTER **18** *Saipan–Tinian*

I have a very good P.P.C. now and he looks after the crew, so maybe I'll get home the last of May like I planned.

Ted, Bill Peoples is back here now. Oh yes, I'm back too. I was with Bill, Ivan Leonard, Jack Fox and Frank White from Woodlawn.

Bill told me about his sister getting married. We had quite a reunion and have planned a couple more. Bob, I'm sending you few more stamps. Hope they reach you in good shape. I have more Jap money to give you too, but I'm bringing that home with me.

Well, I had better sign off and hit the sack. I haven't done anything today, but still I'm tired. I did do a little wash this afternoon. I've been getting my gear ready for a long time—I have ten new white hats now!

Germany should fall soon I reckon? Bad about the President wasn't it?

Your brother Elbert

Elbert Craig was awarded the Air Medal, Asia Pacific Medal with two battle stars, American Defense Medal, and WWII Victory Medal.

I had no illusions about an early relief to stateside. Up to a month or so earlier, I had been the lowest ranking man in the squadron. The fact that I was about the youngest guy in the outfit, lowest in rank, and single, too, assured that I would be among the last to go home.

Prior to the Iwo Jima invasion, many of the Marines on Saipan destined to go ashore on that beachhead began making appearances about the squadron's Quonset huts looking to trade off a Japanese flag or samurai sword for our Smith & Wesson .38s.

A number of our guys did so—until the word got around that no crewman would be relieved for stateside unless he turned in his GI sidearm.

A shipmate who had sold his own pistol to a Marine asked if I wanted to sell my gun. "No soap!" I emphatically answered.

"Look, Klotz," the aircrewman answered, "you won't be going anywhere soon. You'll be the last to go home and you know it. And not having your gun isn't going to put you in jeopardy—but *I've a wife* waiting back in the States."

I sold him my Smith & Wesson for fifty bucks. And true to his prophecy, I was one of the last to go.

Going home! No such luck for me, but the first flight of six VPB-23 planes led by Commander Stevens departed for Kaneohe, TH, on June 20, 1945.

19

Guam

Guam invaded July 21, 1944; occupation completed August 10, 1944. Cost: 7,081 casualties.

VPB-23 detachment at Orote Field, Guam, December 1944.

Admiral Nimitz moves his headquarters to Guam, 1945.

Guam, largest of the Mariana Islands taken by the Japanese on December 9, 1941, was retaken by U.S. forces July 21, 1944. Saipan was secured July 9, 1944, and Tinian was captured July 24, 1944.

Seizure of the Marianas—Saipan, Guam, and Tinian—in July of '44 for B-29 bases completed the first phase of the Central Pacific drive. The second phase would involve U.S. Navy Patrol Bombing Squadron 23.

With the squadron move to Saipan, its crews now reported to CMDR Marine Air Detachment 21, Orote Field, Guam, for air-sea rescue operations. Although airfields and major land area on the islands were reportedly "secured," fighting the scattered remnants hidden in caves and hillside continued on through the war. A notable example was Shoichi Yokoi, a Japanese soldier who hid out in the jungles of Guam until February 9, 1972, when he finally surrendered.

VPB-23 squadron detachments based at airfields on Guam, Ulithi, and Peleliu operated in conjunction with Navy and Marine Corps fighters, dive bombers, and torpedo squadrons—whose missions differed from those at Tanapag Harbor.

The VPB-23 Guam detachment was moved from Orote to Agana Field, operating under air-base command there.

CHAPTER 19 Guam

Officers and aircrews were assigned Quonset huts near the airstrip for quick takeoff, and a large number of the squadron's flights were to escort F4Us, F6Fs or TBFs in air strikes operating from Ulithi and Peleliu.

Occasionally the "hot" pilots being escorted by 23's Black Cats, though very adept at conducting air strikes, did not read their "Dilbert" common sense manuals.

Fran Clifton reports on one such flight of TBMs recorded January 30 from Ulithi to Guam:

> A pilot had become separated and lost from his fellow group. VPB-23 Navy Lt. Charles S. Frantz from the Guam detachment was sent out to find the lost TBM and bring it in.
>
> In spite of poor flying conditions, the torpedo plane was found and Lt. Frantz gave the correct course to the base. However, the TBM pilot thought he knew better, and took leave of his guiding "Dumbo." Unfortunately in doing so, he ran out of fuel and was forced to ditch about 20 miles from Guam.
>
> Search efforts for the rest of that day were unsuccessful. At sunrise on the next day, the search was resumed by VPB-23's Lt. W. B. "Boardie" Jones and crew, who in spite of prevailing adverse weather conditions sighted the two survivors at 1616 that afternoon.
>
> By 1645 the USS *Bailey*, a destroyer called to the scene, completed the rescue. The survivors, Lt. Charles C. Taylor pilot, and his passenger, Lt. J. E. Nafastad, had been in the water over 24 hours!

That was a lucky one. On some searches, we would fly hours on end over the Pacific Ocean and never see a sign of land or life. When on an air-sea rescue mission we would strain our eyes to scan the ocean's foreboding surface in hopes of sighting any kind of little speck that might turn out to be a life raft or reflection from a signaling mirror.

I doubt that any of our aircrews based at Guam ever realized that we were flying over the largest single geographic feature on planet Earth! Totaling an area of 166 million square kilometers, the ocean occupies more than one-third of the globe. Its greatest depth, near Guam, is 11,033 meters—the deepest point on Earth!

Also across this vast expanse of Pacific Ocean, in the path of currents washed by tides, caressed and sometimes mauled by its winds, are more than 27,000 islands. Together sea and land constitute what is virtually an aquatic continent, Oceania. That we were able to navigate these vast spaces, let alone sight and rescue those "tiny specs" spotted in the sea, was a kind of miracle.

Sometimes it was the rescuer that became imperiled. On October 24, 1944, Lt.(jg) Arthur R. McQuiddy, on routine patrol off Ponape Island, lost an engine as a result of a cylinder exploding. Heading for Ngatik atoll, he jettisoned most of the PBY's equipment, some 400 gallons of gasoline, and landed safely in the lagoon. All classified equipment was scuttled.

A plane from the adjacent sector piloted by Lt.(jg) C. B. Phillips landed in the lagoon at about 1600 and made the rescue; no one was injured. The abandoned plane was accordingly sunk, but unfortunately, the "scuttled" plane piloted by McQuiddy was in fact the plane normally flown by "Pop" Decker's crew and had all of the "goodies" aboard.

Harold Moehlman, AOM2/C of the Skipper's crew, recounts:

> My most memorable trip was flying from Guam to Okinawa to make a last weather report to Lt. Gen Buckner from Admiral Chester Nimitz, just before the April 1st invasion. Flew through a typhoon—trip was the worst! Took off for Iwo Jima the next morning in 20-25 foot ground swells—and saw nothing all day but menacing white foam swirling below from the typhoon's southern end.

Lieutenants Decker, Diehl, and Clifton were on Guam when Lt.(jg) Mamer and two other crews appeared with the news that they were there to fly news dispatches and news reel film from Okinawa to Guam after the invasion set for April 1, 1945. The Navy had been catching a lot of flak on the slow release of news from the fleet, so they decided to make an example of the reporting from Okinawa, hence the courier service.

The assigned crews were to fly to Okinawa, land in a bay, pick up the dispatches and film, and return to Guam. There, the material was handled by courier direct to Washington, DC.

Squadron relief crews began arriving in May of '45. Lt. Art McQuiddy reports:

> Our crews at Agana, Guam, were: Kimball, Barton, Bruschk, Phillips, Barnhill, Dwyer, and my crew. By this time crew replacements were in such full swing, I did not even have a chance to get acquainted with the new PPCs or their crews.
>
> Like many other things in life, the new young "hot shots" had little

CHAPTER 19 Guam

regard for the "tired old guard." In mid-August our crew was dispatched to the U.S.—and Phillips, Reeves, Bently, Barnhill and I were assigned to the Instrument Flight Instructors School in Atlanta. Then I was sent to Whiting Field in Pensacola, where I did nothing—until late November when I was released from service.

Reflecting on the daily exchange of official reports both routine and strategic, and the pyramid of paper required for just a relief of a squadron brings to mind the "paper war"—fought in the Pacific on the typewriters of fleet yeomen and/or command officers in the field responsible for reporting their unit's business. There was no "relief crew rotation" for ground personnel attached to the squadron. VPB-23 ground personnel—the three non-flying officers, the yeoman and chief petty officers not regularly attached to a flight crew—were NOT included in this rotational program and the best information was that relief for them would have to be requested and would not be forthcoming until they had passed at least eighteen months out of the States. Here's a salute to those who fought the paper wars in Quonset huts throughout the Pacific—and the mighty yeomen.

Additional comments from Cardoza:

... As to sighting the sub, Decker said the day after our sighting and strafing of it (11JAN45), a destroyer targeted and finished it off about 0200 that morning. I do not know the name or number that got the sub. We were flying plane #46537.

Regarding native girls and in-flight rations: Remember that atoll where we flew over low—to see the native girls and drop Fitch's hair oil and cigarettes that they had ordered by writing on the sand?

As to the "KP" details in prepping for a flight, Cameron and I usually made the coffee and luncheons consisting of canned turkey, canned chicken, Spam (S.C.—guess you know what that means!) We would pick up the lunch fixings at the mess hall in the morning before the hop.

Guam today—once described as the undisputed gateway to Micronesia. An ex-patriot from California who lived on Guam for several years before moving to Ponape described the island territory as follows: "Guam is a K-Mart! Now, there is nothing wrong with a K-Mart but it is hardly necessary for an American to travel halfway around the world to find one. But for the WWII buff or scuba diving, Guam is for passing through ... as fast as you can! ..."

Born and raised in Tacoma, Washington, by Norwegian parents, Clarence Mykland had one brother. He held a newspaper route for ten years and earned his way through the College of Pugent Sound, majoring in chemistry. After graduation in 1938, Clarence decided to do something big with his life and joined the Navy's V-7 "90-day wonder" program designed to make officers and gentlemen of those who entered, while quickly turning out naval officers so desperately needed.

He was soon on orders to Pearl Harbor, Hawaii, via San Diego, and, as a one-stripe ensign, assigned to the destroyer USS *Maury*. The *Maury*'s duty was to provide protective cover, watch for enemy planes and submarines threatening the USS *Enterprise* and its 250-man crew, and also assisted in picking up pilots who missed the carrier and landed in the drink.

After escorting a group of pilots to Wake Island in November of 1941, Mykland's destroyer ran into rough water on the way to Pearl Harbor and had to slow down the pace. The ship was 150 miles from its destination on December 7, 1941.

The *Maury* was able to make it into the harbor the next morning, only to witness the utter devastation. Oil was spilled everywhere—ships were burning and turned over.

The destroyer was given immediate orders to refuel, restock its supplies, and head back to sea to look for Japanese subs.

"To this day I can't believe how they got through to Pearl Harbor," Mykland lamented.

On the USS *Maury*, Mykland was head of the A&R Dept. They participated in all sea battles—Coral Sea, Midway, Guadalcanal, Savo Bay, and other sorties. The thing he most remembered was seeing the Japanese torpedo planes flying so low and going for the USS *Enterprise* EV6. "We were firing our 20 & 40 mm guns at them, but they were not hitting the airmen! It was tough duty at the early part of the war until the great battle at Midway on June 4, 1942. The *Enterprise* was the best ship in the U.S. Navy."

After serving two years aboard the *Maury* and participating in many of the war's major sea battles, Mykland was given the opportunity for flight training. "The Navy wanted aviators, so they gave

CHAPTER 19 Guam   195

those of us with sea duty a chance to go back for pilot training," he said.

He also got another wish. He flew back to Tacoma and married his childhood sweetheart, Barbara. They moved to Florida, where Clarence won his wings, became a flight instructor, and witnessed the birth of his first child.

Then it was back to Pearl Harbor, to join U.S. Navy Patrol Bombing Squadron 23, fly missions over Iwo Jima, and participate in Japan's surrender!

Prior to getting his wings, Lt. Clarence Mykland served in the Pacific, from 1941 to 1943, aboard the USS *Maury*. He joined VPB-23 in '44, as PPC of a relief crew flying ASR and patrol missions from Ulithi, Peleliu. In addition, he experienced some tough duty on Iwo Jima. A special honor came about when he and his crew were chosen to stand by as a back-up and be ready to pick up film and surrender documents of the historic ceremony aboard the USS *Missouri* in Tokyo Bay for delivery to Iwo Jima and final disbursement to the United States.

When the Army Air Force plane first assigned the mission damaged its floats in making an open sea landing, Admiral Halsey ordered Mykland to the task. He proudly remembers talking to the admiral about the rough seas, and his successful landing and takeoff mission. Here are Mykland's recollections as recorded by his granddaughter, Julia Hamlin, for a school project:

> My VPB-23 crew names are: W. J. Gibbons, A. L. Rabellino, Eddie Gordon, Eddie Allen, Irwin Matthews. Peter D. Molthop, John Fijol, Clarence Mykland, and John Flynn. I think we worked well together.
>
> I am now flying in Ulithi, which is an island atoll in the Central Pacific. My crew and I are doing air-sea rescue work. We work with the submarines. We spot planes that are down and U.S. crews that have been abandoned. Then we bring them on board and save them from the dangerous waters.
>
> The following is a picture of Tokyo, Japan, taken on March 30, 1945. We flew over this city many times.
>
> Last week my crew and I participated in the search for the USS *Indianapolis*. It had just delivered to Tinian Island the bomb that would end World War Two. Our search sector found nothing, but one of our VPB-23 planes commanded by Lt. Adrian Marks did. After a first sighting of an oil slick, Lt. Marks was called into the search area. He landed on

the open sea and rescued 56 men, pulling them inside their aircraft or onto the wings. This is an honorable area to work in during this war because we are helping to save lives.

Japanese officials signed documents aboard the battleship *Missouri* in Tokyo Bay surrendering and bringing World War II to an end on September 2, 1945. The first to sign the surrender for Japan was foreign minister Mamoru Shigeitsu. General Douglas MacArthur used five pens to sign the document for the Allies. One pen was given to General Jonathan M. Wainright, another to General Sir Arthur E. Percival. What a relief it must have been to finally sign an official document ending World War Two.

My crew and I were chosen as back-up to pick up films of the signing of the peace treaty aboard the USS *Missouri*. When the army plane damaged floats on an open sea landing, I was then ordered by Admiral Halsey to land and return to Iwo Jima with films. I remember talking to the Admiral about the rough sea and the landing mission.

After trying two rough water take-offs and failing, I then changed strategy and headed downwind at full speed right for shore. To the amazement of the Japanese watching on shore, I made a 180-degree turn close to the shoreline and got enough speed to get on the step and take off.

When we were airborne, I circled over Tokyo to view all the damage and destruction. We flew films back to Iwo Jima and delivered them to the Navy. The films were then flown back to Washington D.C.

I have lived a very memorable experience here in the Central Pacific flying this PBY twin engined airplane.

For eighteen months VPB-23 had flown its last tour of duty on the outer perimeters of hell, encircling Central Pacific battlegrounds and beachheads where waters once washed red from the blood of desperate men. We had scanned vast waters in search of the enemy, plucked comrades from the cruel sea, and performed air-sea rescue for carrier strikes on enemy held islands or the B-29s on their Tokyo runs.

Near war's end, VPB-23 would be destined to participate in the most tragic rescue of the war. After losing a few planes on coral reefs and/or in rough seas, orders were given prohibiting open sea landings. Soon standard air-rescue procedure comprised search aircraft working as a team with submarines and destroyers.

In the early morning hours of July 30, 1945, the cruiser USS *Indianapolis*, having delivered critically secret "Little Boy" atom bomb components to Saipan, was heading toward Leyte. When she was torpedoed by the Japanese submarine I-58, the *Indianapolis* was

CHAPTER **19** *Guam*   197

under strict orders to observe radio silence. She sank rapidly and without sending an SOS. In the oversight, the cruiser was not reported missing until three days later.

As if by God's grace, Lt. Adrian Marks and his crew from VPB-23 were called to the scene. Observing the scattered survivors struggling in the shark-filled waters, Lieutenant Marks without hesitation landed in the choppy waters against orders—to rescue fifty-three men from the ill-fated, torpedoed *Indianapolis*. Other squadron crews also participated in search and rescue efforts over the next few days, including the skipper of the squadron, LCDR Ricketts. Only 316 of her over 1,000-man crew survived.

In the last days of war, VPB-23 and its Black Cats were scattered in twos and threes on a number of Pacific islands—some operating on Guam, others from Saipan, Ulithi, Peleliu, and Iwo Jima. A mission or two was flown to Okinawa, and all the squadron would participate to some degree in the B-29 air war over Tokyo.

On blister watch one clear weather day, circling about as B-29s took off below, I was mesmerized by the sight of cerulean blue waters and dazzling white coral airstrips of Tinian, watching as sleek silver air force superforts took off in endless numbers.

It was a beautiful sight and such a pleasant day. I was proud and happy to be part of it all—oblivious to their mission's intent, which of course was to fire-bomb a death-defying enemy on the mainland into total submission.

The unloaded .50-caliber beside me was indication that the skies were ours and our duty was routine Dumbo. As mother hens we were to keep a watchful eye as our big B-29 birds took off, and be ready to rescue any unlucky crews that might go down at sea.

We were in the last months of war. We had seen the massive build-ups of Navy task force might at Eniwetok, then at Ulithi. We had flown over the invasion fleet at Iwo Jima. And now to be looking all about at the largest air armada of the Pacific War was awesome.

The conflict had moved from the island battles of the Pacific to the Japanese mainland and achilles heel fire-bombing of Tokyo. Then, on August 6, 1945, the first atom bomb was dropped on Hiroshima.

On August 9, 1945, three B-29 superforts flew over Nagasaki to inflict the final "Fat Boy" atom bomb finale on the Setting Sun.

How ironic that the few survivors left of those who, with

prayer scarves wrapped around their foreheads, swooped down one Pearl Harbor morning to inflict burning infernos of black smoke, fire and death, would themselves be recipients of B-29 incendiary attacks with no less purpose than to burn Tokyo out of existence.

As the war came to an end, our squadron was scattered about in small detachments operating from Guam, Saipan, Peleliu, Ulithi, Iwo Jima, and Okinawa. As relief crew replacements arrived, we were singularly detached from the squadron headquarters on Saipan and sent on our way.

Most significant of all was LCDR Clarence Mykland's plane taking off from Tokyo Bay with the USS *Missouri*'s film documenting the Japanese surrender ceremony. After getting airborne and circling over the vanquished city, the black PBY of VPB-23 turned and headed homeward.

In April of '45, relief crews were flying in. The war was coming to a close. President Roosevelt died on April 12—Germany's surrender was eminent—and Japan's surrender seemed soon to follow. Or so we thought!

American troops had gone ashore in the Battle for Okinawa on April 1, and the U.S. Navy would suffer its greatest losses of the war inflicted by kamikaze attacks off the coast of Okinawa.

The planes and aircrews of VPB-23 were kept busy flying routine daily "Dumbo" for the B-29s that were bombing Tokyo from Saipan, Guam, Tinian, and from their new airfields on Iwo Jima airsea rescue missions in and about the Ryukyu Islands. One or two of the squadron's planes even flew "top command" to Okinawa. Another flew into MacArthur's HQ in the Philippines to be assigned a rescue mission for downed pilots. Others made attacks on, and accepted surrender from, Korean troops trying to escape in small boats from further bombardment.

Clarence Cardoza, AOM2/C, remembers: "May 2, 1945, was our last flight with Lt. Willis 'Pop' Decker. Half of the crew—including 'Pop' Decker, Robert Maupin, Max Weaver, and Hollis K. Britt—were sent back to the States. That's when you [Don Klotz] came into our crew along with Tommy Green, a mech, and an ordnance back on a jeep carrier that brought us from Hawaii to San Diego."

Japan surrendered on August 14, 1945, after the Nagasaki atom bomb drop.

20
Ulithi

VPB-23 detachment sent to Falalop Island, Ulithi, December 1944.

As we flew over Ulithi atoll, it looked like the entire U.S. Navy was at anchor! Statistics in mid-March of '45 prior to the Okinawa invasion document some 617 ships anchored there. Ulithi, with its forty-nine islets, including the fourth largest lagoon in the world, became a staging area for the allied invasion of the Philippines.

Falalop, on Ulithi atoll, was the kind of idyllic Pacific island described in travel books or seen in movies. Coconut trees had not been leveled by shelling, and the island was covered with lush foliage—except for the 1,200-yard airstrip that had been carved out by Navy bulldozers.

Asor Islet became the command post for the Navy's advanced fleet, while Mog-Mog, a short distance away, became one of the most important fleet recreation centers in the Pacific. The Seabees took part of Mog-Mog, tore down coconut trees over a vast area, and made ball fields, a prize-fighting ring, and a place you could go swimming.

In 1944 the tiny Yap island of Mog-Mog meant fun to thousands of American servicemen, even if only for two or three hours. After months at sea, ships would stop in this deepwater lagoon surrounded by Ulithi atoll to restock supplies, do repairs, and give their crews a short break. After a few hours, they would gather up their sailors, pull up anchor, and go back to where the war was.

One sailor remembers: "Everyone would get two beers. We

would go over and swim, drink beer, and fight each other to let off a little steam."

In all, about 2.2 million U.S. servicemen visited Mog-Mog in the 373 days the military occupied it. They drank more than 3.8 million beers and soft drinks. A record 20,000 men were entertained there in one day.

On Falalop, from which VPB-23 operated, the natives had been moved to other islands. Their thatched huts were still standing, and native cemeteries were left intact.

Personnel were quartered in tents among the clusters of palm trees beside the 3,500-foot airstrip stretching from one end of the island to the other. VPB-23's Black Cats shared equally in escort duty ferry flights and Marine fighter and bomber attacks on nearby Yap.

In 1944 on Ulithi atoll in the far Pacific, there stood a little grass chapel of driftwood logs and high peaked roof covered with pandanus thatch. In front, a palm-thatched sign hung from an arch of driftwood proclaiming it as "Doughboy Chapel." The chapel, a former "meeting house" originally built by the natives, was now used for Sunday services by the armed forces on the atoll. Furnished with coconut log seats and an altar built by the Seabees, the chapel held services *late* on Sunday mornings by the residing chaplain, a Baptist minister.

Unfortunately, the hour conflicted with Navy chow time. And to make matters worse, "the sinners" who forsook "chapel" for "chow" were often playing poker during that time—with a deck of cards previously provided by the chaplain! This so angered the pastor that he admonished the gamblers, warning that they were all going to hell!

The situation changed a bit when Lt. "Pop" Decker and Ens. Lewis Shepley of the newly arrived VPB-23 detachment approached the angry pastor and suggested he change the service to an earlier hour, thus giving participants the opportunity to attend services and still make the chow line.

He did so—thus tripling the attendance, diminishing Sunday morning card playing, and winning a few better-fed converts!

The talented organist who played in that chapel on Sunday mornings, when he wasn't flying a PBY, was Ensign Shepley. He adds his recollection to the story: "... my main memory was being at Ulithi in '44, where there was no chaplain when we arrived

CHAPTER 20 Ulithi

there—but one did arrive just before Christmas, with a portable Esty organ, which really helped Christmas morale!"

On January 1, 1945, VPB-23's "Ulithi Detachment" was to make squadron history by participating in the invasion of little Fais Island—a mile and a half long, and three-fourths of a mile wide.

Two PBYs under Navy Lt. "Pop" Decker comprised the air detachment flying Army Brig. Gen. Marcus B. Bell as sole command staff overseeing the operation.

Anticipating the invasion, the Japanese had removed all personnel from the island, fifty miles away from Ulithi—except for a corporal's guard to operate the radio station. Natives were to report seventeen armed Japanese on the island.

Accordingly LCDR J. F. McFadden commanded what was known locally as the "Ulithi Navy"(three LCIs, one LST landed the occupation force of 238 officers and men, and five tanks of the "Wildcat" Division, without opposition on the southern coast of the island).

Two days were spent in an unsuccessful search for an enemy hiding in thick underbrush, but on the third day a patrol flushed out eight members of what turned out to be a Japanese "Special Navy Landing Force." The besieged enemy killed three and wounded three more "Wildcats" before being blasted out of a cave by tanks and either killed or taken prisoner.

The American flag was hoisted over Fais on January 4, 1945. Shortly after, General Bell turned over the island government to Mahoru, the native chief, withdrawing his troops and leaving behind a few Marines for liaison with the residing 170-200 natives. Much valuable Japanese radio equipment was salvaged and put to good use by Seabees and Marines on Ulithi. A most precious trophy was a German piano painted red, which was brought back and played thereafter in the Officer's Club on Ulithi. It may be assumed that the co-pilot Ensign Shepley, who flew with "Pop" Decker in the command plane, would also "tickle the keys" on the musical prize of war.

Lt. "Pop" Decker's Action Report:

> Fais Island is a small island some 20 knots southeast of Ulithi Atoll where a Jap Radio Station was reporting our ship movements in and out of Ulithi. It had to be taken out. On 1 Jan 45 an amphibious landing force assaulted the island. I was in charge of 3 crews and 2 planes based on

Ulithi and it was my turn to fly. We took off in plane # 46537 providing the sole air cover for the landings.

Aboard my plane was Army Brigadier Gen. Marcus B. Bell, commanding the "occupation force," Colonel June and a Vice Admiral. The air time was 18 hrs and the operation landing a success—with 30 Japs killed or captured. I have movies of the invasion taken with my 8mm camera.

With Yap and Woleai still in enemy possession, Ulithi could not escape occasional nuisance attacks—or while on patrol, an occasional run-in with a sub! Clarence Cardoza, AOM3/C AB, relates one encounter while flying in Decker's crew.

On January 11, 1945, while flying "Dumbo" out of Ulithi for a Marine TBM, Clarence was beside his gun on blister watch. The bombers had done their job and were heading home. PPC Lt. "Pop" Decker made a final circle over the Jap-held island to see all was accounted for.

Scanning the Yap harbor Cardoza remembers looking out the bow turret and reporting what he thought to be a DE (destroyer escort).

Picking up the mike, Cardoza asked: "What's that DE doing there?"

"Hell man... that's no DE," came an excited reply, "... that's a MEATBALL!"

Cardoza described the ensuing action:

"Pop" Decker turned the plane sharply to Port, and dove downwards for the attack on the sub. Scrambling to battle stations, we manned guns and prepared to fire. On the bow gun, I armed the twin .30s and swung the guns around to the sub which had already begun its crash dive. At approximately 3,000 feet, I commenced firing.

As we closed in "Pop" Decker put the plane into a position where Max Weaver on the Starboard blister gun—and I—could converge our fire... his .50 calibre on the starboard and my twin .30s on the bow.

The ricochet of tracers hitting the submarine's conning tower looked like 4th of July fireworks as the sub disappeared into ocean depths.

We dropped flares to mark the spot, while scanning the surface looking for some effect from our attack. The flares were all we could drop. Our air-sea rescue mission ruled out bombs—but never-the-less we remained on station circling overhead until short on fuel, we were forced to called in relief and return to base.

The next day, we received reports that the sub was sunk at 0200 that morning by a destroyer called in for the hunt.

CHAPTER **20** *Ulithi* 203

Note: Adm. Samuel Elliot Morrison, in *History of Naval Operations in World War II*, "Leyte," reports: "On the 22nd of Jan. 1945, a hunter killer team of destroyer escorts Conklin, Raby and Corbeiser sank submarine I-48 that had been sighted off Ulithi and attacked unsuccessfully by a patrol plane."

"Pop" Decker's crew was: PPC Lt.(jg) Willis B. Decker, Ens. Lewis Shepley, Ens. Don Dutcher, PC Richard Cameron, AMM3/C, Hollis Britt, AMM3/C, Robert Maupin, ARM3/C, Stephen Cigich, ARM1/C, and Donald Max Weaver, AOM2/C.

Clarence adds a related encounter:

> Decades later, while my wife Lucia and I were camping at Elephant Butte Lake State Park in New Mexico, I met a submariner there. Naturally, we ended up exchanging WWII tales. I told him of our submarine incident and asked him if the fireworks that Max and I had rained on the sub could have done any damage to it, such as damaging the periscope or something else... because we rattled the conning tower pretty good.
> Perhaps that is why the sub may have surfaced again as soon as it did. We will never know for certain, but it is nice to know that we may have aided in eliminating one more submarine from the Japanese fleet.

Clarence Cardoza was born August 26, 1923, to Albert and Jewel Cardoza in Seabright, California, about fifty miles south of San Francisco, now considered part of Santa Cruz. The family name, Cardoza, is Portuguese. Clarence's father served in the U.S. Infantry during WWI. Clarence spent his early childhood mostly in the San Jose coastal area. In 1936 he and his family moved to the Yreka area, where he lived and worked on their small ranch until graduation from Weed High School (Weed is a small town south of Yreka). Clarence had been working at Weed Lumber Co. for two years when he was drafted into the Navy on February 3, 1943.

Completing his boot training at NTC Farragut, Idaho, Clarence was assigned to NATTC in Norman, Oklahoma, for ordnance training and graduated with a rating of AOM3/C. Further assignments brought him to NAGS Gunnery School at San Diego, California, and Bombardier School at Hangar 308 in San Diego, where upon graduation he became a bombardier instructor, advancing in rank to AOM2/C.

In March of 1944 he was selected to join the newly re-formed

VPB-23 for its third tour in the Pacific. Participating in the Navy's Central Pacific island campaigns, Clarence returned in September 1945 with a rank of AOM1/C.

Clarence Cardoza, AOM1/C AB, is recipient of two Air Medals and Combat Aircrew Wings. One Air Medal was presented in San Francisco by Capt. John J. Mahoney, USN, Chief of Staff, Twelfth Naval District, San Francisco.

Commenting on his aircrew wings and the sighting of the sub, Clarence remembered: "The day we got off the ship (it was either the *Card* or the *Bogue*—a jeep flat top) they gave us a "chit." I bought my Air Wings at North Island (SS)."

As to the sighting of the sub, "Pop" Decker said that "the day after our sighting and strafing of it (on January 11, 1945) they (the destroyers) got it the following day." Neither the name nor the number of the sub or the ship that sunk the sub is known to this date. The plane flown during this encounter was number 46537. Cardoza adds: "It replaced plane 46571—the plane McQuiddy lost on that atoll where we used to fly low to see the girls and drop Fitch's Hair Oil and cigarettes."

A culinary food-in-flight report by Clarence:

> As to the K.P. details, Cameron and I usually made coffee and lunches consisting of canned turkey, canned chicken, Spam (S. C. I guess you know what this means) sandwiches and fruit. Cameron and I would pick up the lunch fixings at the mess hall in the morning before the hop. The foods that we had over and over again were boll weevil bread, peas in ketchup, orange marmalade, green powdered eggs. Don't forget the boiled mutton cut up with a band saw. Some crews were really lucky to get an innovative crewman aboard who could forage and spice up the menu. We did not have any talented chefs.

Clarence remembers a "wheel shake-down" that got the crew all shook up:

We were coming in on the landing approach when the port wheel suddenly refused to lock. So Lt. Shepley announces his decision on the intercom to go around again and "shake it down." However, Plane Captain Cameron says, "No, never mind—we'll let it down manually."

I was sitting in the port blister getting ready to go forward and help Cameron, when Lt. Shepley suddenly without warning pulled the nose up in the air into a steep climb, and then, noses her over and downward.

CHAPTER **20** *Ulithi*   205

I didn't even get to lock the blister, which flew open—but I had sense enough to hang onto the retractable seat.

When the lieutenant pulled the plane out of the dive thinking he was going to "drop" the wheel, all he really accomplished was to dump everything into the bilge. Coffee and anything that was loose landed in the bilge—and then the seat that I was sitting on flipped up and I hit the deck feeling like I had broken my back.

Soon as I recovered my wits, I ran forward to help Cameron put the port wheel down manually. The next day was "clean-out-the-bilge-day"—coffee grounds and all!

The crew let it be known to Lt. Shepley that he must never do that again. I still wonder how I managed to stay in the plane during that mad roll. (This incident is one of the most memorable things to me about Shepley's command.)

Three destroyers ran smack into the typhoon of December 15-17, 1944, and capsized. Six or seven other ships were seriously damaged, with a loss of 800 officers and men. It was the greatest uncompensated loss since the Battle of Savo Island. Search planes operating from the Marianas, Ulithi, and the Palaus made weather reports but were not much good to the fleet as they avoided bad weather fronts.

Wet was hardly the word! The rain came down in torrents, wind ripping up tents, destroying small craft, and threatening our planes. On the typhoon's edge, our detachments were pinned down. It struck so suddenly, we were forced to lash down our planes at the maximum of the typhoon's ferocity. Many of our tents were blown away, and the shelter we had in the tents that were not blown away was miniscule. Water poured in from everywhere. We lived under ponchos and kept our clothes on for days at a time. The metal food trays filled with water as we tried to eat our chow.

Note: Today, travelers to Ulithi atoll are limited by number and permission from government officials, who might also be able to help with arrangements. Pacific Missionary Aviation flies to Ulithi twice a week. Most people stop here, but with the right pre-arrangements one can get to Mog-Mog, the chief island. A longer field-service will take you to the most remote islands on earth—Woleai (where isolated Japanese starved to death). Satawal is still the center of navigational and canoe-building skills and the lively island of Fais.

21  Peleliu

1st Marine Division and 81st Army Division invade Peleliu, August 1944.

VPB-23 detachment relieves VPB-54 detachment, December 27, 1944.

In August of 1944, the 1st Marine Division was transported some 1,000 miles beyond Truk to invade Peleliu—southernmost of the Palau Islands—and together with the 81st Army Division seized Ulithi, which became the fleet's principal anchorage.

The U.S. Navy VPB-23 squadron PBY detachment at Peleliu lived in tents about fifty yards from the airstrip along with the continuing roar and propwash of planes taking off or landing day and night. Both officers and men "messed" with the Seabees, and later with the Marine air group personnel, getting along well with both groups.

During December '44 and the first two months of '45, VPB-23 operated as standby "Dumbos" for the Marine F4Us whose engine cowlings were painted with a checkerboard pattern and whose pilots were conducting strikes on the enemy-held islands of Babelthaup, Koror, and Arakabesan in the Palau group.

At Peleliu during December 25 and January 25, 1945, were Lieutenants McQuiddy, Barnhill, Baltz, Colvin, Phillips, Scholze, Bentley, Reeves, and Smith.

On January 13, Lt. A. R. McQuiddy, USNR, was notified that a Corsair of VMF-122 had gone down west of Babelthaup Island. McQuiddy's crew was airborne at 11:35 and was led to the downed pilot by another Corsair and a P-38 photographic plane. The ditched pilot was in his life raft in the lagoon, which at that point was only three-fourths of a mile off the enemy's shore and drifting inward. Two Corsairs strafed the Japanese gun positions as McQuiddy made a water landing, and taxiing up to the raft now only one-fourth mile or so away from shore, and under gunfire, he rescued Marine pilot Lt. J. A. Smith. Smith was taken from his raft uninjured and at 1220 returned to base.

On January 14 at Peleliu: Lt.(jg) Clyde B. Phillips, USNR, was on standby Dumbo when he was notified an F4U had been shot down and forced to make a landing only one and a half miles east of the Babelthaup Island airstrip.

In five minutes Phillips and his crew were airborne, and with the help of other Marine Corsairs was in sight of the downed pilot. Standard procedure discouraged open sea landings except in emergency. Though Phillips was aware of this, he also knew the downed pilot appeared not only to be minus a life raft, but was having difficulty with his life jacket—and was unfortunately drifting nearer and nearer toward enemy shores of Koror and Babelthaup.

Deciding to land, Lieutenant Phillips came down on the six- to eight-foot swells with a 16-knot wind, and crewmen threw out a life ring to the downed pilot. Drawing him closer to the ladder, which had been put over the side, it became apparent that the pilot was too exhausted to pull himself up. Plane Captain Robert C. Edge, AMM1/C, then went over the side and pulled him into a position where the rest of the crew could drag him aboard the plane.

The takeoff was rough—the plane bouncing high three times—but finally they lifted off the water. The rescued Corsair pilot, Capt. Warren Fisher of VMF-122, was landed safely at his home base again in a matter of minutes.

Lt.(jg) Art McQuiddy and crew made their second pick-up of the month on January 22. A Corsair of VMF-114 had been shot up, and the pilot, 1st Lt. Richard S. Rash, was forced to bail out three miles east of the Babelthaup Island airstrip. The Dumbo was notified and twenty minutes later was making a full stall landing in the open sea. Swells fourteen to sixteen feet high had made the landing a rough one. Seeing that the injured Marine pilot was unable to open his life raft or help himself, McQuiddy taxied alongside the pilot, and two of the crew, Joseph B. Kocourek, ARM3/C, and

Ellis F. Signorelli, AOM1/C, were able to bring him aboard. The rescue was completed successfully.

On February 1, 1945, Lt. Oscar T. Owre, USNR, was alerted when a fighter pilot was forced to jump from his plane twelve miles off Babelthaup. Owre reached the scene at about 1600. The downed pilot was one and a half miles off the reef when Owre decided an open sea landing was necessary. The plane was put down in a medium swell and 16-knot wind without damage, and the pilot 2nd Lt. J. R. Anderson, USMCR of VMF 114, was quickly picked up. On takeoff, however, the plane, rising over two swells, plowed its nose into a third and tore off both propellers. The port propeller was thrown through the cockpit, missing Owre's face by barely an inch, but hitting his left hand. Windshield glass caused other injuries to Lieutenant Owre, as well as to 1st Pilot Ens. L. D. Bartow, USNR.

A PC boat on the P-Boat's frequency immediately headed for the damaged plane. Reaching the scene an hour and a half later, it took Owre and the rest of the men aboard and placed the crippled plane under tow. The plane's personnel reached base the next morning, but the plane (whose towing had been taken over by the USS *Chincoteague*), sank before she could be reached.

Owre's injuries were severe, requiring immediate return to the United States for hospitalization. Detached from duty February 12, 1945, he was the first man to leave the squadron since its active duty in a combat zone.

"After a thirty-day leave," Lt. Keith Guthrie recalls, "the first pilots of old VP-23 were used to form a new squadron and soon headed out to the Central Pacific." He continues:

> "Bushwhacking" was somewhat limited, especially since "Hove" drew east coast duty—and Washburne was assigned to PBMs, but I managed to get some extra duty.
>
> Eniwetok was a beautiful atoll where the Pacific fleet could be anchored and sheltered behind coral reefs. About the only excursions that could be mustered were two off-limit islands where the natives lived. These, too, proved interesting, but not as revealing or interesting as the South Pacific.
>
> Exploring Peleliu was a bit hairy. When Marines killed off most of the Japs, the Seabees came in and stacked up literally hundreds of Japanese planes in huge stacks. To discourage souvenir hunters ... the authorities posted huge signs, "Beware of booby traps." Enough to fore-

stall much looking. Rumors of Japanese still in the surrounding jungles held expeditions to a minimum.

The colorful parrots on Peleliu rivaled those that inhabited the Solomon Islands. Lt. Oscar Owre, our resident authority on all bird life, had a scenic name for most, but somehow or other would never pronounce the scientific names much less spell them. Oscar, on his return to civilian life, received his doctorate and served as head of the zoology department of Miami University. "Bushwhacking" memories suit me better than Navy citations full of Navy jargon.

While on Peleliu Lt. D. K. Guthrie and his crew took part in two rescue episodes and effected a third by making an open sea landing under enemy fire, in spite of five- to six-foot swells about 20 degrees out of the wind. Keith was awarded the Distinguished Flying Cross, two Air Medals, and was a participant in seven engagements in the Pacific.

January 15, 1945: Lieutenant Guthrie, on Dumbo standby again, flew to the aid of 2nd Lt. C. C. Hawkins, USMCR of VMF-114, who had been hit while on a routine barge sweep and made a water landing thirty miles northeast of Peleliu airstrip. The Dumbo crew found the pilot in his raft with dye marker out, and circled him until a surface vessel picked up the survivor.

The third rescue by Lieutenant Guthrie occurred as an incident in an F4U strike on Yap Island, which Lieutenant Guthrie was accompanying as Dumbo. One of the fighter planes, hit in its engine, went down three-quarters of a mile off the reef on the southeastern side. Following the fighter part of the way down, the PBY's crew dropped a dye marker and a smoke light near it. Because of the proximity of the survivor to the enemy's shore and despite batteries already directing their fire toward him, Guthrie decided to land.

Directed to the downed pilot's raft by Marine fighters overhead, Guthrie landed in 14 knots of wind and five- to six-foot swells, 20 degrees out of the wind, successfully effecting a landing. The raft was quickly brought under the port wing and the pilot hauled to the ladder and attached to the line. As firing enemy shore batteries were getting close to finding the plane's range, the P-Boat's takeoff was started before the ladder was in.

One shell hit the water thirty feet in front of the plane, throwing spray on the windshield. With engines full throttle, three hard bounces later and with some damage to the hull, the plane was aloft and a return to base safely accomplished.

The plane had been hit once; a shrapnel hole was found on the starboard side just aft of the tower window.

The rescued pilot was Marine 1st Lt. S. J. Polluszny of VMF-122.

At Peleliu on February 11, 1945, Lt. D. K. Guthrie, USNR, and his crew took part in two rescues—and then made an open sea third landing under enemy fire.

Guthrie and his crew were flying Dumbo for a Corsair air strike on Yap, when Maj. F. E. Pierce, USMC, CO of VMF-122, developed engine trouble which forced him to ditch his plane ten miles off the southern tip of Yap Island. Learning of the plane's difficulties, PPC Guthrie requested plane relief and a surface vessel from Ulithi to come to the rescue. At 1235, an hour and a half after Major Pierce's successful ditching, Lt. C. E. Wilson, USNR, relieved Guthrie from his sheltering orbit over the raft, remaining on station until 1520. Guthrie, having refueled at Ulithi, returned to take over rescue operations awaiting the arrival at 1610 of USS *Landsdown*, which took the downed flier aboard.

Lt. Wallace Douglas had this report about February 20, 1945:

> VPB-23 flight crews on Peleiu were put to work building a squadron ready room with wood obtained from the Seabees to make a floor and frame for a tent. Fresh water tanks were made from 55 gallon drums for showers.
>
> On the island we lived in tents, but were fed very well. Steaks and fresh vegetables were frequently on the menu because we were dining with a Marine fighter squadron. VPB-23 was flying Dumbo on their strikes against Yap and Babelthaup.
>
> It is believed that the Dumbo flights out of Peleiu helped to earn the Air Medal for the squadron on the third tour. On one flight from Yap, Tenney's plane decided to check out the island of Babelthaup and was immediately fired upon by antiaircraft. Our sightseeing was cut short, for we immediately high-tailed it out of there!

April 13, 1945: Announcement of the death of President Franklin Delano Roosevelt, broadcast over armed forces radio, brought a common sorrow to the nation, its allies, and particularly the multitude of servicemen overseas. He was the commander in chief. He had pulled the nation out of the Great Depression, rallied its people after the attack on Pearl Harbor, and actively participated in forging America into the mightiest war production machine in history. In an address to a Jefferson Day dinner by radio, he said, "The only limit to our realization of tomorrow will be our doubts of today. Let us move forward with strong and active faith."

Three planes and crews were later transferred from Kobler Field on Saipan to Peleliu, allowing continued anti-sub patrols.

This combat activity over heavily gunned enemy territory resulted in several calls on the detachment for assistance to downed pilots.

Lt. Francis Clifton, who later flew with Decker's three-plane detachment out of Peleliu, recalls: "This was about the time that Henry Fonda found his way to our squadron as ACI officer. It took but a week before the Admiral had him back. Our own three staff officers were: Lincoln Brayton, Henry Watson, and Murphy (cannot remember his first name)."

VPB-23 was flying the perimeters of hell. Flying superforts daily wreaked havoc upon the enemy. We all had some apprehension, but knew it was a fight to the finish.

It would be the little known but feisty man from Independence, Missouri, Harry S. Truman, who would so ably take over from FDR. The gathering of an invasion force for the anticipated landing on the mainland of Japan seemed imminent.

ooo

VPB-23 crews scattered over a number of Pacific islands and took on miscellaneous missions. "A brief encounter," as told by Nancy Rider, wife of Lt. William Rider ('44–'45), Ennis, Texas, goes like this:

On 7 DEC '43 Bill Rider joined the Navy's cadet program and was soon flying yellow perils out of Stevensville, Tx., going on to continue his training at the University of Georgia.

Bill, who won his wings at Pensacola in January of 1944, was then ordered to NAS North Island, where as the first pilot reporting in for duty with VPB-23, he was interviewed and welcomed by new Squadron Commander Bill Stevens.

Then he was put to test by PPC W. Boardman Jones, and after performing a perfect full power water landing, he was appointed first pilot in Jones' crew.

In March of '44, he took off from NAS North Island, San Diego, CA, with Lt. Jones for the long Pacific journey to Hawaii. Also on board were: Navigator Ens. Harold Hearon, Plane Capt. AMM1/C Freddie Zaugg, 2nd Mech. Frank Whitey White, AOMC Bomber Day, AOM Frank Watson, 1st Radioman 1/C "Boo" Booher and 2nd Radioman Don Klotz ARM3/C.

From there, the squadron went on to the Central Pacific flying Patrol, Reconnaissance, Anti sub, Air-sea Rescue, and Dumbo missions.

Bill took over as PPC in August of '45, after Lt. Jones left for home ... and while we haven't all the particulars (Bill lost his Log Book, too), he remembers being sent from Peleliu with sealed orders to report to General MacArthur at his headquarters on Leyte.

Upon landing, Lt. Rider was confronted by a young army officer who came angrily running up to him, waving frantically as he was disembarking.

"Get this goddamn plane outta here!" the red-faced Lieutenant yelled.

"I've orders to report to General MacArthur," drawled Rider.

The red-faced lieutenant shot back: "Well, give me those goddamn orders and get this Navy plane outta here!"

"Negative, Lieutenant!" replied Rider. "I've orders to report to the general, and that's what I'm gonna do!"

Turning to one of his men, the disgruntled officer ordered, "Bulldoze the damned thing off the runway!"

Rider looked up to Plane Captain Freddie Zaugg, who was leaning on the .50 caliber in the port blister. "Freddie, man the .50 ... if one of these bastards tries to move this plane, shoot 'em! I'm gonna find the general!"

Looking back to his men, the young lieutenant threw up his hands, withdrew his order, and ran after Rider, who was then heading for MacArthur's HQ. Finding the Quonset hut by the many officers milling about, the PBY pilot was soon being escorted by the flustered Army officer into the general's headquarters.

There, among the many sharply attired staff officers, Rider was suddenly confronted by an immaculately dressed and precisely pressed ramrod figure of a general—pipe clenched tightly in his mouth. Sizing up the the shabbily dressed Navy pilot in front of him, the general frowned disapprovingly and growled: "Who the hell are you and why are you out of uniform?!"

"Sorry, sir, I had to dump my gear overboard on an aborted mission, and all I've got are these CB greens."

Agitated, the general took the corn cob pipe from his mouth, angrily articulating, "Don't you know you're supposed to salute an officer!"

"In the Navy, we don't salute while uncovered, sir," replied Rider, cap in hand.

CHAPTER **21** *Peleliu*   213

"Where's your insignia? How can you command men?" barked the general.

"We're a small crew, sir ... my men know I'm in command! That's what matters, sir."

"Give me those orders!" said the general, snapping open the envelope.

Lt. Rider's mission was to pick up a couple of P-38 pilots downed in an enemy-held shoreline jungle in the Philippines. He was to fly over a designated spot where the downed pilots would then flash green lights signaling an O.K. to land—or red lights to warn the plane off.

After a couple of runs over the next three days, Rider was given the green light. He made a water landing, picked up the stranded pilots, and after dropping them off, returned to Peleliu. He never saw the general again.

When first contacted by me, Bill Rider was asked what he did when he got home from the war. A man of few words, he replied in his distinctively slow and easy Texan drawl: "Well, Don ... I bought me a bank ... and settled down in Ennis, Texas ... where I've been ever since!"

Bill's had his full share of health problems, but he still enjoys hunting with his two sons, and regularly goes into town to play dominoes with his friends. He's got many more stories yet to tell. (He flew into Iwo on D-day-4, swapped stories with Henry Fonda, and remembers Carol Landis!)

ooo

At fourteen minutes after midnight, on July 30, 1945, the heavy cruiser *Indianapolis* was torpedoed in the South Pacific by a Japanese submarine.

Within twelve minutes, in an inferno of choking smoke and blazing fury, she sank. Hundreds of men went overboard, most without life rafts or any means of survival except gray kapok life jackets which the Navy required each to wear. No distress message got out, and by some cruel turn of fate and error the Navy was totally unaware of the calamity. Of the crew of 1,196 men, 800 went over the side, with only their life jackets. Of the 800, only 316 of those men survived.

On August 2 a Ventura land-based patrol plane piloted by Lt. Wilbur Gwinn sighted some survivors. It could not land. To make matters worse, its radio antenna had tangled and fouled. The message sent, though garbled, did indicate a life raft had been spotted.

A second plane, a huge Martin Mariner, arrived a little after noon. Having lost several seaplanes in futile attempts at open sea landings, CINCPAC had issued orders prohibiting such landings, and instead required calling in surface vessels. The Mariner dropped three life rafts and then proceeded west to the Philippines. Then a Catalina PBY amphibious patrol plane from the VPB-23 detachment on Peleiu was sent out to investigate. What Lt.(jg) Adrian Marks found was the greatest naval disaster in American history!

Quickly sizing up the situation, the lieutenant ignored standing orders and successfully landed to pick up fifty-six survivors. Though later forced to sacrifice his airplane damaged in the rescue effort, he succeeded in calling in ships from the Western Pacific to complete the rescue of the 316 men who had survived a four-and-a-half-day swim. (Of the *Indianapolis* crew, 980 perished.)

The survivors of this tragedy meet every five years in the city of Indianapolis.

One year a VPB-23 rescuer in Marks' crew, Donald Hall, attended the ceremonies. Lt. Cmdr. Adrian Marks had returned home to Frankfort, Indiana, after the war to become a successful attorney. Until he was hospitalized in 1994, Marks addressed the survivors and many other *Indianapolis* groups over the years with the following speech:

I'VE SEEN GREATNESS!
By Adrian Marks
Addressing a group of *Indianapolis* survivors

I met you men 40 years ago—on a sparkling, sun swept afternoon of horror. I have known you through a balmy tropic night of fear. I will never forget you. But the memories which surface in my retrospection are not of horror, blackness, or fear, but of things as small as honor, courage, and simple honesty.

Small, yet so great, that they form the cornerstone of our society. I am humbled by thought that I have seen true greatness in my time.

The computer alongside my desk is a never-ending source of astounding revelations. These miracles I have come to accept and even understand. But there is a miracle, which is beyond all my powers of understanding. It is a miracle that you are here today.

In training, I flew many air-sea rescue missions searching for men

CHAPTER 21 *Peleliu*

deliberately placed out in the water to test various survival techniques. It was axiomatic that you could never find a lone man floating in the ocean. He might be seen only if he had some sort of survival aid.

The best aid was a mirror. A mirror catching the sun and flashing in the pilot's eye. So too, were dye markers to color the water, or bright yellow life rafts.

But you survivors had none of these aids ... and were simply out there, unknown and unmissed, floating in dull gray lifejackets. A man's head is but six inches tall. A pilot flying a search mission at ten thousand feet, as Wilbur Gwinn, was looking down an angle at the water about four miles ahead ... and a span of vision about five miles.

I turn on my computer and find that there are 6,080 ft. in a nautical mile. There are thirty-six million, nine hundred and sixty-six thousand, four hundred square feet in one square mile. Three quarters of a billion feet in one twenty-square-mile glance!

A floating man will occupy less than one square foot of that space. A search mission went out 600 miles to make a visual search of ten miles on each side of this track. A radar search, as Wilbur Gwinn was making, would be much wider.

I type these figures into my computer: 600 miles by 20 miles, 12,000 square miles on each pass—it would take 5 passes to visually search a 100-mile wide strip. A pilot and air crew normally looking out at an angle of water searching for ships and the sky for aircraft won't see a man swimming in the water unless he happens to look right straight down on him.

Straight down on one of you? Not a chance in a million. I know most of you prayed a lot; and that made some of you feel that it made a difference.

Wilbur Gwinn is a wonderful man—a fine pilot. He never said he heard a voice speak to him—but was there an unseen hand on his shoulder? Did he find you by pure chance? The odds against it are one in a million—nay, one in a billion.

But somehow Wilbur Gwinn did look down ... at that split second that would become one of the great moments in history. Any sensible person knows that no one can swim for four and a half days—and yet you did.

For forty years, I have reflected upon the blind courage and the unbelievable greatness of spirit that I saw when each survivor was brought aboard my plane. I have been compelled by that sight to believe in miracles.

But I am digressing—let me share my memories. I am sitting in the wardroom of the USS *Doyle*. It is all over, and we're heading back to Peleliu. Over the wardroom transom, the bravest man I ever knew was crying. Between sobs he talks, in a voice so hoarse from exposure that it croaks, rasps, and it breaks.

The voice was Lt. Cdr. Lewis L. Haynes, senior medical officer aboard the USS *Indianapolis*. Awakened after too few hours of sleep ... and with a sudden release of emotion and nervous tension the Captain is off on a talking jag. Though asked to rest, he will not be stilled. Exhausted, dehydrated, sleepless and shaking with fever, he strains to talk.

"Why didn't they know we were missing? Why weren't they looking for us? Why? Why? Why?" the voice rasped on. I listened but could not answer him ... I still can't today.

He continued: "I have known some monumental foul-ups in the Navy ... cases of mistakes, of negligence, of equipment and communication failures; but what malevolent fate caused all to befall on one ship at one time."

It was the next day and I was again sitting in the warm ward room of the *Doyle* feeling the throb of the screws pushing us back to Peleliu. Down in the crew's compartment, the fifty-six survivors from my plane, together with thirty-seven more the USS *Doyle*'s crew had fished out of water, were being tenderly cared for. Every member of the ship's company had become a hospital corpsman primarily responsible for the survivor occupying his bunk.

Each sat beside his patient, bathed him, brought him water, kept a doctor's alert and felt the satisfaction of seeing the transformation a few hours of water, rest, and care could bring.

In the wardroom we had our survivor, too. Before Dr. Haynes awoke, I was writing my official report, reviewing with my co-pilots the fateful decisions made. I felt that most of them were right. Though we had broken radio silence, we had stirred up action. We had landed in open sea violating orders, but the landing was a success. We had destroyed our aircraft; but no one would question its expenditure.

But other decisions would continue to haunt me.

Upon landing, we realized that we couldn't rescue everyone. There were heartbreaking decisions made as we were forced to pick and choose among survivors! We saw the clustered groups of ten or more men, clinging together. But outside these groups were many lone swimmers floating in their life jackets. Most were seemingly alive, others obviously dead, including those whom we had seen molested by sharks.

I decided the men in groups had the best chance of survival, as they could splash and scare away the sharks and provide group moral support and encouragement. But single swimmers alone in the water were most likely to succumb to the despair of the night. I therefore decided that we would concentrate on picking up the single swimmers.

But now back in the wardroom I realized the full gravity of the men's condition, and was beginning to doubt the wisdom of my decision. Could I ever be forgiven for passing any of these men by? Dr. Haynes had been with one of the largest groups of survivors. They had no raft, but the doctor had organized them to look after one another and day after day had administered the injured, the demented, and the dying.

Finally after four long days of torment, he had seen my airplane slowly taxiing toward him. As we approached, he and his fellows had waved, screamed, and cheered; we waved back in recognition but deliberately passed them by.

To them it was simply incomprehensible. They shouted, shook their fists and wept tears of black despair as they were left to shiver yet through a fifth night until the near morning, when found by the *Doyle*.

Now, as I listened to the Doctor's recount of the horrors experienced, my decision to pick up the lone swimmers first weighed heavily upon me—had I been wrong? True, we rescued fifty-six men, but darkness stopped our rescue operation, and there was still room on our plane's broad wing. Had I gone after the groups, would I have been able to take on more men in the time available?

I realized how bitter his disappointment must have been to see the plane deliberately taxi away. Explaining my decision to the Doctor, I asked him if I had made a horrible error—should I have taken his men aboard? In a voice that was scarcely more than a whisper, he looked at me and rasped, "Lieutenant, you were right! You did right to pass us by!"

His answer showed the magnitude of character and courage summoned forth in times of crisis.

My co-pilot and I taxied the plane, while Navigator Ensign Morgan Hensley was in charge of fishing out survivors from the water. As we approached each man, a life ring with a line attached was thrown out. The men grabbed the ring and thusly were hauled aboard.

One of the survivors slipped out of his life jacket as we threw him the ring. Knowing that if we missed him in passing, he wouldn't have the strength for a second try, Morgan reached down from the Port Blister, grabbed the man under the armpits, and then straightened in such a way as to enable him to lift the man out of the water and pitched him over his head into the airplane.

Morgan later said he didn't know where he got the extra strength to do it.

But then, I don't know what gave those men in the water that extra strength to swim for four and a half days either.

Our plane carried but four water containers containing four and a half gallons each. As each survivor came aboard, he was given a half a cup of water each, then minutes later, when his stomach was settled, he was given another half cup.

Afterwards they usually collapsed into a deep sleep, periodically waking to cry out of thirst.

The old PBY soon filled to capacity, two men to each bunk. We tried to sit them on the floor but they would collapse and soon pile on top of one another. It was impossible to walk through the airplane as more and more survivors were brought aboard.

I shut down the engines and we started to haul men out on the wings. They were too exhausted to help themselves, and trying to pass these badly burned men up to the wing and keep balance on the bobbing plane was sometimes a dreadfully painful maneuver. The wing, while broad enough, had a decided slant to the stern requiring each man be secured with a piece of parachute shroud to prevent him from sliding off.

The darkness came quickly in the tropics, and we streamed a sea anchor from the bow and drifted. I had hoped to use our landing lights and Aldis lamp to continue the search, but found the plan to be impractical. The little water left was passed up in a kettle and we groped our way in the darkness, giving each man a sip or two more. The method was slow, requiring many attempts.

But as we passed these exhausted and dehydrated survivors in the darkness, voice after voice would say "I've had mine" which would enable us to find the next crewmate who hadn't. A measure of supreme character was evident as each man, though still burning of thirst, asked for nor no one took an extra ration! Such conduct is not indoctrinated through military training. It is learned at an early age—-in Sunday School and in a home where honesty is a way of life.

In an operation where so many things went wrong, where so many people didn't get the word, or if they did, failed to respond, the perception of Lt. Cdr. W. Graham Clayton CO of the USS *Doyle*, was a shining exception. Steaming to the scene a hundred miles away, he intercepted a conversation between me and the Ventura search plane. Sensing the desperation of the men in the water, he threw away caution against enemy submarines in the area, to light up the night sky with the *Doyle*'s big twenty-four-inch searchlight! Pointing it straight up to reflect off clouds two thousand feet up, it offered a beacon of hope that help was on the way and summon the last ounce of courage of helpless survivors to hang on a just little longer in night's darkness.

I'll never forget sighting that first light in the sky. How dark the night without moon or stars obscured by clouds. We had dispensed the last drop of water, and the wind was whipping up a chilling cold. Scores of badly injured men stacked in the fuselage and ranged far out on the wings were softly crying with thirst and pain ... and then there was that light!

Look! See the light! The destroyer is on the way! There's water and doctors and rescue coming soon! Turning on that light took that measure of character ... and the measure of courage proved proudly true of the Navy that night!

I've seen greatness in my time. Not of some political leader or popular hero, but the greatness of an entire crew of a great ship. And while that crew will always be something special to me, I know that it was drawn at random from all the servicemen in our country. I've seen the greatness of America!

That morning following our rescue, I climbed to the destroyer's bridge and with a swift salute, requested my Catalina be destroyed by gunfire. She had done her job well.

Lyle Pasquet reported for duty aboard the USS *Indianapolis* sixteen days before it was torpedoed! He spent some 104 hours in the water before being rescued. An honored guest of VP/VPB-23's 2nd Reunion in Minneapolis, the aircrew vets of VP-23 warmly adopted this wonderful man, whom we hope to see and hear more from.

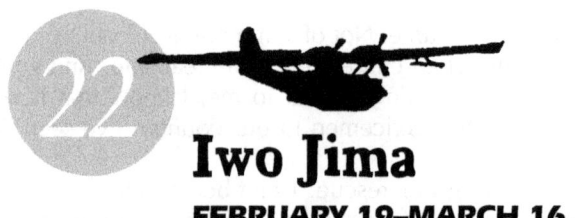

22

Iwo Jima

FEBRUARY 19–MARCH 16, 1945

VPB-23 detachment on Iwo Jima, Nanpo Shoto.

At Iwo Jima on March 6–April 16: CMDR Stevens, Larson, Decker, Crook, Phillips, Scholze, Bentley, Barnhill, Baltz, Colvin, McQuiddy, Reeves, Smith, Bartow, Murphy, and Brayton.

The squadron participated in patrol and search-and-rescue missions out of Saipan, Guam, and Peleliu, and on D-Day+9 he flew in a three-plane detachment to Iwo Jima.

Capt. Robin Larson writes of his Iwo experience:

> It was my first real taste of war on the ground. We were told to "dig in" to foxholes and spend the night there. We dug and dug but the volcano ash didn't hold up and so we slept on top of it.
>
> That night a large number of Air Force pilots and aircrewmen were killed when a Japanese group tunneled into their detachment. The same night a Japanese missile of some type exploded and I still have the piece that wound up in my plane.
>
> I say again, that we Navy pilots do not really know what war on the ground is about.

"Moose" Van Matre, ARM3/C, a radioman in Lt. Art McQuiddy's crew, remembers:

> Lt. McQuiddy volunteered us to go to Iwo—as he had volunteered

CHAPTER **22** *Iwo Jima* 221

us for everything else. Signorelli, an ordnanceman in our crew, refused to go—as did another AOM. Maybe they were smart to do so. Our crew had to "dig themselves in" on airstrip with Japs sneaking all about and mortars exploding. Not too far away from us, Japs did get through, slitting the throats of a few P-51 pilots before being dispensed with.

My first night on Iwo, someone else had dug my foxhole to sleep in, and a rock was in my ribs all night. The next morning I dug it out and it wasn't a rock ... but an elbow of a Marine or Jap!

We played poker every night on Iwo ... we were too scared to sleep but no one would admit it.

LCDR Clyde Reedy ('44-'45) had this memory:

Harold Marks, Pitts, Tanzman and myself were assigned to VPB-23 for the Iwo Jima run. Attached to the Seaplane Tender *Chincoteague*, we spent a difficult night or two on the wing of one of our planes.

We were tied up to a buoy, just below Mt. Suribachi, and the Japs would send an occasional mortar our way. One night without telling us, the Navy command sent the USS *Pennsylvania* and *Pensacola* in behind our ship. (We were aboard our PBY tied at buoy.) Asleep on the wing, I woke up as the first shot went whistling over our heads and realized I was but six inches off the wing. Pulling myself back, I joined the others in watching the ships pump a helluva lot of shells into the side of that mountain, trying to still the mortar and machine gun fire that the Japs were shooting at the Marines on the beach.

We could actually see the spin of the shells as they went over our heads.

John Fijol, ARM2/C in Lieutenant Mykland's crew, remembers:

We arrived on Iwo Jima on April 8, 1945, from Saipan. We landed near Mt. Suribachi, the only airstrip at the time. The first few days I was sick from the stench of dead bodies which were piled up in heaps. A few days later bulldozers dug deeply into the volcanic dirt, shoved the dead Jap bodies in, and covered them up.

Some of the Marines were still mopping up at the far end of the island. The Japs were forever coming out of the deep caves looking for food and fighting to the bitter end. The first few days we were there, we had to find the tent which contained Army K rations to eat. About three days later we received a hot cup filled with what they called coffee. The water was undrinkable. It was hot but had a strong sulfuric [taste]. We had a blister bag in the tent area from which you were allowed to fill up your canteen once a day with water to brush your teeth and take a short drink. We slept in tents, the days were comfortable and the nights were cold.

Everyone with the squadron was issued a .38-caliber pistol and it had to be carried at all times. At the entrance to our tent we had to step over a 500-pound bomb that had been dropped by an American plane that had never gone off. The first few days were scary because we had to step over the bomb, fearing it may go off if we hit it somehow.

In a few days it was business as usual. We flew air-sea rescue missions covering the B-29s on air strikes to Tokyo, Honshu, Osaka, Nagoya, and Kobe. The P-61 Black Widow, P51 Mustangs, and the P38 Lightnings from the Army Air Corps were based with us on Iwo Jima. They flew escort for the B-29s also on the above mentioned strikes.

The Navy Seabees did miracles with their hard work. They built a second airstrip to accommodate emergency landings for the B-29s and other planes shot up over enemy territory who could not make it safely to Guam or Saipan.

They erected hundreds of tents for us to sleep in and latrines so we no longer had to use the pipe with the big funnel (so we wouldn't miss the target). They also built Quonset huts ... and then the Seabees did what the Japs said was impossible. They built a road to the top of Mt. Suribachi, never realizing that the Japs still were holed up in their caves! During the month of April we received the sad news over the loud speaker that President Franklin D. Roosevelt died. We were all saddened by that announcement.

On May 11 we got called back from a Kyushi air strike because the weather got bad. It took five approaches to find the airstrip because of the heavy fog and heavy rain.

On June 2, Lt. Mykland's crew and Lt. Mann's crew took off a few minutes apart to cover a Tokyo raid, and we were also alerted to a Jap submarine that was spotted near Iwo. It was a 10-hour flight for us and when we returned we were informed that Lt. Mann's crew was missing.

June 3—A severe thunderstorm hit Iwo Jima.

June 4—We searched for Lt. Mann's crew.

June 18—We left Iwo Jima and returned to Saipan.

June 27—Left Saipan to take up residence at Ulithi.

June 28—Flew a night patrol; during the flight the fuse panel began to smoke. Eddie Allen, our first radioman, pulled the fuse out of the panel as it caught fire. Ensign Peter D. Molthop, our navigator, put out the fire with a fire extinguisher.

We returned to base with our electrical system completely out, and as base put flares and runway lights on to light the runway, Lt. Mykland made a beautiful landing without any real problem.

August 3—We flew a 6-hour patrol searching for survivors of the

USS *Indianapolis*. Lt. Adrian Marks' crew rescued 56 survivors. During the night they were all picked up by the USS *Doyle*, a destroyer, and taken to Guam. The next day our squadron CO, Max Ricketts, and his crew picked up nine survivors.

August 15—President Truman announced Japan's surrender.

August 22—Left Ulithi, went to Guam. During the month of August our great skipper Lt. Mykland promoted to Lt. Cdr. We were all happy for him.

August 25—LTCMDR was informed that Admiral Halsey had chosen him to fly to Tokyo Bay to fly the surrender documents from the USS *Missouri* to Iwo Jima. An Army pilot chosen by General Douglas MacArthur damaged the floats on his during a practice landing in Tokyo a few days previously.

August 26—We flew from Guam to Iwo Jima The Army replaced the marines and was conducting a tour of the caves on the far end of the island, when we landed. We joined a group of soldiers and went into the entrance of a large cave and what we saw was unbelievable. The cave was about a half a mile long, large rooms with radio equipment in some of the rooms. Large bottles of saki and other drinks. It was unbelievable that hundreds of Japanese soldiers were there and we didn't know such large caves existed.

August 28—We flew to Tokyo to familiarize with the route LTCMDR Mykland was to fly and where to pick up the documents.

September 2—Flew to Tokyo Bay and picked up 250 pounds of press material and surrender documents from a dock alongside the USS *Missouri* which was anchored nearby. There was a huge crowd gathered there with news photographers taking newsreels. After being airborne after a difficult take-off, Admiral Halsey contacted Lt. Cmdr. Mykland to fly over Tokyo and witness devastation that the Army, Navy, and Marine pilots had done. Tokyo was in complete ruins. After circling Tokyo, we flew back to where the documents were transferred to a waiting B-29, which was to fly to Hawaii and then to Washington.

September 3—We flew back to Guam.

John Fijol was active in sports as a youth playing baseball, football, and basketball. He was scouted by the Boston Braves just before the war broke out. When Pearl Harbor was attacked, he was working at Curtiss-Wright Aircraft Co., building the P-40 fighter for the army. John further recalls:

> I had several 2B deferment because of working at Curtiss and it was time when the American youths were enlisting in record numbers to join

their favorite branch of service. I told my parents I was going to enlist in the Marines. My father encouraged me to join the Navy instead.

I enlisted in the Navy and left home October 29, 1942. I took my boot training at Sampson, NY. After completing boot training I was assigned to aviation radio school in Jacksonville, FL, then to aerial gunnery school in Yellow Water. After gunnery school we were assigned to San Diego. I met Eddie Allen on a troop train on the way to the West Coast. There was no air travel at that particular time. It was a five day trip to the West Coast!

The train made frequent stops all through the midwestern states and the people along the way were really great. At each stop we would be allowed to go out on the platform and stretch. The women and children would come out in large numbers with coffee, soda, pastry and candy. At that time the people in America showed great respect for the men in service.

Henry I. Aries, ARM2/C ('44-'45), a radioman in Lt. Mykland's crew:

Our three crew detachment arriving on Iwo came into possession of a Coleman Stove—the Marines who were dispensing had scrounging bread somewhere. Anyhow Eddie Allen, our 1st Radioman, was out drawing midnight small stores from a stacked pile of K-rations when a Jap jumped out and threw a grenade. He missed and Eddie emptied his carbine and .38 pistol—and would still be shooting the Jap had he not been stopped! Don't know who was more scared—Eddie or the poor Jap!

Eddie was from L.A. and a good friend of mine. I was always a bit jealous that they got to land and taxi up to the Battleship *Missouri* during surrender ceremonies!

At Iwo I remember you had to have a password to be out at night because Japs were still slitting tents and tossing in grenades, etc. The Marines were a little jumpy—like BANG!—"who goes?" We had to be on our toes. Also remember having to sleep in the plane as watch. Didn't sleep too well—must have been rough on the first crews arriving there.

When we weren't flying or watching B-29s make emergency landings, we had an "ongoing poker game" in our tent. The night before the typhoon hit, we were up late so Leroy Penton got disgusted and went to another tent to get some sleep. Anyway, I woke up to find someone shaking me to get up. Our tent was gone—and my shoes were full of water!

We ran down to the line and our plane had broken all the control blocks. Murphy, our plane captain, came up with a block and tackle and

CHAPTER 22 Iwo Jima

hooked it to the yoke and we kept the old boat on the ground! It was flying standing still!! There were lots of Army Air Force planes destroyed and wrecked ships all over.

Duty in the South Pacific was exciting. The weather for the most part was great for flying. The weather was just the opposite from what we had in the Aleutians, and we had a happy crew and a great pilot.

Lt. Clarence Mykland was great to all of us—and to this day, those of us who remain are forever grateful to him. It was a pleasure to serve with him.

In our tour of duty we were stationed on Saipan, Guam, Ulithi, and Iwo Jima. We flew bombing runs, particularly over Yap, and patrol duty when alerted that Jap subs were in the area. Also air-sea rescue covering B-29s when they returned from bombing various Japan targets.

Sgt. Jack Finn, an army photographer from Brooklyn, was on a good number of flights with us when we were on Iwo Jima. He really liked our crew and spent a lot of his time visiting with us in our tent area. We would kid him to get rid of his army uniform and we would outfit him with a Navy one, including a flight suit. I think if there was a chance, he would do so.

On the morning of June 2, 1945, prior to take-off, Lt. Mann's crew and Lt. Mykland's crew (my crew) had about a half hour wait at the airstrip on Iwo before we boarded our respective planes for take-off and we were all standing by and shooting the breeze.

Mann's Plane Captain Pat DeLoughary, AMM3/C, was from Detroit, Michigan. Others I knew in Mann's crew were: John Briggs, ARM2/C, from Oklahoma, with whom I went to radio school, and my best buddy, Mike Kubovchik, AMM2/C, from Cleveland, Ohio.

When I was on Saipan, many days were over the 100-degree mark and I picked up a skin rash. Every evening I had to go to sick bay and have it treated. It persisted to give me a problem even when we got to Iwo Jima. The weather on Iwo was much more comfortable than Saipan. The days were warm, around 70 degrees, and the nights were much cooler. In the evening when we went to the movies, we sat on long boards of lumber which rested on sand bags. Mike Kubovchik would save me a seat because I was always late. Every evening I had to report to sick bay and get the rash painted up.

We got the go-ahead and as we were boarding our respective planes to fly an air-sea rescue mission, we knew the B-29s were to fly a massive air strike over Tokyo, and we were also alerted that a Jap submarine had been spotted.

As Mike headed toward his plane, his last words to me were: "See you at the movies tonight, John. I'll save you a seat—and don't forget the poncho."

Our planes took off minutes apart, and we never heard from them again. Two days later, on June 4th, we flew a 10-hour search for Lt. Mann's crew, but without any luck. The day before we were hit on Iwo with a torrential rainstorm. That wouldn't have helped Mike and the crew.

Over fifty years later Jim Sawruk, a historian searching out status reports, noted that three of the crew members previously listed as "Presumed Dead" were as of February 20, 1947, listed as "Determined dead by enemy forces." Cause of the casualty listed only that the plane failed to return from air-sea rescue search.

The historian reports that records noted it was not due to enemy action and was almost certainly weather related. Location of the casualty was reported in the Nanpo Shoto area.

On August 3, 1945, we flew a similar search mission. This one lasted for seven hours as we searched for the survivors of the ill-fated USS *Indianapolis*.

One of our VP-23 Catalinas, piloted by Lt. Adrian Marks, made history by picking up 57 survivors from the torpedoed cruiser. In spite of orders to the contrary, Lt. Marks made an open sea landing to rescue survivors who had been in those those shark infested waters for five days after their ship had been sunk by a Japanese submarine.

Donald Hall, AMM2/C, was the plane captain in Lt. Marks' crew. Unable to attend our reunions because of health problems, he lives in Dayton, Ohio, and attends the USS *Indianapolis* reunions which is only an hour from his home. He was awarded an Air Medal pinned on him by LCDR Max Ricketts on Guam.

Regarding Mykland's spectacular takeoff in difficult waters from Tokyo Bay Harbor, with surrender film from the USS *Missouri*, there were no citations from Admiral Halsey. I honestly feel Mykland deserved one for his courage to turn that plane 180 degrees and take off practically by himself to get the plane airborne. (There are some dark secrets I have to share with you—there was very little co-operation from the co-pilot on that take-off—Myk did it himself!)

This is a recount of the air-sea rescue of the B-29 "Jackpot" crew, as reported by Sgt. Finis Saunders:

On March 20, 1945, approximately 160 miles north of Iwo Jima, a Catalina from your organization found an Army Air Force crew adrift in a very rough Pacific Ocean. I was a 19 year old radar operator on that crew. Also here today is Ernie Fairweather, who was CFC gunner on that crew. We are here some 55 years later to pay tribute to you for making our rescue possible. This had to be one of the greatest events in our lives and one which certainly we will always remember. We would like to tell you of the events leading up to this rescue as we recall them and have learned from others in our discussions over the years.

This bombing mission to Nagoya, Japan, was the 9th mission for our crew and our faithful B29 which was named Jack Pot. It was thought this name "Jack Pot" might somehow make our bomber harder to hit. On this particular mission it didn't seem to help. This was a low level night mission and we were carrying incendiary bombs.

As we started our bomb run up Nagoya Bay we were picked up by search lights, and anti-aircraft fire was intense. We lost our #3 engine to anti-aircraft fire just before bombs away. Since we were so close to the dropping point our pilot decided to carry on. Just as our bombs were away, our #2 engine was hit and caught fire.

A hole was blown in the left side of the fuselage, by the Navigator position, and some of the glass panels in the nose were shattered. Our #2 engine was shut down but continued to burn. With cowl flaps full open our pilot put the bomber in a diving turn. Luckily this blew the fire out. Fortunately for us, the searchlights and anti-aircraft fire was pulled off of us and redirected toward other incoming planes. We limped away on our two remaining engines.

Iwo Jima had not yet been declared secure, but the airfield was in our hands and emergency landings could be made there. We got no response from the radio in our attempts to tell someone of our problem. It, too, had been damaged by anti-aircraft fire. After flying several hours it became apparent that a third engine had been hit and was running out of oil. With the loss of this engine and only still running our pilot announced we would have to ditch. Ditch we did, in a very rough ocean at approximately 6 AM on March 19th.

Our airplane broke in two on impact with the water and remained afloat for no more than two or three minutes. We were all able to man rafts, which had been popped out and inflated just as they were intended to do. But for the skill of our pilot, copilot, and considerable help from God, none of us would have survived this crash landing.

Here we were in a very big and rough ocean, our airplane was gone, and we believed, because of our radio, no one knew of our problem. This proved not the case, since we learned later that our radio was transmitting but not receiving. This, too, was a blessing because we were being advised the ocean was too rough for ditching—and we should bail out! Had we done so, it's doubtful we could have survived.

The day was cloudy and sea very rough. Riding the waves was like riding a crest of water up a mountain, and then falling back into a hole with the water seeming to be pulling in all directions. We tied the two rafts together so we could not get separated, but we had some difficulty. The rough water kept tearing them apart. The waves were continually breaking over us and so we were bailing water most of the time. When night came we were wet and cold.

The next day dawned sunny and seemed to lift our spirits a bit. The sea was still very rough. Good news, at about three in the afternoon someone thought they heard an airplane. Sure enough, off to our east was a Navy PBY Catalina. Our pilot fired off a flare and immediately the Catalina turned toward us. What a feeling! What a beautiful airplane! We had been found and somehow things were going to be all right. The water was too rough for the catalina to land, but they did make several passes over us, dropping a sea marker dye and also some other supplies. Paddle as we would, we were not able to get any of the supplies. They just drifted away.

Finally they made a pass dropping a peanut can with a long white streamer which we were able to retrieve. Inside this can was a note saying a ship was on its way to rescue us; also on the note was a score of a ball game which had been played that day. As darkness approached the PBY dropped some more flares on the water near us. Later our PBY turned away and was leaving. What an awful feeling—until we saw another PBY approaching.

This one stayed with us and it, too, kept replacing the floating flares as needed. The only light we had was a one-cell flashlight. When the flares burned out our pilot would turn on this little light. The PBY would then drop more floating flares near us. We could not believe that the Catalina crew could see such a small light, but the system seemed to be working and we certainly did not want to mess it up, so we dutifully turned it on each time.

Well into the night, we were suddenly aware of this monstrous ship about to run us over, or so we thought. The ship with no lights was difficult to see. It was headed direct toward us and was already quite close. Our pilot grabbed the flare gun and shot off a flare.

We were being bounced around so by the rough watter that the flare didn't go straight up as intended but at an angle up through the rigging of the ship. This illuminated the ship as well as the many sailors who seemed to be hanging from everything and staring at us. A loud voice boomed over the PA system: "Cease Fire! Cease Fire!"

They knew exactly where we were and not about to run over us, but we didn't know they knew. The ship was a destroyer, the USS *Gattling*. Not a big ship, you say. Well, it sure looked big to us when compared to our little rubber life rafts where we had spent the last two days. We made another blunder a short time late while trying to retrieve the lines being thrown to us through the rough wind and water. After several unsuccessful attempts one of our crew yelled over, asking if they could get their boat a little close. A sailor yelled back, "What do you think we have, a row boat?" It's a wonder they just didn't turn around and leave us right there. We didn't know it was an insult to call a ship a boat.

Finally, we were able to grasp the rope and were pulled over close to the ship. The ship was rolling so badly that one minute its railing would be in the water and the next instant it seemed twenty feet in the air. Our attempts to grasp the net which hung down low over the side and climb up on board just didn't work. When the ship jerked upward we could not hang on and fell back into the water. We had been secured by rope so we could be pulled back to the ship each time.

This problem was solved by a sailor on each side grabbing us as the ship's rail came down to our level and heaving us on board one at a time. In my case a sailor grabbed me as I landed on deck, then walked me through darkness to what I later learned were Chief's quarters. What wonderful hosts they were, even after we had called their ship "a boat."

We had showers and some food. Their people stayed up so that we could sleep in their quarters. Our clothes were taken away while we slept and returned laundered and pressed.

The next morning we said goodbye—and expressed our sincere thanks as we were put ashore at Iwo Jima. As we walked on to the beach there was a newsreel crew taking our picture. Being all starched and pressed, I'm sure no one would have believed we had spent two days lost in a very rough ocean.

On Iwo we were able to meet and express our thanks to some of the Catalina people who found us. To me, it is unbelievable how well the various branches of service worked together in Air Sea Rescue and to what lengths they went to rescue survivors. This navy air crew had flown hundreds of miles looking just for us, one Army Air Force bomber crew of 10 men. The USS *Gatling* had been called off shelling of Iwo Jima and travelled 160 miles through enemy waters to pick us up and then return 160 miles to Iwo Jima. We do indeed live in a wonderful country. Thanks to the Navy and VPB-23 we survived this mission.

With a new airplane and under the guidance of our pilot Warren Shipp, we were to fly 18 more missions before the war ended. Today six of the men you helped rescue are still living. So, from the crew of the "JACK POT"—Thank you, VPB-23!

Ens. Clyde M. Reedy ('44-'45):

Howard Pitts, Herb Tanzman, and I are the only surviving members of our crew. (We can't find a trace of Keith Kummer, so assume he's passed on.) We lost several fellows late in the war north of Saipan. I have checked my data, mostly log book stuff, with Herb and Howard.

My mother had asked me to write down some material circa 1946, but at that time we were trying to erase most of it out of our memories. So I had a few notes written.

"There will come a day," she told me, "when you may want to read this to your grandchildren," was her way of manipulating me into writing some of this.

In October 1944 our PBY "Catalina" crew was assigned to Fleet Air Wing 6 stationed at NAS Whidbey Island, Oak Harbor, WA. Crew members were as follows: Lt.(jg) Robert Nicholas PPC; Ens. Alfred Johnson; Ens. Clyde Reedy; John L. McDonald AMM1/C—Crew Chief; Herbert M. Tanzman ARM3/C; Howard Pitts, AOM2/C; David L. Cox, ARM2/C.; and Keith Kummer, AMM3/C.

On December 20, '44, we flew PBY #44244 to NAS North Island via San Francisco. At North Island and from there to Kaneohe Bay, HI. After a simulated TransPac flight (a distance halfway between San Diego and Hawaii), we took off for the real thing on Jan. 12, '45 flying PBY 08133 to NAS Kaneohe Bay in 19.1 hours.

While based at Kaneohe, we did some routine training flights, including an overnight trip to Johnson Island. On Feb. 9th, we were assigned to VH-2, a unit of FAW-1 as a replacement crew. VH-2 was already based at Tanapag Harbor, Saipan, and flying PBY5s, assigned to do air-sea rescue work. Our crew was assigned routine patrol and air-sea rescue flights in and around the Marianna Islands, flying as far east as Truk. All of these flights could be considered routine with no enemy contact made nor air-sea rescue attempted.

Our crew was just settling in, and getting comfortable with one another when, on Feb. 12, 1945, we were detached from VH-2 and assigned to temporary duty to VPB-23. Sent to Guam, we boarded the USS *Chincoteague*, a seaplane tender that was part of the U.S. 5th fleet. The ship comprised a massive attack group heading for Iwo Jima, some 750 miles north of the Marianna Islands.

Arriving off Iwo Jima on Feb. 16th, "D-Day minus 3," we took up position off the southeastern point of the island, a few hundred yards from the foot of Mt. Suribachi. Our plane, PBY 46470, was at a buoy, in open waters just below the mountain. We made no flights during this, our first visit to Iwo Jima, remaining as a stand-by rescue plane and crew.

The *Chincoteague* remained in position from Feb. 16th until March 14, 1945, when the seaplane tender was dispatched to Guam and our crew was returned to Tanapag harbor still attached to VPB-23.

On March 21st our crew was ordered to fly PBY 46490 from Saipan to Iwo Jima landing on air strip #1 near the foot of Mt. Surabachi. We began to see action almost at once. On March 24th, we accompanied an Air Force P-51 fighter squadron on an attack aimed at the Bonin Islands.

CHAPTER 22 Iwo Jima   231

On March 28th while on routine patrol in the Bonin Island area we drew heavy AA fire from the Japs on Ha-Ha. Though our plane was rocked by the explosives we were not hit and returned to our base on Iwo Jima without further incident.

President Bush, then Ens. George Bush, did not fare out as well. A few days earlier he had been shot down and picked up by an on station submarine.

On March 31st, we were scrambled to Kita Iwo Jima, about 200 miles north of Iwo. ("Kita" in Japanese translates to "small" in English.) An Army Air Corps plane was shot down in the area just east of Kita Iwo Jima, approximately 200 yards from shore.

We flew around the north end of the mountainous island, to create an element of surprise. The P-61 night-fighter was still partially afloat. We sighted a small craft with five or six Japs on board, about halfway between the downed aircraft and the Island's shore. When our plane came into sight they reversed course and headed back to shore.

The 50 cal. mounted in the starboard blister was manned and as we drew on a line with the small craft, we commenced firing. The boat made for shore and the men raced for cover of the island. We believe that three or four japs were hit by our 50 calibers.

Radio contact with our base had been maintained and we were advised that a submarine in the area was proceeding at flank speed to pick up the downed pilot and sink the P-51. We were ordered to return to base.

In early April, still based on Iwo Jima, we conducted several flights to the Japanese homeland, accompanying Army Air Corps fighter squadrons or B-29 Superforts enroute to their targets. The much faster planes would leave us, to be accompanied by a large number of submarines stationed as pickets along the way.

On April 4th we again drew anti-aircraft fire, this time from Kita, Iwo Jima. And again from the same island on April 12th. Intelligence reports indicated the Japs on the tiny mountainous island were serving as lookouts, radioing the impending arrival of American aircraft to the homeland. The large number of Army Air Corps planes, and virtual elimination of any effective Japanese air power made the Kita, Iwo Jima operation almost a sham. Nevertheless, the Japs did their best at harassing them, inviting our air-sea rescue station to make a pass as the AAF planes went on to the Japanese mainland. While the enemy had good shots at us, indeed almost dead aim in a couple of cases, they were unable to hit us even once.

More routine patrol flights, without occurrence, took place between the 1st of April, the date of the Okinawa invasion, and the 19th of April, when we were detached from VPB-23 and returned to VH-2, landing our plane on Kobler Field Saipan. Our Black Cat Days were over—we went back to the PBYs painted blue.

23
Going Home

"There were no parades to welcome us..."

My original crew, the aircrew I had come out with from NAS North Island, had all been sent back to the States. Reassigned to Lt.(jg) Lewis Shepley's crew during the last month or so of the war, I was in one of the last crews to be relieved.

I had been out of the States some fourteen months! Flying out of seven Pacific Islands! And participating in some form or other in that many battles. We received stars for only two: Iwo Jima and Okinawa.

We packed our gear in a parachute bag, were handed our orders, and without any fanfare were flown back to Hawaii, put on an escort carrier with a few other squadron-mates, and returned to North Island, San Diego.

As we walked down the gangplank of the jeep carrier USS *Card*, I don't even remember a coffee and donut greeting, although I'm sure the USO provided some goodies on the way back. I heard there was a big blast back in Hawaii for some of the guys, but I missed it.

I remember going into San Diego with a few of my crewmates to celebrate soon afterwards. Wearing campaign ribbons and feeling like old salts, we swaggered into one of the many bars for a farewell drink before leaving our separate ways. I was immediately approached by two Navy shore patrolmen and asked to show my ID card. It was but a few short weeks from my twenty-first birthday—and of course, by Navy regulations, I was not of drinking age. My buddies attempted to plead in my defense, emphasizing we had just returned from the islands and were just saying a last good-bye. It was by now an old story. There had been hundreds of vets returning home before us and there was no compassion felt here. These stone-faced Shore Patrol sailors would not even allow me to sit there with a Coke!

I went outside to linger while the guys finished their beers. Afterwards, we talked and laughed a bit on the sidewalk in front of the bar. And, after shaking hands and giving friendly pokes, we waved our good-byes and I went back to base.

Clarence Cardoza, AOM1/C, remembers:

We went back on the jeep carrier—the USS *Card*. There were at least three other crews that made that trip. The people in our crew were: Tommy Green, Mech2/C; Richard Cameron, AMM1/C, crew chief; Stephen Cigich, ARM 1/C; Lewis Shepley Lt.(jg) PPC; Don Dutcher, Lt.(jg), first pilot; Clarence Cardoza, AOM1/C (AB); and of course you [Don Klotz].

There were two more ordnancemen whose names I do not remember. The relieved aircrewmen flew from Guam 1 Sept. 1945 in the PBY Baker 46465 (recorded in my flight log book).

1st day—Guam to Eniwetok; 2nd day—Eniwetok to Tarawa; 3rd day—Tarawa to Canton across the Equator; 4th day—Canton to Palmyra; 5th day—Had to lay over in Palmyra due to magneto problem; 6th day—Palmyra to Oahu. Bussed from Kaneohe to Pearl Harbor to board a jeep carrier, the USS *Card*.

Our original crew were: Clarence Cardoza, AOM2/C AB, flew with Pop Decker's crew; PPC Lt.(jg) Willis B. "Pop" Decker; Ens. Lewis Shepley; Ens. Don Dutcher; PC Richard Cameron, AMM2/C; Hollis Britt, AMM3/C; Robert Maupin, ARM3/C; Stephen Cigich, ARM2/C; and Donald Max Weaver, AOM3/C.

Fifty-three years later, Clarence Cardoza's wife, Lucia, wrote:

Clarence has no pictures from his boot camp days—and the only part of his dress uniform that he has is the blouse. Of course, that is now too small for him. The pants were commandeered by his daughter while she was in high school. At that time that type of trousers were a very hot thing for teenagers to have in their wardrobe, at least in this area of the country.

From the relocation center in San Diego, I was put through the necessary processing and paperwork, and eventually was sent off on a one-man detail by train back to the Great Lakes Naval Training Station, where it all started. There, after more Navy procedure, I was given $300 mustering-out pay, an honorable discharge from the Navy, and finally headed homeward to Chicago.

After flying in immense open sky over vast blue ocean and remote white coral pacific islands, returning home to Chicago brought me back to the crowded, noisy, and smoke-filled industrial complex I had left behind three years earlier. Returning to a small third-floor apartment on Kildare Avenue in a crowded west side sector of two- and three-family rental apartments brought the dark reality that while the world had changed drastically, little physical change had taken place in the neighborhood.

There was also little fanfare upon my arrival home. In fact, my mom and sisters were all out shopping, my brother was working, and as I had no key, I headed over to my grandmother's. Dad, separated from Mom, lived with my grandmother and after a nice visit I headed back just in time to greet my mom and sister Anna Mae arriving home with the groceries. There was the initial happy talk and interest in where I had been, but conversation of life and times and what was happening in Chicago soon prevailed. Each member of the family was looking in different directions. My brother was discharged from the Navy. My brothers-in-law were home. Bruce was back home from the Pacific; Jim was back from Okinawa. The war was over. There were jobs to go back to, homes to start, babies to be born—and a new world to aspire to.

Fate had timed it well. I had signed up at seventeen for a three-year hitch—a "kiddie cruise," the Navy called it. The war ended three years later. Had I signed on at eighteen, I would have had another three years to go before being discharged!

Anxious to get back into civilian life and make up for lost time, I had already done my paperwork for the GI Bill and enrolled in the Chicago Academy of Fine Arts. I was discharged from the Navy on a Friday and started school on the following Monday. The high road was out there—I was determined to take it!

(Left) *Donald Lewis Klotz (in ROTC uniform) left Austin High School in Chicago, Illinois, to join the United States Navy on January 18, 1943. Don would later be assigned to VPB-23 for duty in the South Pacific.* (Don Klotz Collection)

(Below) Radio School ARM/AR-6 Sec. F, N.A.T.T.C. Memphis, 1943. Don Klotz is at left end, middle row. (Don Klotz Collection)

Ordnance School, FAW14, Air Bomber Class. Three who went on to VPB-23: Art DelRey AOM3/C sitting sixth from left, Clarence Cardoza AOM2/C, crouching second from right, and Charles Chollet AOM3/C, sitting front row, third from right. (DelRey Collection)

(Clockwise from top left) *Awaiting assignment. Aircrewmen Eddie Allen, Harry Blenco, unknown, and Don Klotz in San Diego.* (Don Klotz Collection)

Don Klotz hitching to L.A. on famed Coastal Highway 101. (Don Klotz Collection)

Cover illustration by Don Klotz, S1/C ARM, appearing in base publication North Islander. *Don had already left for the South Pacific.* (Don Klotz Collection)

Don Klotz, S1/C ARM—Cartoonist for North Islander, *before shipping out.* (Don Klotz Collection)

(Clockwise from top left) *Lt. Cmdr. William M. Stevens at Squadron Headquarters on Saipan. In March of '44, "Skipper" Bill Stevens assumed command and reformed VPB-23 at North Island NAS. The squadron was soon deployed to the Central Pacific, participating in a string of island offenses, including Iwo Jima and Okinawa.* (Don Klotz Collection)

Harold Moehlman, AOM2/C (in Skipper's Crew), on the squadron's motor scooter at Eniwetok, wearing island attire. (H. Moehlman Collection)

Squadron headquarters. Quonset huts under palm trees built by "Seabees" (Navy construction battalion). (Don Klotz Collection)

The Foxhole Gang at Saipan, 1944. L-R, back row, VPB-23 pilots Phillips, Guthrie, Clark, and Decker; front row, McQuiddy, Barnhill, and Ben. (McQuiddy Collection)

(Top of page): *"Boardie" Jones' crew No. 9, Eniwetok, 1944.* (L-R, standing) William Booher, ARM2/C; Ens. Hubert Hearon, Navigator; Lt. W. Boardman Jones, PPC; Lt.(jg) William Rider, 1st pilot; and Capt. Fred Zaugg, AMM1/C; (kneeling) Robert Watson, AOM3/C; Art Hernandez, AOM2/C; Frank White, AMM2/C, and Don Klotz, ARM3/C. (Don Klotz Collection)

(Middle): *Baker-33 ready for takeoff.* (Don Klotz Collection)

(Bottom): *"Fran" Clifton's crew at Eniwetok, 1944:* (L-R, back row) First four unidentified, "Slim" Hallas, Burrough; (front row) David Parks, Francis Clifton, Bartow Brown. (Clifton Collection)

VPB-23 Aircrews on Midway. (Fetty Collection)

(Clockwise from top left) *Craig's crew at Eniwetok in undress uniform of the day. (L-R) Gene Brock, E. N. Shagnea, C. M. Westley, E. B. Craig and* (kneeling) *Joseph F. Maney.* (E. B. Craig Collection)

Francis Carbine, ARM3/C, with mascot, "Sack Time." (Don Klotz Collection)

Ens. Herbert Hearon, 1st pilot, at the controls. (Don Klotz Collection)

Ulithi atoll: Assembly area for Task Force 58 and operations for VPB-23 detachment. The limited size of the airstrip provided a challenge to pilots. (Don Klotz Collection)

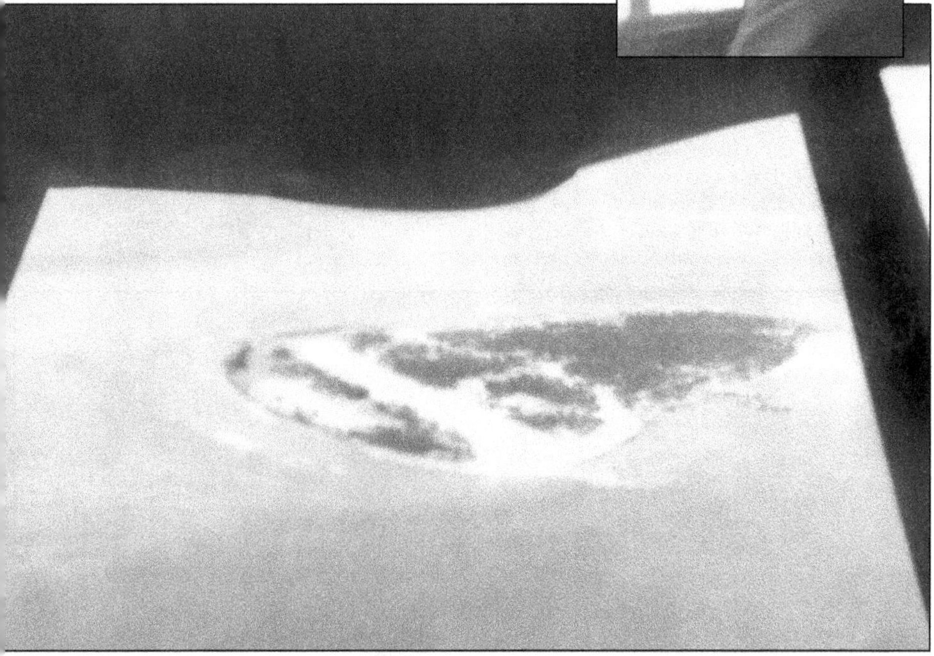

(Top left): *Home Sweet Home. Don Klotz outside underground revetments on Midway.* (Don Klotz Collection)
(Top right): *Showers at Eniwetok.* (Don Klotz Collection)
(Middle): *Squadron tents at Eniwetok.* (Don Klotz Collection)
(Below): *Chow line: Some "C" rations!* (P. Williams Collection)

(Top): *VPB-23 aircrewmen in personnel carrier on Eniwetok.* (L-R) *Kimbrough, Friddell, Midaugh, unknown, Cameron, unknown.* (P. Williams Collection)

(Right): *B-29s over Guam heading for Tokyo, 1945.* (Wise Collection)

(Above): *VPB-23 Skipper Bill Stevens pins medal on Lt. Phillips, Saipan.* (P. Williams Collection)

(Top) *Downed pilots spotted in open sea by Lt. Jones' crew VPB-23, who called in team destroyer to complete rescue.* (Don Klotz Collection)

(Below) *"Pop" Decker's crew—* (L-R, back row) *Ens. Don Dutcher, Navigator Hollis Britt ARM2/C, Ens. "Shep" Shepley, PPC Lt. "Pop" Decker;* (front row): *PC Clarence Cardoza AOM1/C, "Max" Weaver ARM2/C, R. Maupin ARM2/C, Steve Cigich ARM1/C, and Tommy Green AMM3/C. Accredited with sinking Japanese sub. Flew "command" PBY for U.S. Marine invasion of Fais Island.* (W. Decker Collection)

Now, Voyager! Ens. Wallace Douglas and Lt.(jg) Al Snedeker getting ready to set sail in homemade sailing rig made of airplane parts, salvaged materials and a little Yankee ingenuity. (Douglas Collection)

No, Voyager! A beautiful boat but most unseaworthy. Sad sailors after being towed back when bottom of boat rips against coral. (Douglas Collection)

(L-R, top photo, back row) *A. "Smitty" Smith ARM3/C, Charles Chollet ARM3/C, and unidentified;* (front row) *Clayton Dewhirst ACMM, and two unidentified.* (Dewhirst Collection)

(Middle left photo) *Gunner E. B. Craig AOM3/C on bow turret gun.* (E. B. Craig Collection)

(Middle right photo) *Cartoon for "Smitty" ARM3/C by Klotzie.* (Don Klotz Collection)

(Bottom left photo) *A dog's life on Guam.* (back row) *"Rocky" Cameron AMM2/C, E. "Murph" Pasquariello ARM3/C, Bob Watkins AOM2/C;* (front row) *unidentified, Tommy Green AMM3/C, F. "Whitey" White AMM2/C.* (Don Klotz Collection)

(Bottom, right) *Aircrewman Don Klotz on blister watch somewhere over the South Pacific.* (Don Klotz Collection)

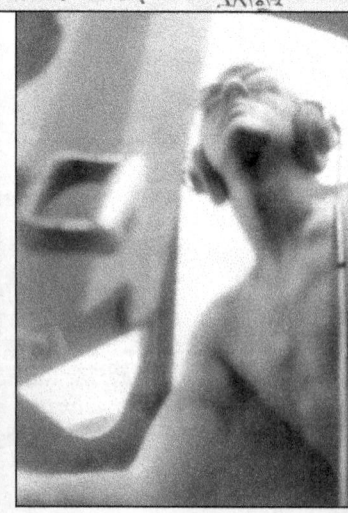

(Top left) *William "Boo" Booher, ARM2/C, at radio controls.* (Booher Collection)

(Top right) *Lt. Clarence Mykland and bride Barbara cut the wedding cake. The lieutenant would fly with VPB-23 on its last tour in the Pacific.* (Mykland Collection)

(Bottom) *VPB-23 aircrewman John Fijol, ARM2/C, with two native tribesmen in front of Quonset hut on Peleliu.* (J. Fijol Collection)

(Top left, L-R) *Tom Kimbrough AOM3/C, Ens. L. Crook, Walter Jakiela ARM2/C.* (Don Klotz Collection)

(Bottom left) *Bob Hope trouper Carol Landis entertains at a USO show in Eniwetok, October 1944.* (Fridell Collection)

(Middle right) *PBY bomber's wing over enemy shores.* (Snedeker Collection)

(Bottom right) *PBY on Saipan prepares for takeoff.* (Ricketts Collection)

(Top) *VPB-23 flight line.* (Wise Collection)
(Bottom) *"Red Beach" on Saipan.* (Aries Collection)

(Top) *Lt. Willis "Pop" Decker and Ens. Don Dutcher on Peleliu.* (Decker Collection)

(Middle) *Going home! Aircrew loading baggage for homeward flight.* (Douglas Collection)

(Right) *Captured Japanese air control tower on Saipan.* (Don Klotz Collection)

(Below) *VP-23 "Cats" on way to target.* (Snedeker Collection)

(Top) *VPB-23 contingent helping to erect tents on Iwo Jima.* (Douglas Collection)
(Middle) *VPB-23 tent area on Iwo Jima. Mt. Suribachi in background.* (Douglas Collection)
(Bottom) *Chow line at Iwo.* (Aries Collection)

(Top) *Lt. Adrian Marks* (front row, second from right) *and crew. They made an open-sea landing to rescue fifty-three survivors from the USS* Indianapolis. (D. Hall Collection)

(Middle) *Don Hall, ARM3/C in Lt. Adrian Marks' crew receiving citation at Peleliu.* (D. Hall Collection)

(Bottom) *Japanese fortification, Saipan.* (Don Klotz Collection)

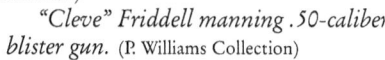

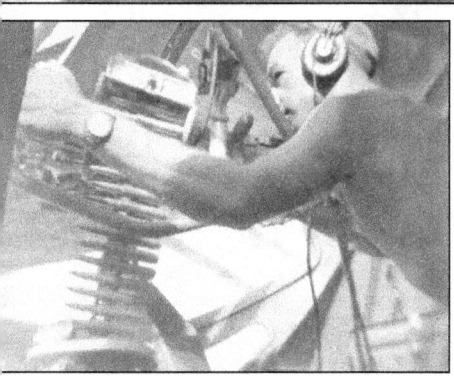

(Clockwise from above) *Lt. Marmon's crew.* (L-R, back row) *W. Murphy AMM2/C PC, Ens. James, Ens. Gurry, Lt. Marmon PPC, R. Cranston AMM2/C;* (front row) *L. Penton ARM3/C, H. Aries ARM3/C, W. Leird AOM3/C, J. Weir AMM2/C.* (H. Aries Collection)

Commander Ricketts, skipper of VPB-23 (center), *at Iwo Cemetery, with Lt. Frayer* (left) *and unidentified officer on right.* (Ricketts Collection)

3rd Marine Division Cemetery, Iwo Jima. (Aries Collection)

"Cleve" Friddell manning .50-caliber blister gun. (P. Williams Collection)

(Top) *VP/VPB-23 squadron detachment at Ulithi.*
(Ricketts Collection)

(Middle) *Lt. Clarence Mykland's crew:* (L-R, front row) *Ens. P. Molthop; J. Fijol, ARM2/C; Lt. Clarence Mykland, PPC; Lt.(jg) Flynn;* (back row) *A. Rabellino AOM3/C; W. Gibbons AMM2/C; I. Matthews AMM1/C, Edward Allen, ARM2/C, E. Allen ARM2/C; E. Gordon AOM2/C.*
(Fijol Collection)

(Bottom) *Receiving a "Well done" from Admiral Halsey for picking up surrender documents from USS* Missouri *for delivery stateside, Lt. Mykland was given permission to fly over devastated city of Tokyo before heading on.*
(Fijol Collection)

VPB-23 Squadron on Peleliu at citation ceremony for crews participating in search and rescue of survivors off the torpedoed USS Indianapolis. (D. Hall Collection)

VP/VPB-23

REUNITED
1941-1995

VP/VPB-23—1995 Reunion: L-R, front row, kneeling : *W. B. Jones, D. Klotz, P. Landry, C. Mykland, J. S. Layman, A. Medeas, A. DelRey, J. Jared, G. Friddell, R. Kottner, J. Watters, T. Benton.* Middle Row, L-R: *Unidentified, W. Ondrejcka, C. Horowitz, W. Decker, B. Geritz, S. Cigich, Unidentified, D. Weaver, R. Reed, H. Pitts, E. E. Laughlin;* back right: *L. Penton, A. Rabelino, H. Dickerson;* back row, *C. Chollet, C. Dewhirst, M. Offen, R. Charles, L. Shepley, D. Dutcher, L. Waslov, E. B. Craig, W. Douglas, C. Reedy, A. Wilkerson, P. Williams, B. Kelley, W. Moehman, C. Cardoza.* (Cardoza Collection)

24 The Reunion

"It was you and t'was me—in old Twenty Three—That flew those Black Cats ... to Pacific Victory!"

They had not met in over fifty years! Wearing new Navy blue and gold polo shirts and baseball hats designed for the occasion and embroidered with "WWII PBY VET" and "VP/VPB-23," they glanced about the Grant Hotel lobby looking for a comrade they once knew on some Pacific atoll over half a century ago.

Some made instant recognition as they came up to the hotel's registration desk; others, upon entering the "Squadron Headquarters" room. And still others would meet as strangers for the first time, for they had served in the same squadron but on another tour or on another island.

Their manner of approach was most always the same. These now gentle, white-haired men and their wives made their way through the hotel lobby, glancing about with a gingerly reticence, then a surprised animation upon recognizing an old comrade—followed by a jubilant cry of elation and outreaching embraces.

The historic coming together was truly an act of providence. It brought together this group of destiny's children in a common bond, reflecting a time, circumstance, and participation in one of our country's finest hours—and in proudest tribute to comrades who made the supreme sacrifice.

But it was so much more, for with the passage of time, each smiling weathered face, walking now with a senior's gait, gave witness to the great American tapestry—woven together on the edge of a millennium, and with their love and courage, sacrifice and perseverance, tragedy and triumph, reflected our nation's brightest colors in its greatest victory over the darkest struggle for freedom.

Greeted by the brightly colored, smiling-faced PBY cartoon poster in the main lobby, arrivals were directed to "Squadron Headquarters," a large and spacious room furnished comfortably with sofas, armchairs, tables, podium, video viewer, and flags. They came into this room truly as members of a family coming home and soon were drawn into events remembered so many years ago.

The Navy's cooperation played a vital role in bringing it all together through the great help received from the National Archives, Navy Historical Department, and the U.S. Naval Academy. An excerpt from an outgoing letter of thanks I wrote to the Navy reflects the wide scope of our singular event:

> On behalf of VP/VPB-23 Veterans Association, I convey our grateful appreciation and heartfelt thanks to the fine officers and enlisted personnel, men and women, serving the Department of Defense and Department of the Navy: CHINFO, COMNAVAIRPAC, CHC, NAVSTA, MCRD, U.S. MARINES, COMNAVBAS, NAS, NORTH ISLAND, NAVY/BAND SAN DIEGO, and The USS *KITTY HAWK* for their extraordinary efforts and participation in making our first VP/VPB-23 Squadron Reunion and Memorial Tribute held 2 Sept. '95 at NAS North Island and 3 Sept. '95 aboard the USS *Kitty Hawk* a big success!
>
> Thanks to the U.S. Navy and the DOD our first reunion was unanimously acclaimed one of the most memorable of our lives. The memorial services, reading of names, and wreath ceremony aboard the USS *Kitty Hawk* culminated a grand tribute to all of our comrades and a long healing overdue.
>
> Accompanying tours following the service gave all of us a feeling of great honor and proud history as well as a job well done by our contemporary counterparts now manning our first line of defense, in proud tradition of the U.S.Navy.

VP/VPB-23's historic reunion magic prevailed from the first arrivals as they gathered at the majestically beautiful U.S. Grant Hotel to the last toasts of farewell. Elegant ambiance, a welcoming warmth extended by a most cheerfully accommodating hotel staff, assured a happy reunion takeoff from the start.

CHAPTER **24**   *The Reunion*

A Farewell to Comrades

For it's Toasts up, and Floats up—and NAVY Anchors aweigh!
We're heading our sights towards good homeward bay
Having shared our great tales of a war time gone by.
We'll meet again next year... and again reason why,

It was you and t'was me—in old Twenty Three—
That flew those Black Cats... to Pacific Victory!

So ended the first World War II U.S. Navy VP/VPB 23 squadron reunion in over fifty years! More than sixty pilots, aircrewmen and their wives—some 120 in all—gathered in instant compatibility and warmest congeniality as they recognized and greeted former comrades with embraces, hugs, and tears. It was truly a great event. And to the many who were unable to attend, glasses were raised on high.

CHIEF OF NAVAL OPERATIONS

**A MESSAGE TO THE MEMBERS OF THE
VP/VPB-23 VETERANS ASSOCIATION**

Best wishes on the occasion of the VP/VPB-23 Veterans Association Reunion.

As you all know, Patrol Bombing Squadron 23 is a unit with a special place in Navy history. The first to make a mass flight of airplanes from the continental United States to the Hawaiian Islands, and the first to make a complete and accurate report of the Japanese fleet attacking Midway Island. The squadrons accomplishments were many, including countless bombing, search and reconnaissance, and "Dumbo" air/sea rescue missions from the many island bases that supported the unit throughout the war.

Although our ships and aircraft have changed over the years, one thing has not. That is the tremendous quality of our people. We owe much of our current success to you, the past members of VPB-23. The pride and dedication of Navy men and women on duty today reflects your many accomplishments. You have greatly enriched our Naval heritage.

This reunion is very important for another reason. Such gatherings ensure that we do not forget the service and sacrifices of our Navy veterans. On behalf of the men and women who proudly serve in the U.S. Navy today, please accept our thanks and best wishes. We salute you!

J. M. BOORDA
Admiral, U.S. Navy

2001 Reunion of VPB-23, under PBY at Aerospace Museum in San Diego. (L-R, standing): J. Jared, C. Chollet, H. Dickerson, A. Medeas, W. Decker, B. Geritz, C. Mykland, E. Gordon, J. Fijol, L. Penton, C. Horowitz, E. B. Craig, C. Dewhirst, R. Reed, B. Ondrejcka. (Kneeling): R. Brucksh, D. Klotz, B. Kelly, A. Smith, W. Douglas, A. Rabellino, A. Del Rey, D. Dutcher (sitting), and C. Cardoza. Missing from picture: G. Burkey, G. Blackman. (Cordoza Collection)

BLESS 'EM ALL

They say there's a squadron just leaving the States
Coming to be our relief....
The boys on the staff say, go pack up your gripes—
You're leaving September fifteenth!
But listen my lads, here's a warning to heed;
Ere starting too soon celebrate;
It's happened before, it can happen again—
Reliefs have been known to be late!

Bless 'Em All, Bless 'Em All ...
The long and the short and the tall—
Let's leave this commotion, this side of the ocean,
Go back to the States—Bless 'em all!

Our Planes are all bettered, they're old and they're worn,
But we wouldn't part with a damned one,
Our old PBYs they will see a man through—
And take him back home for some fun!
There is just one big trouble with sending us back
That trouble is easy to see;
They'll break up the gang which we'll never forget—
The gang in VP-Twenty Three!

Bless 'Em All, Bless 'Em All!
The long and the short and the tall;
Let's leave the commotion on this side of the ocean,
Go back to the girls—Bless 'em all!

We've mothered the Army, saved men from the deep
We even tried bombing Nauru;
We've sat in our foxholes, been shot at by Japs—
Now we'd like to get something that's new.
For over a year we have flown this big sea
Looking for enemy ships;
I've had it with water and glare of the sun
I want to start looking at hips (and have fun!)

Bless 'Em All, Bless 'Em All!
The long and the short and the tall;
Let's leave the commotion on this side of the ocean,
Go back to the girls—Bless 'em all!

Submitted by Robert Elberg
from *Hubers' Songbook*
(with a little change in words and tempo from Don Klotz).

Index

A
Abele, J., 99
Ady, Howard P. Jr., 9, 28, 29, 30, 43, 44, 47, 49, 51, 74
Aebischer, Bruce, 116, 163
AKA *Kenmore*, 185, 186
Akagi, 161
Allen, Eddie, 195, 222, 224, 237, 254
Anderson, J. R., 208
Andrews Sisters, 166
Aries, Henry, 224-226, 253

B
Baker, ———, ix
Baltz, ———, 206, 220
Barnhill, Whit, 157, 171-172, 192, 193, 206, 220, 238
Barthes, August A., 47, 49
Barton, ———192
Bartow, L. D., 208, 220
Bayler, W. L. J., 28, 30, 31
Bell, Marcus B., 201, 202
Bellinger, Patrick, 6, 7, 8-9, 10, 11, 12, 43, 44, 45
Ben, Frank, 71-72, 152, 157, 163, 238
Bennett, Clyde, 184-186, 187
Bentley, ———, 180, 193, 206, 220

Benton, Thomas, 59-62, 69-70, 98, 99, 258
Berens, Mr., 116, 123
Binkley, ———, 36
Blackman, Geoffrey "Blackie," 44, 263
Blenco, Harry, 146, 237
Bligh, Captain, 75
Bonner, Malcolm, 77
Booher, William "Boo," 148, 157, 173, 175, 176, 212, 239, 247
Boorda, J. M., 262
Booth, Mrs., 116, 123
Brady, ———, 47
Brady, A. P., 108
Brady, Norm, 59
Brandley, Frank "Buck," 46, 47, 66, 77, 89, 93, 131
Brayton, Lincoln, 211, 220
Briggs, John, 225
Britt, Hollis, 198, 203, 233, 244
Brock, Gene A., 168, 241
Brown, Albert L., 19
Brown, Bartow, 239
Brown, Bert, 70
Brown, Ed, 101
Brucksh, R., 192, 263
Buckner, Gen., 192

Bueler, A. R., 130-131
Burkey, Gale, 9, 17-18, 44, 107, 263
Burrough, ———, 239
Bush, George, 231

C

Cameron, "Rocky," 246
Cameron, Richard, 193, 203, 204-205, 233, 243
Carbine, Francis, 158, 241
Cardoza, Albert, 203
Cardoza, Clarence, 168, 170-171, 193, 198, 202, 203-205, 233-234, 236, 244, 258, 263
Cardoza, Jewel, 203
Cardoza, Lucia, 203, 233-234
Carmichael, ———, 173
Chamley, Howard, 73, 102, 103, 152, 157, 163, 174
Chaney, Howard, 152
Charles, R., 258
Chase, Bill, 13
Chase, W., 35, 48
Cheney, ———, 28, 31
Chennault, 4, 5
Chenowith, Ray, 184
Cheverton, M., 59, 68-69, 92, 97, 105
Child, ———, 50
Chittengen, ———, 108
Chollet, Charles C. "Chuck," 159, 168, 236, 246, 258, 263
Churchill, Winston, 5
Cigich, Stephen, 203, 233, 244, 258
Clark, ———, 69, 238
Clark, B., 99, 167
Clark, G. W., 163
Clayton, W. Graham, 218
Clifton, Francis, 90-91, 103, 149, 154, 163, 167, 171, 186, 191, 192, 211, 239
Colonna, Jerry, 166
Colvin, ———, 206, 220
Conlin, ———, 69
Corrigan, Jerry, 63
Cox, ———, 102
Cox, David L., 230
Cox, Mike, 57, 58

Craig, Elbert B., 167-170, 188-189, 241, 246, 258, 263
Craig, Robert, 188-189
Craig, Ted, 188-189
Crane, Roy, 167
Cranston, R., 253
Crocker, Albert M., 163, 220, 248
Crook, Leslie H., 184, 220, 248
"Cuccias," 128, 129
Cunningham, W. S., 27, 29

D

Day, Robert C., 149, 158, 173
Decker, Willis "Pop," 157, 163, 170, 171, 174, 192, 193, 198, 200, 201-202, 203, 204, 211, 220, 233, 238, 244, 250, 258, 263
DelRey, Art, 236, 258, 263
DeLoughary, Pat, 225
Denaree, ———, 61
Devereux, James P., 27, 29, 31
Dewhirst, Clayton "Dewey," 172, 173-174, 187, 246, 258, 263
Dicken, Neil, 184
Dickens, Tad, 82
Dickerson, Howard, 50-51, 62-63, 85, 86, 86-87, 258, 263
Diehl, Franklin, 157, 163, 171, 192
Douglas, Wallace, 94, 174, 210, 245, 258, 263
Doutt, Richard, 58-59
Duncan, Sherman L., 49
Dunn, A., 99
Dunn, S. M., 143
Dutcher, Don, 203, 233, 244, 250, 258, 263
Dwyer, ———, 192

E

Earnest, "Bucky," 12-13, 53, 55, 184
Eckel, Al, 71
Edge, Robert C., 207
Elberg, Robert, 72-73, 74, 76, 102, 264
Elrod, Hank, 31
Eniwetok, 162-177
Espiritu Santo, 78-88

F

Fairweather, Ernie, 226
Fijol, John, 195, 221-224, 247, 254, 263
Finn, Jack, 225
Fisher, Warren, 207
Fleming, ———, 62
Flint, V., 99, 101
Flynn, John, 195, 254
Fonda, Henry, 166, 211, 213
Ford, ———, 72
Ford, John, 45
Fox, Jack, 189
Franco, General, 4
Frantz, Charles, 157, 163, 172, 191
Frayer, ———, 253
Friddell, "Cleve," 243, 253, 258
Fuchs, Bernie, xi
Fujisawa, Mastaka, 70

G

Gamblin, ———, 158, 173
Garcia, Bebo "The Message," 68, 70, 72, 75, 89, 92, 94, 105, 131
Geritz, William J. "Sabu," 70, 71-72, 98, 99, 100, 105, 258, 263
Gibbons, W. J., 195, 254
Gibson, ———, 55
Gibson, P. L., 143
Girard, Bernie, 82
Goodlett, G., 99, 101
Gordon, Eddie, 195, 263
Gottsch, "Salty," 168
Gragg, ———, 34
Great Lakes Naval Training Station, 115-124
Green, Tommy, 198, 233, 244, 246
Greenlee, ———, 34
Guam, 190-198
Gurry, ———, 253
Guthrie, Keith, xi, 65-68, 163, 181-182, 208-210, 238
Gwinn, Wilbur, 213, 215

H

Hall, Donald, 214, 226, 252
Hallas, Taras "Slim," 40, 62, 239
Halsey, Adm. "Bull," 19, 21, 67, 76, 90, 97, 164, 195, 196, 223, 226, 254
Hamilton, ———, 28
Hamlin, Julia, 195
Hampy, Art, 28, 31, 55, 62
Hansom, James, 101
Hawkins, C. C., 209
Haynes, Lewis L., 216
Hearon, Harold, 148, 174, 212, 239, 241
Hecker, George A. 184
Hendee, David, 82
Hensley, Morgan, 217
Hernandez, Art, 149, 168, 239
Hill, Ed, 101
Hiryu, 161
Hitler, Adolph, 1, 5
Hoagland, Ken, 49-50, 54, 64, 99
Hofheins, Marion "Lee," 38, 61
Holden, Glen L., 49
Hood, Jeff, 80
Hoover, Vice Admiral, 166
Hope, Bob, 166, 248
Hopkins, G. T., 71, 101
Horowitz, C., 258, 263
Horstman, Herbert, 32
Hoverston, Morris, 66, 67, 68, 208
Hubbell, M. Chuck, 20-21, 38
Huber, Joe, 102, 166
Hughes, Bill, 101
Hughes, Massie, 6, 9, 12, 18-19, 29, 30, 43, 44, 45, 46, 47, 48, 49, 53, 54, 55

I

Imus, Charles I., 32
Isaacs, H. W., 71
Iwo Jima, 220-231

J

Jacobs, Richard W., 32-33
Jakiela, Walter, 248
James, ———, 253
Jamieson, William, 47
Jared, J., 258, 263
Jennings, Minuard, 45
Johnson, ———, 55
Johnson, Alfred, 230

Johnson, Lyndon, 66
Jones, Becky, 179
Jones, Chuck, 44
Jones, W. Boardman Jr., x, xi, 34, 35, 65, 73-76, 108, 109, 144-145, 147, 148, 149, 152, 153-154, 157, 159-160, 161, 163, 169, 174, 175, 178-179, 191, 211, 212, 239, 244, 258
Joy, Bernie, 102
June, Colonel, 202

K

Kaga, 161
Kai-shek, Chiang, 4, 5
Kaiser, ———, 185
Kaltenborn, H. V., 3, 23, 62
Kaneohe, 152-156
Keene, ———, 28
Kellam, Joe, 18, 59
Kelley, B., 258, 263
Kelso, ———, ix
Kennedy, John F., 91
Kimball, ———, 192
Kimbrough, Tom, 173, 243, 248
Klotz, Ann, x
Klotz, Anna Mae, 2, 23, 116, 150, 234
Klotz, Don, 113-124, 125-142, 145-149, 152-156, 157-166, 172, 175-177, 180, 182-184, 187, 197, 198, 212, 213, 232-234, 235, 237, 239, 242, 246, 258, 263, 264
Klotz, Genevieve, 1, 2, 23, 116
Klotz, Jack, 2
Klotz, Harry Adams, 130
Klotz, Mrs. Harry, 130
Knight, Harry, 38
Kocourek, Joseph B., 207
Kolb, H. C., 71
Kosich, John, 53, 55
Kottner, Ralph A., 168, 258
Kubovchik, Mike, 225, 226
Kummer, Keith, 229-230

L

Landis, Carole, 166, 213, 248
Landry, P., 38, 258
LaPlant, L., 34

Larsen, Carolyn, 161
Larsen, Tom, 161
Larson, Robin, 5-6, 43, 45, 54, 55, 144, 157, 163, 184, 185-186, 220
Laughlin, Elmer, 55, 101, 258
Layman, J. S., 258
Lee, ———, 38
Leik, Frank, 101
Leird, W., 253
Leonard, "Red," 57
Leonard, E., 99, 101, 102
Leonard, Ivan, 189
Lewis, Donald, 130
Lilian, Ed, 101
Linn, Walter, 87-88
Lough, Hal, 12, 37, 44, 46, 60, 61, 62
Luberti, H., 35

M

MacArthur, Douglas, 196, 198, 212, 223
Mahoney, John J., 204
Mamer, ———, 192
Mandgroc, Paul F., 71, 72
Maney, Joseph F., 168, 241
Mann, ———, 222, 225, 226
Marks, Adrian, 195-196, 197, 214-219, 223, 226, 252
Marks, Harold, 221
Marmon, ———, 253
Marshall, Chester, 178
Maslanksi, ———, 35
Mason, ———, 108
Matsen, Axel E., 181
Matthews, Irwin, 195
Matthews, L., 254
Mauldin, Bill, 147
Maupin, Robert, 173, 198, 203, 233, 244
McBride, Jerry, 36, 103, 106
McCain, ———, 59
McCarthy, Charles, 77
McClinton, Rudy, 73
McCoy, Clyde, 129
McDonald, John L., 230
McFadden, J. F., 201
McGarry, Jack, 35

McGee, "Gunner" Tony, 101
McKelven, ——, 44
McKeon, Thomas J., 163, 168
McQuiddy, Arthur, 46, 99, 143, 152, 157, 163, 166, 180-181, 192-193, 204, 206, 207, 220-221, 238
Medeas, A., 258, 263
Middaugh, Glen E., 168, 243
Midway, 43-51, 157-161
Miller, Romayne, 176-177
Miller, Roy A., 184
Miller, Stuart "Chippy," 175-177
Mitchner, ——, 165
Moehlman, Harold, 184, 192, 238, 258
Molthop, Peter D., 195, 222, 254
Mooney, Jim, xi
Moore, Baxter, 35, 44, 53
Moore, Jack, 101
Morrison, Jim, xi
Morrison, Samuel Elliot, 203
Mulroy, Thomas, 91
Murphy, James "Murph," 28-29, 30, 43, 44, 47, 55, 56, 74, 211, 220, 224
Murphy, W., 253
Murrow, Edward R., 3, 23
Mykland, Barbara, 195, 247
Mykland, Clarence, 21, 194-196, 198, 221, 222, 223, 224, 225, 226, 247, 254, 258, 263

N
Nafstad, J. E., 179, 191
Naval Air Gunners School, Hollywood (FL), 132-135
Naval Air Technical Training Center, 125-131
Newell, Dick "King," 133, 135
Nicholas, Robert, 230
Nichols, Horace E. "Nick," 44-47, 53
Nimitz, Adm. Chester, 58, 69, 143, 166, 180, 192
Nixon, Richard, 72

O
O'Dowd, ——, 44
Obee, Don, 133, 135
Offen, M., 258

Ogden, James, 7, 12, 44, 45, 47, 53, 54
Ogden, Mary, 7
Ondrejcka, B., 64, 258, 263
Operational Training Unit, Jacksonville (FL), 136-142
Osborne, Baxter, 82
Osborne, Clifford, 81, 82
Osborne, Harry, 81
Osborne, William, 78, 81-82, 104
Owens, ——, 173
Owre, Oscar T., 99, 152, 163, 175, 208, 209

P
Padaskowski, ——, 108
Parker, Julian, 19
Parks, David, 239
Pasquariello, Elmer "Murph," 170, 246
Pasquet, Lyle, 219
Pearl Harbor, 9-33
Pearson, Jim, 39, 49, 65, 78, 82, 104
Pederson, Ernest, 35
Peleliu, 206-219
Pennock, Glenn E., 7, 15-16, 17, 28, 30-32, 107
Penton, Leroy, 224, 253, 258, 263
Peoples, Bill, 189
Percival, Arthur E., 196
Perry, ——, 158
Peterson, Warren E., 39
Phillips, Bobo, 157
Phillips, Clyde B., 143, 163, 180, 192, 193, 206, 207, 220, 238, 243
Pierce, F. E., 210
Pierce, James, 77
Pindell, Clifford, 78, 104
Pipes, Barbara, 84
Pipes, John, 83-84
Pipes, William, 78, 83-84, 104
Pitts, Howard, 221, 229, 230, 258
Plank, Dormas "Doc," 91-93, 94, 102
Poenack, Harvey, 146
Polluszny, S. J., 210
Powers, Tyrone, 166
Powlison, Jim, 14
Powlison, Nani, 14-15

R
Rabellino, A., 195, 254, 258, 263
Ramsey, Logan, 6, 11, 45
Ramsey, Thomas W., 49
Rapley, Walt, 77
Rash, Richard S., 207
Rath, ———, 181
Redhage, R. J., 36, 60, 61, 71
Reed, R., 38, 258, 263
Reedy, Clyde, 176, 221, 229-232, 258
Reeves, ———, 180, 181, 193, 206, 220
Reister, "Pappy," 47, 53, 54
Rendal, ———, 107
Rich, C., 99
Rich, Merlin, 78, 82, 101, 104
Richards, K. F. Jr., 91
Richardson, James O., 8
Rickard, Glen, 19
Ricketts, Josephine, 188
Ricketts, Max, 187-188, 197, 223, 226, 253
Rider, Nancy, 211-213
Rider, William, 148, 179, 211-213, 239
Riepl, Edward "Rip," 38, 63, 64-65, 78, 80-81, 84-87, 104
Riepl, Helen, 97
Riepl, Jerry, 81, 87
Riepl, John Edward, 87
Riley, Francis C., 28, 29-30, 44, 53-54
Robinson, N. L., 71
Roche, Jim, 116
Rochester, Eddie, 35
Rodgers, John, 1
Roosevelt, Franklin Delano, 22, 24, 198, 210, 222
Roosevelt, James, 54
Rowlan, ———, 72

S
Saipan-Tinian, 178-189
Saunders, Finis, 226-229
Sawruk, Jim, 32, 70, 226
Saylor, Morgan, 46, 105
Schneberger, W. A., 168
Schneider, Tony F., 49
Scholze, ———, 180, 206, 220
Seaton, Earnest Thompson, 57-58

Sessions, ———, 108
Shacklett, Frank, 18-19
Shagnea, E. N., 241
Shepley, Lewis, 85, 86, 200, 201, 203, 204-205, 232, 233, 244, 258
Shigeitsu, Mamoru, 196
Shipp, Warren, 229
Signorelli, Ellis F., 208
Slater, Bob, 45, 55, 56
Smith, "J. J.," 175
Smith, A. "Smitty," 246, 263
Smith, George E., 80
Smith, Harold J. 174
Smith, J. A., 207
Smith, Maurice "Snuffy," 47, 52, 53, 63, 65, 78, 79-80, 81, 86, 87, 104, 180, 181, 206, 220
Snedeker, Albert C., 54-57, 58, 94, 98, 99, 102, 245
Snedeker, James, 55
Snedeker, W. "Bill," 174-175
Solomon Campaigns, 52-94
Soryu, 161
Spencer, C. E., 71
Spraggins, J. A., 28, 29, 47
Stark, Admiral, 7
Steck, Fred, 83
Steck, Ruth, 82
Stevens, Jimmy, 88
Stevens, William M., 88, 143-144, 145, 152, 157, 163, 184, 186, 187, 189, 211, 220, 238, 243
Stewart, Glen, 6, 39
Stillwell, ———, 35
Stolz, Earl, 83
Stolz, Ray, 83
Stolz, Vernon, 78, 82-83, 104
Sustae, Frank, 36, 47, 48
Swan, ———, 35
Sweeny, ———, 167

T
Tallman, Humphrey F., 45
Tanzman, Herbert M., 221, 229, 230
Taylor, Bing, 80
Taylor, Charles C., 179, 191
Tenney, Brad, 93

Index   271

Tenney, David B., 92, 93-94, 102, 152, 161, 163, 210
Tharin, ———, 31
Theuson, Swede, 44, 49-50
Thomas, Jane, 39
Thomas, Pres, 36, 38, 47-49, 63-65, 85, 86, 115
Tinker, Clarence, 43
Titinsom, Luke, 88
Trout, Robert, 23
Truett, ———, 69-70
Truman, Harry S., 211, 223
Turner, ———, 54
Turner, Kelly, 45

U
Ulithi, 199-205
USS *Arizona*, 16
USS *Bailey*, 191
USS *Ballard*, 56
USS *Ben Franklin*, 142
USS *Bon Homme Richard*, 47
USS *Card*, 232, 233
USS *Chincoteague*, 108, 230
USS *Curtiss*, 52, 53, 59, 60, 69, 87, 108
USS *Cimarron*, 51
USS *Detroit*, 44
USS *Doyle*, 215, 216, 217
USS *Enterprise*, 21, 27, 194
USS *Gatling*, 229
USS *Grant*, 54
USS *Grayson*, 174
USS *Hammon*, 51, 161
USS *Indianapolis*, 68, 195, 196-197, 213-219, 224, 226
USS *Kitty Hawk*, 260
USS *Landsdown*, 210
USS *Langley*, 1, 8
USS *Macfarland*, 53
USS *Mackinac*, 47, 53, 54, 56, 69, 78, 87, 108
USS *Maury*, 21, 194, 195
USS *Missouri*, 196, 198, 223, 224, 226
USS *Monahan*, 51
USS *Pennsylvania*, 221
USS *Quincey*, 56
USS *Ranger*, 8

USS *Saratoga*, 30, 56
USS *Saufley*, 70, 71
USS *Utah*, 12
USS *Vincennes*, 56
USS *Wasp*, 53
USS *Wisconsin*, 68
USS *Wright*, 8, 9, 68
USS *Yorktown*, 49, 51, 161

V
Vaatvert, A. R., 99
Van Matre, Lois, 181
Van Matre, Robert "Moose," 180, 181, 220-221
Vance, ———, ix
Vandergrift, ———, 72

W
Wainright, Jonathan M., 196
Wake Island, 27-33
Waldren, ———, 73
Ward, Del, 45
Washburn, Judith, 72
Washburn, Langhorn, 66, 67, 68, 72, 208
Waslov, L., 258
Watson, Bob, 149, 158, 239, 246
Watson, Frank, 212
Watson, Henry, 211
Watters, C. James, 6-7, 12-14, 37, 46, 51, 56, 258
WAVES, 127-128
Weaver, Donald Max, 2-3, 133, 198, 202, 244, 258
Weir, J., 253
Weiss, ———, 38
Wesley, Charles M., 168, 169, 241
White, "Red," 184
White, "Whizzer," 91
White, Frank "Whitey," 148, 151, 153, 158, 159, 173, 189, 212, 239, 246
Wilcox, Bob, 53, 54
Wiley, ———, 69
Wilkerson, ———, 38, 258
Williams, P., 35, 56, 107, 258
Wilson, Charles, 163, 173, 174, 210
Winn, Bob "Windy," 147

Winters, Bob, 6, 43, 44
Winters, Hugh, 12-13, 19
Woods, L. E., 172

Y
Yokoi, Shoichi, 190

Young, ———, 144
Young, J., 99

Z
Zaugg, Fred, 148, 153, 158, 173, 212, 239

www.ingramcontent.com/pod-product-compliance
Lightning Source LLC
Chambersburg PA
CBHW050549160426
43199CB00015B/2590